RAKING LEAVES IN THE WIND

A Memoir

Catherine Miller Hahn

Copyright © 2022 by Catherine Miller Hahn.

First Printing.

ISBN: 979-8-9870724-1-7 (hardcover)
ISBN: 979-8-9870724-2-4 (paperback)
ISBN: 979-8-9870724-3-1 (eBook)

Library of Congress Control Number: 2022918916

Printed in the United States of America.

Published by Irish Giants LLC. Prescott, Arizona.

Please direct all correspondence to:
  Irish Giants LLC
  PO Box 10302
  Prescott, AZ 86304

catherinemillerhahn.com

In the Wind Series

Raking Leaves in the Wind
Chasing Balloons in the Wind*
Counting Butterflies in the Wind*

---

*Forthcoming

For all my children.

Dan and Mary
My Four Roses
Dylan
Kristi and Chad
Duncan and Reese

Let all that you do
Be done in love.

1 Corinthians 16:14 (ESV)

CONTENTS

∅

AUTHOR'S NOTE

God can bring good from all things, even the worst things, such as abortion. I know from personal experience that this is true. I learned to trust the Lord and discovered He was always waiting for me to seek His forgiveness and heal me. Healing from abortion was never about who I was but who God is. I have read fine memoirs about the lives of many people, some from women who had abortions, but I did not find a memoir about how long the path can be that leads to abortion for some women, women like me. As a lifelong pro-life woman, I did not decide to have an abortion on the spur of the moment; it was a lifetime of moments that pushed me in that desperate direction; some may have happened before I was born. Statistical estimations cite that over forty percent of American women have abortions, and seventy to eighty percent of those women regret them. I began to understand what regret was doing to me when I went to a small, new church in Prescott, Arizona, on a warm Sunday morning in the spring of 2018.

I sat down on a hard chair to listen to the vocals of the African American members of the Mt. Zion Church choir. I was never in the church before that morning. Still, I was there hoping there might be soulful singers who would join the cast in our community theater's production of *Big River*, Roger Miller's musical version of Mark Twain's *Huckleberry Finn*. It was a musical I loved and wanted to stage since I first heard the original Broadway recording in 1985 while working on my master's degree in theatrical direction at the University of Kansas. That morning, I planned to slip out the church door right after the choir sang and before the actual service began.

The members were singing praise and worship songs full of hope and happiness. Their songs were not repetitive dirges like the ones I grew up listening to in the Catholic church. Everyone was on their feet, singing, clapping, and praising the Lord. The African Americans in the congregation were dressed in their Sunday finest, the men in nice suits and shined shoes, the women in pretty dresses, sparkling jewelry, and high heels. Others in attendance were of mixed races: Hispanic, Asian, and American Indian, but primarily Caucasian. Some people came from blue-collar homes dressed in jeans and work shirts; others came from nearby ranches dressed in southwestern clothing, the women in denim skirts and starched print blouses, the men in cowboy boots and plaid shirts with snaps for buttons. There were also homeless veterans dressed in washed shirts, jeans, or overalls, cleaned and given by church members.

I looked around the room for the closest exit as the choir finished singing, but as I got up to leave, people shook my hand and welcomed me to the service. It was clear I either had to stay or be rude and walk out of their church. I smiled, sat back down, shifted my weight on the chair, and watched their pastor walk to the front of the church. He was a middle-aged man on the young side, tall and handsome in his tailored olive-green suit and crisp white shirt. He looked at his congregation, then grinned before he spoke. "I'm Pastor Mike," he said. "Welcome newcomers to Mt. Zion Church; welcome back to those joining us again this morning to praise and love the Lord."

I wondered what kind of sermon I would hear at this church. Would it be fire and brimstone? Pastor Mike was quite a contrast to the elderly wrinkled Catholic priests I remembered, priests dressed in ceremonial vestments and standing at their podiums droning on about shame and guilt. Instead, Pastor Mike's words were gentle and poetic, often humorous. His preaching was colorful, animated, and soulfully couched in an undeniable love for Jesus Christ.

"Brothers and Sisters," he said, with his long arms extended and masculine hands raised toward heaven, "Don't go another day without making Jesus the center of your life! Hear me now. Listen to me, dear people! Without making Jesus foremost in your hearts and minds, you are on a sure-fire path toward an eternity of fruitless work, like you are rakin' leaves in the wind! Do you feel me? Hear me now! Glory to God! Trust in the Lord. Make today the day you throw down those sorry rakes and tell Him your secrets, even the secrets you might be keepin' from yourselves!"

Pastor Mike's sincerity struck me as entirely authentic. He was no puppet, showman, or holy roller, no TV evangelist with Hollywood hair who rained down woeful words upon his congregation. Pastor Mike was a man of God, one of "the only three real men of God" my mother promised I would meet in my lifetime. I thought, how is it that this man, a man I had never met or seen before, how could he be so accurate in describing my decades-old, anxiety-ridden exhaustion with such laser-sharp accuracy? "Rakin' leaves in the wind," he said. Yes, it was a perfect description of how I was living.

Pastor Mike drew me to God with his booming, magnetic voice. He opened my doctrine-clogged ears with that simple phrase. This pastor's earnest jubilance, his genuine reverence for Jesus Christ, pierced through my resistance to formalized religion. With his powerful and abiding love, Pastor Mike awakened my dormant mind and spoke directly to my heart. I was so moved by Pastor Mike's bold determination and unselfish desire to reach his flock that he challenged me to know Jesus and find my way to be fully present in my skin for the first time in my life.

"Hear me now," Pastor Mike concluded. "Put down those heavy, sad ole rakes and develop personal relationships with God. Come to Jesus, give Him your weariness. He is waiting for you; He has always been waiting for you. The energy in the Father, Son, and Holy Spirit is pure and true. Make the journey to everlasting peace and joy."

Pastor Mike's message echoed in my mind for the thirty-five-minute drive home. Secrets. Had I been keeping secrets from myself? I sat at my desk when I got home and started writing. Four hours later, I realized I had not only begun the challenging task of writing a memoir but also the painful process of healing from abortion.

Memoirs open secrets. Writing a memoir illuminates fallibilities during its treasure hunt; it helps sort out who I was and whom I became. My goal in this first memoir was to discover greater truths about myself when I was a child and face them as an adult. *Raking Leaves in the Wind* is the first step in a series of three that combined tell the complete story of the accumulative problems I encountered and needed to understand to find the courage to ask God and my unborn children for forgiveness.

The values and heritages in my life shaped this memoir, not just facts. Facts don't breathe like the stories from people who helped me on my journey to meet myself. My truths are bound to differ from those that figure prominently in this book. The actual truth is probably a composite of their truths and mine.

No memoir is based merely on memory. I needed to dig deep enough inside myself to awaken my mind to the purpose of an examined life. Memoir writing is not a process for the faint of heart. There is pain involved, a necessary self-surgery on wounds that, in my case, required God's oxygen, His abiding love, and forgiveness to heal.

The assembling of memory puzzles requires trust between readers and writers of memoirs. Writing a memoir is a tentative process, not a form of twisting the truth. The reconstruction of the dialogue in this book came not only from my memories and diaries but also from those shared with me by others. There are scenes I did not witness but only recount as if I were there. Mary Karr, an outstanding memoirist, says, "A good story told often enough puts you in rooms never occupied." Karr also suggests, as do many excellent authors of memoirs, not to give correct names for all people but to assure readers that all the people are honest and not composites. I follow her advice and warnings to avoid exaggeration.

Mark Twain said something to the effect that the only reason a book is finished is that the publisher wants it finished! This must be especially applicable to a first book. I wanted to keep making corrections and changes forever, and probably would still be doing both were it not for Pastor Mike's words still in my mind from that spring Arizona Sunday. It was time to let this first book go, put down my heavy rake, and begin clearing my spiritual path to God's amazing grace. It was time to open my secrets and bring God's revelations to light, the only light in which the true self can be seen.

Catherine Miller Hahn
Prescott, Arizona
August 2022

PROLOGUE
THE PIE

There were five women seated at the round table. I was the oldest, fifty-eight years old, and retiring that month from thirty-five years of high school and college teaching. Taylor was the youngest; she was in her early twenties. She was married, had no children, and was in college. Lisa was in her thirties; she was married, had two young children, and worked as a secretary for a law firm. Jocelyn recently turned fifty. She was divorced with three children and worked for the local school district as a cook in an elementary school. The four of us shared one thing: we were weary and too old for our ages. The fifth woman at the table, Karen, was ageless. She was our soft-spoken counselor from the Crisis Pregnancy Centers of Greater Phoenix, Inc.

All of us were present at the Prescott crisis pregnancy center to continue our post-abortion grief work in the *Forgiven and Set Free* program. We were assigned *The Pie* exercise at our previous meeting. Karen handed us each a sheet of paper with a vast circle on it. The instructions on the top of the page said: *Who Is Responsible?* The assignment asked us to think about our abortion experiences and divide the "pie" into pieces that showed the proportion of accountability for those we believed responsible for our abortions.

Examples suggested were God, yourself, your parents, the baby's father, the doctor, the clinic, etc. The last instruction was to bring our completed papers back the following week.

I knew who was responsible; I knew immediately when Karen handed me the exercise to take home. I thought this assignment was the easiest one given to us thus far. The minute I got home, I wrote in the middle of my pie; *I alone am responsible.* I believed, was confident, I had the brave answer, that my pie displayed my total admission of guilt. Abortion was my fault; it had to be my fault alone. I was thirty-nine years old when I panicked. I was too old to be that weak and sinful, too submissive to judgmental people and the liberal voices in the university atmosphere where I lived. I was lost in fear; I could not find my voice, intelligence, or morality. I caved into my alarm and their rationalizations.

"Everyone, we will just go around the circle," Karen said on discussion night; "one-at-a-time show the names you wrote and the portions designated. Let's go youngest to oldest tonight."

One at a time, we each put our assignments on the table and did as Karen asked us to do. Taylor had a big slice of pie for her boyfriend, a larger one for her father, a thin piece for her mother, and the rest had her name on it. Lisa's pie had the words *father of the baby,* written on one-fourth of her pie, about an eighth for a female friend's name, society for another fourth, and the rest of the pie for her name. Jocelyn's pie was divided into two halves, one with the word husband and the other saying "me." My heart hurt for the other women I thought had not come as far as I had in their grief work. I placed my assignment on the table; sure, I was light years ahead in my healing process. Everyone stared at my pie, said nothing, and

Karen took an audible breath. "Oh Cathy," she said, tears in her eyes, "dear heart." She got up from her chair, came around the table, and put her arms around me. Lisa and Jocelyn patted my hands. "Oh Cathy, how God loves you," Karen said, "but you have so much work to do."

"I don't understand, Karen," I said as I began to weep; "how could anyone else except me claim responsibility for my abortions?"

Karen brought her chair beside mine, sat down, and looked at the four of us. "The forgotten women in the issue of abortion are the walking wounded, the traumatized women who have had abortions," she said. "The women in this category, like you, fear that their selfishness and lack of morality forced them into traps, then, like animals, they chewed off their legs to free themselves. These wounded women wear self-hatred with far more pain than the scarlet letter others paint on them."

"Some people asked me," I told her, "How is it that a woman with your education, credentials, and upbringing be so stupid?"

"Since my two abortions," Jocelyn said, "I am asked, 'Can't you figure out what is making you pregnant?' Each time I hear that question, I get angrier at myself for divorcing my abusive husband and how that makes me too poor to give birth to more children than the three I already have."

"I am asked the same hurtful thing, too," I told her, usually by some of the female teachers I thought were my friends. They laugh when they say it; they are oblivious to why it is no laughing matter."

"My mother tells me," Taylor whispered, "'You know all women who have abortions go to hell!' What hurts me the most is that she says it aloud for all to hear, fully understanding my abortion."

Taylor's words brought back a time when my mother said the same thing to me in front of two of my closest friends, two good friends who knew too well of my pain and guilt over abortion. The four of us were having wine one night when she brought the subject up out of nowhere. "Women who have abortions will all go to hell," she said. The memory of my mother's judgmental face and the sound of condemnation in her voice from almost twenty years before flooded through me again as though that moment had just happened. Sitting with the other women at the crisis center table, I had no breath; all I could do was squeeze Taylor's hand.

"Women who have babies are heroes, but we are sinners doomed for hell," Lisa added to the conversation, weeping. She looked at us and said, "I believe that."

"Yes, they are heroes," Karen counseled, "but most women who have babies have support systems; most do not reach the levels of loneliness and panic that other pregnant women experience. The trauma endured by abortion is a primal one. It is a near-fatal wound that victims of abortion continue to relive to punish themselves with self-hatred in the hope it lessens any pain their babies experienced."

We sat in tearful silence until Jocelyn got up and went outside. Karen, afraid we might lose her from the group, got up and followed her. A few minutes later, they both came back inside. Karen was holding Jocelyn's hand.

"We have much to cover in all our grief sessions, much for you to learn about your abortions other than the fact you had them. When women see the truth of their actions, they stop running from God and seek Him with all their hearts. We will acknowledge all your emotions and face them together, and I promise they will lead to the joy of God's forgiveness."

That evening, the rest of the class consisted of Karen sharing enlightened studies with us. The four of us listened and passed the Kleenex box around and around. Every sentence she spoke described me and had my name on it. She explained how the abortive mother's mind becomes so fragmented and warped from the guilt that often multiple pregnancies happen because of the mental illness created from the first one. The woman loses control of reality and her behaviors to the point her brain twists until she believes she deserves more pain and guilt and that maybe, her first baby will not hate her so much if they are not alone." It was determined when I was very young that I was hypersensitive (HSP). Karen explained how hypersensitive women feel abortion trauma more deeply than those who are not and why this makes their way out of the mental and behavioral abortion darkness even more difficult. "If current research estimates are right and some forty percent or more of women in America have had abortions, you are not alone in your grief and regret," Karen said.

We concluded the meeting with prayer, and then Karen gave us our assignment for the following week. We were told to make a list of questions that would make us aware of any emotional or physical responses we were having from our abortions and record them as honestly as we could. "It puts you in touch with areas of your life most affected by your abortion experience," Karen said. I looked at the other women's faces; it would be another challenging exercise for all of us.

We left that night knowing our lives had grown dark after our abortions. Our decisions to wipe our children from our bodies also wiped the sun away from the earth. We grew cold inside and out; we were the walking wounded, women just not quite dead. I knew that I entered the program because I felt my physical and mental health in my fifties were deteriorating as fast as cold winter winds bleed the colors from trees in autumn. I believed the other women also felt the same debilitations at their ages. The four of us hugged each other in the parking lot. Two of us cried; two of us didn't. Our minds were full of all we heard, and our hearts were heavy with all we were afraid to face. We were not modern women who "hear us roar." Instead, we were just four women falling apart.

I thought about other women as I drove home, women who appear to lack regret about their abortions and believe they have no apparent signs of physical or psychological side effects. I knew in my soul I wasn't one of those women. These thoughts became determination to do the work Karen told me I needed to do if I was going to heal for my husband, my family, and myself. The journey to forgiveness was going to take time, emotional pain, and complex psychological challenges to understand why I chose abortion. Still, I knew that until I did it, there was no life worth living for me.

ℒ

PART ONE
HERITAGE

Memory is history recorded in our brains,
Memory is a painter; it paints pictures of the past
And of the day.

- Anna Mary Robertson Moses (1860-1961)

CHAPTER ONE
HANK AND MARY

I learned in public school that nature and nurture contributed to my composition as a human being. I later learned that the Bible says my Father (Abba) in heaven created me long before I was knit in my mother's earthly womb. To know myself and God as my first parent, I needed to learn more about my mother and father before I existed on earth. Alfred Lord Tennyson wrote in Ulysses, "I am a part of all that I have met." That idea intrigued me when I first came across it in school. It made me wonder if there was an ultimate connection between what my parents experienced in their life journeys and mine. How could there not be?

Mary Ida Kelly, my mother, was born at home in 1920, and Henry Richmond Miller, my father, was born at home in 1916. They grew up, met, and married within twelve shady blocks of one another in Webster Groves, Missouri. In 1925 a five-year-old blonde, bushy-haired Mary Ida stood on Lockwood Avenue and firmly protected her hopscotch chalk lines from "Hank" Miller. With her hands at her waist, she swung her hips and said, "Listen here, Henry Miller. You and your friends cannot play marbles on my sidewalk! Go home!"

"Aw, you go home, Cotton Top, and quit bossin' us guys around! You don't own this sidewalk!" he responded.

It was not exactly the best start to a friendship, much less a future marriage, but fourteen years later, bossy Cotton Top grew into a radiant young woman. She was a golden beauty who needed no makeup except for a bit of red lipstick. Willow slim, a model perfect five feet, seven inches, 120 pounds, Mary Ida Kelly, made for a breathtaking future bride for the tall kid. My mother was barely nineteen in February 1940 when she married all six-foot, seven inches of my father.

"His infectious charisma, perfect teeth, and gleaming smile rivaled any movie star," my mother said.

They wed in Holy Redeemer Catholic Church right behind her hopscotch sidewalk. My Scottish/French/English father was a former Presbyterian who converted to Catholicism to marry my half-Irish, half-German mother.

"I had to kiss the ring," my father told me. "I needed to qualify to marry your mother."

My father was a lover, not a fighter. He was an impeccably clean young man when my mother married him. He wore starched white shirts and tailored suits, barely long enough for his height. My father and mother moved to Wichita, Kansas, after their wedding because my father was a traveling salesman working from the headquarters of Socony-Vacuum Oil Company, Inc., later changed to Mobil Oil Company Inc. in 1955. My parents were at home on my mother's twenty-first birthday when the Japanese bombed Pearl Harbor on December 7, 1941. This tragedy sent my father straight to enlist in the Air Force, the Navy, the Army, and the Marines, but all refused him. No branch of the Armed Services accepted a man of his extraordinary height. My father was discouraged that he was turned down in his effort to help his country and that he and my mother had to remain in their "dusty cracker box apartment."

"There were so few trees around us in Wichita," my mother said, "when the Kansas dust winds blew, we had to push sopping wet sheets and dish towels into the cracks around the windowsills and under the doors to keep everything inside clean."

The Army needed more recruits, so they raised the height requirement a year later. This time my father successfully enlisted in the Army Corps of Engineers and earned the rank of Sergeant. His job during the war was laying pipes in France and Africa. My mother did not see my father once for almost four years. She fell into a deep, clinical depression. Her parents, Daniel and Claire Kelly worried about Mary's health and insisted that she return to Webster Groves to live with them until my father came home from the war. My mother got angry at her parents and insisted that, as a married woman, she should be allowed to live on her own.

"I don't care that 'it just isn't done!'" she told her stoic German mother and her gentle Irish father. She did move back home with them, but to exert some independence, my mother dropped the "Ida" part of her name. "I am Mary Kelly Miller now," she told them in defiance.

My mother was a fighter, not a lover. She was a lifelong escape artist. She got through the war, her fight with depression, and any problem she ever had by burying herself in books. She spent her wartime career as a sales clerk for Doubleday Books, Inc. in nearby Kirkwood. Whenever community members saw her sitting at Woolworth's lunch counter or in a chair at the library after work, she was riveted to books. My mother was known around

Webster as "the pretty blonde woman who always has a book in her lap."

By age twenty-five, my mother had already buried her favorite Aunt Kate, who died of cancer, and her older sister, Margaret Mary, who died of scarlet fever. "Claire Kelly loved my older sister, Margaret Mary, more than me," my mother said about my grandmother, whom she always called by her first name. "Claire loved my sister more than my brother, Jack, too. I was the youngest child, years younger than my sister and brother. My mother ignored me so much that when I was little, I wished Margaret Mary would die; I even prayed she would. Then, she did die. "Cathy," my mother said, "never be jealous of anyone. That green-eyed monster kills you from within."

My mother loved her brother, Jack, and spoke of him often. "He took me to the St. Louis hockey games and wherever else he could," she said. "Jack was a severe alcoholic and not dependable, but I didn't care. I loved him for loving me."

My mother's most significant loss was when her father died. Daniel Joseph Kelly died of heart disease in his early sixties. "I wish you could have known him," she said. "He was a true, right-off-the-boat immigrant and a sweet man with a heart too soft for his own good. He was a full-blooded Catholic Irishman with red hair!" Mother was proud of her father, who worked for the Missouri Pacific Railroad. "My father played a large part in starting Boy Scouts of America in St. Louis," she told me. "When my father died, over two hundred Boy Scouts came to his funeral." A dark melancholy always came over my mother whenever she spoke about my grandfather. "I think something died in me when he died," she said.

My grandmother, Claire Paffhausen Kelly, was German Catholic, exceedingly intelligent, disciplined, and extremely strict. "She could have been a lawyer in another day and age," Mother said. "I think she was in love with a judge in town and never with my father at all." My mother resented my grandmother for the way she treated my grandfather. She struggled with loving her and only claimed the Irish half of her heritage. One day in her forties, my mother took my grandmother's picture off her bedroom wall and put it in a drawer. I asked her where it was only one time. "I took it down and put it away; it caused me bad dreams," she said.

One afternoon when my mother was very young, she played in the basement of their family home and found two large oil portraits of my Irish great-grandparents under a dusty cloth. "I wondered why Daddy's parents' portraits were in the dirty basement while the portraits of Claire's parents were in prominent places on the living room walls. "My father's parents were considered shanty Irish by Claire and her friends," she said; "they were considered undeserving of being upstairs."

My mother held a great deal of anger inside that centered around the strict Catholic boarding schools where her mother sent her from kindergarten through two years of college. She experienced years of loneliness and fear, having been kept so far away from her family. The Catholic schools were in sooty downtown St. Louis. Sometimes my mother alluded that a few nuns were cruel and some priests got "handsy" with her. "All men should be allowed to marry," she said as I grew up more times than I could count.

My mother was considered an ice queen in many ways. There were only a few times I could recall her touching my brothers, my father, or me. She may have had good reasons for her coldness after all her isolated years away from affection, but we never discussed it.

My mother wanted to go to Washington University in St. Louis for college, but my grandmother made her go to another women's boarding school, Maryville College, in St. Charles. "At least there I met Mother Callan, the first kind nun who understood me," my mother said. She loved Mother Callan so much that she often took me to Maryville on Sundays to visit her when I was a little girl.

"Does God bring our bodies back to our souls when we go to heaven?" I asked Mother Callan.

"Oh, my dear child, I hope not!" she answered. "I want to be finished with this old carcass of bones once and for all!"

I think my mother escaped her loneliness at Maryville to marry my father. "Your father was fun to be around; we laughed all the time," she said. "But Hank is also a hopeless dreamer and a poor provider who is always waiting for his ship to come in. But your father breathes charm and humor and is always positive. Even though his family lost all their money in the depression, your father believes he can get it back easily." I learned at a young age that my father was a gambler; he bet on poker, horses, dogs, sports, or that it might rain tomorrow, but he was also Santa Claus, and the Pied Piper rolled into one. "Your father loves children and adults, and they both adore him," my mother told me, "But he dances from job to job, always believing there are magical ways to avoid working."

My mother loved my father for his ability, in an instant, to make her laugh. I often thought my mother experienced little laughter when she grew up. It delighted me to see her laugh with my father. It struck me ironic, even at my youngest age, that my mother's laughter made it difficult for her to maintain anger at my father over our family's continuous financial instability.

Everyone loved my father. No one was more fun to be around or make laughter erupt in any room faster than my father. But as my parents' marital years together multiplied, so did my mother's silent anger and the number of family financial burdens thrust upon her. Divorce was never an option in my mother's Catholic faith. She may have contemplated it as her hunger for independence and incessant worries grew. As I got older, my mother became more of a distant chaplain toward me, a kind of martyr who desired but never quite achieved sainthood. My father was more than a prince in dented armor to me; he was my soulmate, my supportive spine that held the weak rest of me together.

Hank Miller was the baby in the Miller clan, spoiled by most of his relatives. The Millers had Black servants, including a Black nanny, Luisa, whom my father adored and who loved him with equal affection. Luisa traveled with the Miller family whenever they left their Sherwood Drive home in Webster Groves for their summer home in Ashville, North Carolina. Luisa left the family's employment when she grew too old to care for him, and another Black woman, Sophie, became my father's nanny. He loved Sophie as much, if not more than Luisa. My father grew up with ponies, toys, recurring gifts, and about everything a little boy could want. He had an older brother, Lucian, and two sisters, Jeanette and Gladys, who doted on him too.

I was fed stories as a child about who I was because of who everyone else was in at least two generations of my father's family. Henry Claudius Miller, my grandfather, was born in 1881. He was of Scotch-English heritage and married a wealthy French-English woman, Katherine Blackmer, born in 1883. The Blackmer family owned the Blackmer and Post Company in St. Louis, which made sewer pipes. Katherine (Kate) Blackmer's side of the Blackmer-Miller union started the Webster Groves Building and Loan Association in 1884 and lived on Marshall Place with a 10-acre lawn and a winding drive that led down Swon Avenue to the thick stone walls surrounding their property. Blackmer Place, a street on part of this land, was named for the family. Because of them, I was in the social register.

Claude and his family lost their affluence when the Blackmer and Post Company went bankrupt. The depression hit in the dirty thirties, and the Miller family was not spared. This time in my father's life was challenging, including his relationship with his father. "Though Claude was proud of me when I made Eagle Scout, I was not close to him," my father told me about the man who insisted all his children call him by his first name.

"Claude was a toucher," my mother said about her father-in-law after she joined the family in 1940. "Binks (Lucian's wife) and I used to call him the lint-picker because he 'picked lint' off my legs and her breasts. Whatever happens when I die," my mother said, "don't bury me on top of Claude!"

We called Daddy's brother, Lucian, Uncle Lou. He and Aunt Binks, along with my mother and father, took care of Grandma Miller, "Kate," after Claude died in 1951. My mother and Aunt Binks were the only ones who took care of her until she died in 1965 in the small studio apartment they rented for her on the corner of Lockwood Avenue and Rockhill Road. My father's sisters, Grandma Miller's daughters, were married and lived elsewhere, so Kate's care fell to her two daughters-in-law, though not without complaint.

"How is it that with four children, including her own two daughters, we are the lucky ones who must care for Kate?" my mother often asked of Aunt Binks. "For fourteen years, we have been cleaning her apartment, bathing her, and having her over for dinner every other Sunday."

"Kate is a cold, helpless woman," Aunt Binks responded. "She has been an old woman since thirty-five years old!"

My father told me one story about Grandma Miller that stunned me as a child. "This story is about my pet chicken," he said. "One day when I came home from school, I asked my mother, 'where is Pecky?'"

"He is in the refrigerator, Henry. We are going to have Pecky for dinner," she told him without looking up from her sewing. "I didn't eat meals with the family for many days after that," my father said.

All the stories about the Kellys, the Paffhausens, the Millers, and the Blackmers before I was born helped me know them as people, not only as mothers, fathers, and grandparents. Their stories were great insights into my hypersensitivity toward everyone and everything around me. My father was easy to know and even easier to love; his family stories described him exactly as I knew him, affectionate, naughty, full of fun, and a fine teller of tall tales. My mother was more challenging to know and love; her stories from either side of her family were few and far between and often mournful or bitter. I once gave her a grandmother book when I was an adult to write her memories for her grandchildren. Under the third prompt, she wrote *none of your damn business!* She never wrote another word in the book after that entry. I guess that's why I called my father Daddy and addressed my mother as Mother, never Mommy.

✍

PART TWO
CHILDHOOD

We could never have loved
The earth so well
If we had had no childhood in it.

- George Eliot (Mary Ann Evans)

CHAPTER TWO

MOUNT VERNON, ILLINOIS

My father loved Grandma Kelly. My parents moved to Mount Vernon, Illinois, when Daddy came home from the war and went to work for Pontiac. Daddy was delighted to have Grandma Kelly live with them after Grandpa Kelly died.

"Of course, he loved Claire," Mother said. "Together, they got in trouble with me often. One time it happened over raising chickens and turkeys and selling eggs. Every time I walked up our sidewalk, I was embarrassed by the clumsy red painted signs on scrap boards that the two of them nailed to the trees in our front yard: *1 doz fresh eggs, only 25 cts!* Claire loved your father more than she ever loved me," Mother said.

Daddy nicknamed everyone, relatives and friends; he called my older brother "Hero" or "Nick." Rick was born on April 12, 1947. Mother was supposed to be induced to deliver the baby on April 13th, but Daddy was very superstitious and told the doctor, "No baby of mine will be born on the 13th!" Mother was induced the day before.

"There are twins," a surprised Dr. Joseph Hardy told Daddy in the hall outside the delivery room, adding, "I can save Mary or the babies, Hank, but they are in such distress, I cannot save them all."

Daddy, shocked and frightened, said, "No, Joe, I need my wife to walk out of this hospital!" Dr. Hardy understood that demand and Daddy went to the chapel to kneel beside Claire. "We waited eight years and through a world war to have a family; this cannot be happening," he told her.

"Just pray, Hank; St. Mary's is a good Catholic hospital, and Dr. Joseph Hardy is a good Catholic doctor," she said, "just kneel and pray."

Several hours later, when Dr. Hardy entered the chapel, he spoke to them. "I was able to save Mary, but only one of the baby boys. The umbilical cord wrapped around the neck of the second baby and cut off his air supply during the birth. I am so sorry, Hank; I tried to save him, but you can go to the nursery window and see your new son now. Mary is sleeping and must not have any visitors until tomorrow. It was a complicated birth for her."

At first, Daddy couldn't move, but Grandma Kelly got him up and guided him to the nursery. "There he is," she said, "Henry Richmond Miller, Junior. His name is longer than he is!"

"I just stared at him," Daddy said. "He was so long and red that I was terrified he would not live either. He was as skinny as a snake. I went straight to the bathroom and threw up."

The next day after seeing Mother, Grandma Kelly and Daddy arranged a burial for little Joseph. On the day my mother was discharged, the three held a small funeral and buried Rick's twin in the Cemetery of St. Peter and Paul next to Grandpa Kelly, his namesake. At the gravesite, Claire told Daddy, "Now the little one will be in Limbo forever since he died before he was baptized."

"Like hell, he will be!" Daddy bellowed. "Our baby is in heaven; little Joe went straight to God in heaven! Straight to God, damn it!"

Daddy hired Georgia, a Black woman, as a nanny to help Mother with baby Ricky while she recovered. Mother loved Georgia dearly, so much that she never lost contact with her until Georgia died many years later. Proud, sad, and grateful, Daddy drove Claire, Mother, and their miracle baby boy back home to Mount Vernon.

Children need to hear stories about their births. There are countless celebratory books for children written on the subject, but none of Mother's pregnancies were easy, so our stories never had celebrations. "I almost died with all of you," she told us. The fear of death during pregnancy was planted in my brain often and early. I was the only girl born to my parents. I absorbed Mother's stories like a sponge soaks up liquids three times its weight.

I was born on April 29, 1949, two years after Rick was born. "I had six blood transfusions during your delivery!" Mother said. "You were my biggest baby at six pounds, but I was happy to have a girl. I wanted a girl." I was named after my two grandmothers, Katherine and Claire. Mother was not happy to have Grandma Miller's name any part of mine. She wanted to name me after her favorite aunt, Cate, so she changed the "K" to a "C," hoping people would call me Cate. Catherine Claire Miller, then, was the final decision.

There are no pictures of anyone but Grandma Kelly holding me as a baby. She rocked me and read to me. She stood Rick on a chair on one side of her and placed me on top of the table in an infant carrier on her other side while she baked cookies, streusels, cakes, and pies until, like snow, the flour covered us and every surface of the kitchen. "Claire was a better grandmother than a mother," Mother told us.

Daddy nicknamed me "Munker" because I had a pronounced overbite, even without teeth. Twelve years later, I was written up in an orthodontic journal as one of the worst malocclusion cases ever recorded. "How's my little chipmunk?" Daddy said to his baby girl. Later, Mother changed my nickname to "Tatter;" after the sound my hard baby shoes made on the wood floors. It was my good fortune that Tatter stuck.

Sunday, August 29, 1949, was a beautiful summer day with a break in Illinois' dog's day heat and humidity. It was perfect weather for a drive in the Pontiac around Mount Vernon. Our car was sitting at a stop sign when a drunk driver roared over the top of the hill and slammed into the back of us. Grandma Kelly sat in the middle of the back seat holding me; Daddy was at the car's wheel, and Mother was on the front passenger side; two-year-old Rick stood between them. The fast-moving car pushed the Pontiac across the intersection, where we were hit again in the rear passenger door by another oncoming car to the right. Mother and Daddy put their arms across Rick to stop his fall through the windshield. The clasp of their arms saved him from fatal injury. Grandma Kelly clutched me to her chest as she slid across the backseat and hit the armrest in the door behind Daddy. The blow to her side was so intense that it opened the door, and she fell into the street, still holding me. Mother rushed around the front of the car and reached my grandmother just moments before she died.

"Something happened at that moment when I watched Claire die," Mother told me. "I know that because I saw it happen. I cannot describe it, but something went from your grandmother into you." Mother never defined if what went into me from Grandma Kelly was good or bad; I just carried the question mark inside me.

∅

CHAPTER THREE

WEBSTER GROVES, MISSOURI: GRANT ROAD

My father bought a little yellow house after Grandma Kelly died. He was happy to move Mother back to Webster after another funeral experience for her. It was on Grant Road near Highway 66 in Webster Groves, Missouri.

"We got a terrific deal on this house!" Daddy said, but they learned the house didn't have a furnace when winter came. It had the surroundings for a furnace, but there was none inside.

"Leave it to your father," Mother said, "to buy a house without a furnace!" It was a new home for Rick and me, but without a furnace, it was just another expense to Mother and not be the last of Daddy's "good deals."

Medical studies explain how babies are not simple beings but are complex and ageless. Many doctors consider babies small creatures with big thoughts which can have some memory of their births. Imaginings are not memories, however. I imagine in the hospital when I had no language and was wrapped too tightly in the pink blanket that it felt good to scream because once I could talk, I couldn't form a word without flailing my arms. The poop and pee smell from my bleached, diapered bottom could not have been as comfortable as swimming naked in my mother's womb's safe and heated pool. It was so pleasurable in that moist darkness with Mother's heart beating close to me; I was not ready for the glaring lights and hard slap that made me cry.

My earliest memories were of my first bed. It was a blonde wooden crib with Mary, and her Little Lamb painted on the outside panels of the headboard and footboard. The railing had a thin plastic cover to keep me from biting into the soft wood. My first playmates were the spinning pastel balls on top of the footboard, one pink, one blue, and one yellow. I remember spinning them and thinking they were friends and were alive.

My crib was also my playpen. I spent hours in it the first few years while Mother's health improved from my difficult birth. My earliest image of Mother was watching her follow Rick around the small rooms of our house. I recall standing and shaking the railing of my crib to make it rattle. I sang, "Ride the horsey, ride the horsey, yeeha!" Sometimes, redheaded Rick toddled into my room and visited me. He poked his pink face between the crib slats, pointed, and said, "Baby Caffey," before Mother came and whisked him away.

My future beds after my crib became my sanctuaries, personal cathedrals to me. I felt the safest and most secure in my bed, given to anxiety from birth and the accident. I always needed to be the last one to go to sleep. Sleep wasn't possible if anyone was awake in the house. Everyone I loved needed to be home, safe and sound asleep, no longer needing anything from me. Only then could I close my eyes and go to sleep. It was my "restless imagination," Mother said.

Pat the Bunny was my first book; I learned the five senses sitting on Mother's lap when she read it. I touched the daddy's scratchy face; I smelled the sweet, powdery-scented flowers; I saw my hazel eyes in the cloudy mirror; I heard the creaking of Grandma Kelly's old rocking chair against the hardwood floor, and I tasted the bitter corners of the little book's pages before Mother pulled them from my mouth.

"No baby," she said, "pat the bunny, pat the soft little bunny."

I learned life's five senses quickly enough, but it took over forty years to understand the depth and consequences of my emotional sensitivity, which felt more like a bully than a blessing. My emotions were acute, raw, and as fragile as a porcelain doll that breaks into a million pieces if clumsy hands drop it on the floor. I absorbed all energy around me; I was a radar disc, an overloaded circuit that crackled and sparked from too much voltage. The only antidote for my (HPS) hypersensitivity was Daddy. It felt like it took forever for him to come home each day, an eternity, before he lifted me high in the air, and I heard him say, "Grrrr, grrrr, gobble, gobble when he kissed my tummy.

"Daddy is home!" Mother announced each night. She clapped her hands when she said it, but her glad actions never felt out of joy for seeing my father, more out of relief from her long days as a 1950s stay-at-home mother. Daddy's arrival from work was a celebration for Rick and me. He grabbed Rick and gave him multiple squeezes, and then it was my turn to experience Daddy's magic. I waited all day to hear his lionhearted voice and see his smiling face peek around the corner of my room.

"Where's my Munker?" he said. "Where is she?"

Presto, liberation from daytime jail! I loved to smell his well-groomed, shiny Vitalis head when he hugged me and said, "How I missed my little chipmunk today!" My father always smelled like he had just stepped out of a shower twenty-four hours a day. The fresh, clean mixture of Mennen Skin Bracer and Ivory soap radiated from his neck, no matter how hot or humid the St. Louis day. The entire atmosphere of our house brightened the minute my father walked through the door. I lived two lives in those early years – one when Daddy was home and the second when I was waiting for him to come home. His presence meant freedom and the absence of loneliness.

"In you go, Munker," Daddy said when he tucked me in my crib at night and kissed my forehead. "Night night, sweet dreams; I will see you in the morning."

My father and I played a game for eighteen years until I left for college in 1967. We called it our Chicago game. Daddy pretended to leave my room, and I covered my head with my blanket. "Oh no! Where did Cathy go?" Daddy said when he came back into my room. "I hope she didn't go to Chicago! I would miss her way too much if she went to Chicago!" Then, he sat on my bed, pretended to put all his weight on me, and pretended to cry in wailing sobs on my pillow. This never failed to start my giggles; I laughed under my covers and popped my head from beneath them. "Whew! There she is!" Daddy said. "Thank you, God; I never want to be without my Munker!" The last part of our goodnight ritual when I was still in my crib was when he made all three colored balls on the footboard spin at once. No one ever told me for sure, but I believe that "Daddy" was my first word.

Rick and I got older, and once I was liberated from my playpen for good, I found him to be much more fun than pastel spinner balls. We sat beside each other on the floor and watched the Cisco Kid or the Lone Ranger on our nine-inch RCA black and white television in the living room. If Rick felt generous toward me, he took his favorite 45 rpm record, *Cruising Down the River,* off his blue-striped suitcase player and let me play my favorite song, Roy Rogers and Dale Evans singing *Happy Trails to You.* It was a rare occasion because when Rick wanted to play with his toys, it meant I needed to hit the trail. Rick was the only non-stuffed guest at all my tea parties, though, and he was always the good big brother cowboy to my Indian.

There were no girls in our neighborhood when we were old enough to play outside, so I was a tomboy, complete with scabby knees and bruises dotting my long, gangly legs. I wore Rick's hand-me-down overalls and tee shirts, a financial necessity for our post-WWII mother who counted every penny, especially living with Daddy, who sometimes made no pennies to count. Many of the mommies on Grant Road happily shed their Rosie the Riveter outfits for the new 1950s trendy dresses or feminine and beautiful blouses atop bouffant skirts with wide belts that make their waists look small. These pretty clothes were moved to the backs of their closets when they needed spacious, shapeless maternity clothes to produce more of our baby boomer generation.

I was happy to be a tomboy because of the freedom it gave me when I played with the boys in the neighborhood. I felt like one of them. I rode down the streets on my green Schwinn bike, not wearing any top, just like the boys did during the hot suburban St. Louis summers. No one could tell I was a girl In Rick's clothes, with my short, cropped hair and flat chest. It was sweet equality until the day I wanted to pee standing up. "The boys don't go home to potty," I said to Mother; "they just throw their bikes down on the grass and pee on a bush or someone's grass." I practiced peeing standing up at home in our bathroom. I stood in front of the toilet instead of sitting on it. I was sure I could accomplish the boys' feat, but the pee ran down my legs toward the floor and into my red Keds tennis shoes. "I can do it, Mother!" I pleaded as I looked at her disapproving face in the bathroom doorway.

"Honey," she said, "all women wish we had one of those handy things to take on a picnic, but God gave them only to boys. Like the rest of us girls, you will learn that God made us special in other ways."

I was blessed with the time on earth God gave me to be alive. Nobody knew of transgender changes in the 1950s, or someone on Grant Road might have thought I was a strong candidate for an operation. Mother knew, though, that inside my tomboy, I was all-girl. I realized years later that my conversation with Mother in our little bathroom was meaningful. It was her way of preparing me a bit for the limitations the women of her generation encountered in life while at the same time teaching me to try and love myself and love how God made me. I could have saved myself years of heartache and therapy if I had learned her lessons that day, but the only lesson I learned was that life was much cleaner if I gave up the desire to pee standing up.

No matter how hard I tried to fit in with the boys, they excluded me. "Go home! Boys only!" they yelled. I never let them see me cry, but when I got home to my sanctuary and climbed onto my bed, I avoided crying by losing myself in the pictures in my books and the words I could read. Cross-legged I sat on the riverbank and made friends with Mole and Mr. Toad or Caddie Woodlawn. I soothed my rejection sorrows with story after story. I galloped away from loneliness on the back of Black Beauty and fell down a rabbit hole with Alice. I loved my paper friends; they had time for me.

"Why don't the boys like me?" I asked Rick one afternoon.

"You're crazy; we like you. It's just us guys who want to do guy things. Sometimes, you're just not tough enough. Mother says you are too sensitive for your own good, that you wear your feelings on your sleeve."

"That's not true. Daddy says I play too hard and get overly tired, and that's why I sometimes cry," I told him, hoping Mother was wrong and Daddy was right.

The adults on Grant Road were much nicer than the boys to me. Their lives looked much more fun, anyway. On the Fourth of July, our Miller family had barbecues with the Biederman family. Mr. and Mrs. Biederman had two sons, Rossy, my age, and Bobby, who was the same age as Rick. Our parents met the day chubby Rossy hit Rick in the head with a brick. Nobody got mad; Mr. Biederman and Daddy chalked it up to 'boys will be boys." Mr. Biederman was mostly stomach and smelled like warm beer. He wore an undershirt with no sleeves, and when he barbecued his famous chicken with his secret sauce, he had more sauce on his shirt than on the chicken.

Mrs. Biederman had long, thick, curly brown hair like Rita Hayworth and wore Ragin' Red Revlon lipstick. She wore so much perfume; "You can smell Bea before she comes in the door," Daddy said. I liked the sound of her gold bracelets clanging together whenever she waved her arms, something she did a lot when she talked. Mrs. Beiderman wore bright-colored circular skirts with low-cut white blouses she pulled onto her shoulders. I wished Mother always wore brighter colors instead of tan or dark green.

"I bet Bea wears all those bracelets to bed," Mother told Daddy.

"Maybe Beiderman has to wear earplugs in case they hit the headboard," he said. Mother burst out laughing and left the room.

After our Fourth of July supper and all our red, white, and blue sparklers were burned out, the kids went to bed, and the grownups sat outside in our backyard beside Daddy's tomato plants. "There is nothing, not even in Italy, I bet, like a Missouri homegrown tomato," Mother said. The adults swatted mosquitos and drank beer while they talked. Mr. Beiderman's chair had the most beer cans around it. Daddy and Mr. Biederman sang army songs, *over hill, over dale, as we hit the dusty trail* and shot off bottle rockets and cherry bombs to celebrate America's freedom. Rick and I listened for the ka-booms in our beds. On the Fourth, Daddy and Mrs. Biederman got their rifles and shot out the windows of the deserted Grant School next door. Rick and I jumped up and ran into the living room to look out our picture window when the police car roared up our short, steep driveway. The red lights on top of their vehicle bounced off the walls and our faces.

"Officers, we're not sure who did it, but it looked like some pretty rough teenagers," Mrs. Biederman said, waving her arms and clanging her bracelets on the front lawn. "I think they took off down Grant Road, that way, toward Highway 66."

Daddy loved to make friends with policemen and firemen. "They are great guys," he told us. "Hey guys, come back when you get off duty and join us for a Fourth of July beer," Daddy said as their car backed away from our house.

It was a mutual friendship because the Webster policemen and firemen loved my father too. Later that same Fourth of July night, the two officers came back. Daddy got two more green and white webbed lawn chairs out of the garage so they could sit down. Rick and I watched from our back screened porch as they joined the adult celebration; it was fun to listen to how they all laughed at Daddy's jokes.

"I wish your father handled money as well as he handles people," Mother said. "One time after the war, your father was offered rock bottom stock in Polaroid right before they came out with the sixty-second picture development camera. 'Who in the hell cares about getting a picture in sixty seconds?' your father said. He loved cameras, but he had no financial vision for the future of photography."

One Halloween, on heavy, perforated, tightly rolled Kodak film, Daddy took a curious picture of five-year-old Rick and three-year-old me. Daddy took most of the photographs in our family because Mother never centered us in the lens. Mother took crooked photos of only parts of us, an elbow or kneecap beside an empty swing, a foot in a puddle, or the backs of our heads. Daddy's pictures focused us dead center. He always saw all of us.

In one photo, Rick was dressed as a little Irish cowboy with freckles so pink on his cheeks and hair so red they were visible in black and white. His sweater had six horizontal stripes and was too short; it did not cover his tummy. His white undershirt showed above the gleaming six guns draped down both sides of his no-hips little boy body. He was wearing long pants tucked into black cowboy boots, each with a white stripe forming a "v" on the top. His black hat was pulled tight under his chin with a white cord held fast by a little bead. He was grinning right into the camera, standing knock-kneed with both feet solidly planted. Rick was dignified, even at five, all good guy, all confident, all hero with kindergarten cinema star appeal. He was the one playing dress-up. I was in disguise.

Standing to Rick's left, I wore a crumpled paper grocery bag on top of my almost curly but only wavy hair that was neither blonde nor brown. A faded scarf was fastened to the paper bag draping down the sides and back of my head. Rick's old plaid cardigan sweater was buttoned at the top, forming my own "v" but upside down against Rick's outgrown baggy corduroy overalls. One sleeve fell over my closed hand; only my fingertips showed. My other hand was free of its sleeve, visible with wide open fingers fully extended. My pant legs were too long and hid my feet. I was an odd little creature, all luminous eyes with deep circles beneath, just standing there waiting for someone to tell me who or what I was.

∅

CHAPTER FOUR
BEAUTIFUL BABY

Mother was told not to have any more children after I was born. Dr. Hardy gave my father strict Catholic instructions, "No more children, Hank. Do you understand what I am saying? Mary must not have more children." It was a sin for a Catholic woman to use other birth control methods other than the rhythm method in the early fifties.

"I obeyed Dr. Hardy's warning," Daddy said to me. This was the first time I heard the words hell, pregnancy, and love connected. "We used the rhythm method, but all the Catholic fires of hell or the threats of Dr. Joseph Hardy could keep me from making love to my wife, the woman I have loved since she was five years old."

Four years after my birth, my mother was pregnant again and feared for her life a third time. "God forgive me, Hank, but I don't want this baby," she told him. "I know I will die this time, but if I get an abortion, I will go straight to hell. I am so scared; who will care for Rick, Cathy, and the new baby if I die having it?"

"You are not going to die, Mary," Daddy told her. "I love this baby too much already; this is the only child I've ever wanted!" That last part wasn't genuine because Daddy loved all children and wanted more, but his emphatic statement helped Mother calm down and believe God would take care of her. Daddy said every day of her pregnancy, "It is all going to turn out fine, Mary; I know it." But he was on his knees every night, praying to God that it would be fine. I heard his prayers and loved to touch Mother's stomach whenever she let me. I loved the baby, especially when it moved inside her.

On the day of the scheduled cesarean delivery, Daddy turned to Dr. Hardy before taking the elevator back down to St. Mary's chapel for his third time. "You must save them both, Joe! You must!" Again, on his knees, he prayed for Mother, the baby, our family, and God "to find something better than the damn rhythm method!"

On August 7, 1953, James Blackmer Miller was born, though not without some complications. Three days later, Daddy took his six-year-old son and four-year-old daughter to stand on the grass outside the hospital to see Mother and the baby. We could only wave to our new brother in the nurse's arms when she held him up to the window of Mother's room. She was in a special care unit, and no children were allowed there, so we stood outside below her third-story window. I remember Rick clapping and how tiny Mother looked when she came to the window and waved back at us. I remember Daddy's big smile as he looked up at her.

My mother suffered a lifetime of repressed guilt when she lost baby Joseph. She was haunted by it. She worried about Rick and whether he felt part of himself was missing. I often wondered if she ever enjoyed sex with my father or if she only equated sex with pregnancy and possible death. Mother told me about her friend, Emmie Wynn, from college. Mrs. Wynn had six children, one right after another, and ended up in a mental institution.

"What happened to Mrs. Wynn?" I asked.

"She had too many children," Mother said.

Another of Mother's friends she told me about was Jane Weiss, who died of ovarian cancer. "Why did Mrs. Weiss have to die so young?" I asked Mother.

"Her husband would never leave her alone sexually, so after her third baby, she took birth control pills, and those gave her cancer," Mother said. What I understood then was that sex plus birth control equaled cancer.

My mother took full responsibility for any emotional problems or learning disabilities Jimmy had as a child or adult. She experienced more guilt over saying she didn't want to have him. Those fears plagued her, too. Mother was in a perpetual state of atonement. The counselors at Bristol and Clark public schools where Jimmy went told Mother that she should place Jimmy in a particular school for more academic help. "No!" she told them. "My son will learn how to survive in the real world, not from someplace that will teach him how to hide from it. Jimmy will stay in public schools, and I will help him do it!"

Jimmy had two children with his beautiful second wife in the 1980s. One afternoon when he came home from work, Jimmy found her in their bed with another man. Their divorce was ugly, one where the court eventually awarded Jimmy the primary custody of their two small children. The two toddlers were his pride and joy, and his court battle was arduous. That January, on a brittle cold, snowy night as only Kansas can deliver, he took his children for a visit with Mother, their "Yaya Mary." The snowstorm that raged outside Mother's apartment had strong, biting winds that made large, ice-topped snowdrifts. Mother called me on the phone just after Jimmy left to take his children home.

"Cathy," she said weeping, "it broke my heart to watch Jimmy trudging to his car through this storm. He was carrying baby Christopher in one arm and holding little Jacque close to him with the other. He fell into the snow and pulled both children down with him. Somehow, he managed to get up, brush the children off, and get them inside the car. I closed my eyes and prayed to God, 'Please, please help him!' Oh Lord, Cathy, how in the world will Jimmy manage as a single father? You must promise me that you and Rick will always stay close to Jimmy if anything happens to me. Promise me."

I promised, but neither Rick nor I needed to promise; it was a given that we would watch over our younger brother; we loved him; we were Millers.

Jimmy was born a clone of Daddy. It was impossible not to love him. Rick and I were more father and mother to Jimmy than brother and sister. We learned to be his parents while we were still children ourselves. Mother, ruled by fear and guilt, always saw the future like movie previews that ruined the movie by showing too much. Rick and I shared this cinematic way of visualizing life with our mother; it was just that Mother's movies were always Irish tragedies that featured Daddy, Rick, Jimmy, and me in the leading roles.

After convalescing in the hospital from her distressed third birth, Mother and Daddy brought baby Jimmy home to Rick and me. "He is my most beautiful baby of all of you!" she said to our waiting faces and outstretched arms. Daddy was so happy about the birth of his newest son that he nicknamed Jimmy twice "Reed because he was long and thin like a blade of grass and "The Kid" because Daddy knew this baby was to be their last child; he knew the Hank and Mary Miller family was as complete as it would ever be. I knew it too.

ℒ

CHAPTER FIVE
WOODLAWN AVENUE

The time our Miller family spent in our Woodlawn house was too brief, though we were there for ten years. The five of us had enormous, even embarrassing, love for one another. We had our language adapted from listening to my father's way of talking about life. A person didn't fall if he lost his equilibrium, Daddy said, "he took a dive." Words like "large" or "huge" didn't exist, only Daddy-words, "giant" or "gigantic." People didn't die; they "kissed off." We didn't make a mistake; we "blew it!" I was raised in a family of gigantic exaggeration. Every Sunday evening, when Daddy started the charcoal fire in his Weber barbecue, he used so much gasoline that there were deafening explosions with flames so high the neighbors ran to their windows to be sure World War III hadn't started.

Some people couldn't get enough of the Millers; others didn't know how to take us, while still others ran away, often as fast as they could. We were intimidating, sometimes crazy, and often a moody family, but we cared about each other. Bad dispositions and pouting were not tolerated in our family. Daddy would say, "Put a smile on your face or go to your goddamn room! An attitude like that deserves a hard slap!" Those remarks would scare people who heard them when they were visiting, but Daddy never scared any of us. The feigned military sound of his voice just made us laugh. All those threatening orders in our Miller's language boiled down to three things: "Go to your room, find your sense of humor, then report back!"

We were a family of big and tall people, except for Mother, who insisted she was also big and tall but was nothing close. Normal-sized people liked it best if we sat down to have conversations because their necks ached less from looking up when talking to us. Our family was sensitive over almost anything and everything, except for Mother, who was pragmatic. I was the only hypersensitive member, followed distantly by Daddy and Jimmy. Rick was more like Mother in temperament; he was only self-conscious about his weight, but then, so were the rest of us. No doubt, though, all the Millers responded intuitively to each other's vibrations. Mother used to whisper, "If any of you kids get diarrhea, do *not* say the word out loud, or your father will immediately get it too!" My hypersensitive triggers were so apparent that many family issues were not shared with me for fear I would cry or fall into depression. Everything in our family was done with love, even when it was done clumsily, seemed scary, or ridiculous to others.

The depth and source variations of our Miller affection for one another were confusing for me as I grew up. Mother's affection came from her fear that if we were not tough enough and non-emotional, then harm would come at us from all sides of life. Her words and tone were usually harsh. Rick's affection came from his forced roles as our family's oldest son and replacement father; his communication often came as dutiful warnings rather than gentle, brotherly advice. Jimmy's interactions were always playful and happy; I never doubted how much he loved me; I was his sister, even if I had to be maternal with him.

There was a pressured urgency about everything said and done to show love in our Miller house, so many mixed messages in our efforts that it felt like a burden on me, as the middle child and the only girl, to provide the glue needed to keep us stuck together; I had no energy left to love myself. My family was a personal mystery to me. Recollections of our Miller family time together unlock secrets as to why I took a gigantic dive into suppressed maturity in my thirties on my way up the adult ladder.

My brothers and I still talk about when we lived in our Woodlawn house. I was invited into the house in the early 2000s when my husband and I went on a road trip through Missouri. We parked outside and looked at the front for a while. I wanted him to see the place that held many of my family's stories. "Can I help you?" the current owner asked when she drove up beside us, returning from an errand.

"I lived in this house from 1954 until 1964," I told her.

"Well then, by all means, please come inside and walk through it," she invited.

The house proper was the same but much smaller than I remembered. The present owner was the third family to own the house after my family sold it. All the subsequent owners made additions to the home, but the place I lived in was still complete. The longer my husband and I walked through the house, the more my childhood giddiness melted into adult melancholy, and the more my remembrances of my family's time there seemed built on nostalgic re-imaginings. I kept thinking, how did all five of us live in this tiny house and not fall over each other in every conceivable way?

My husband and I thanked the owner for her generous hospitality and returned to our car. I realized as we drove away that it was never the house I loved so much, but it was the last place where all five of the Millers lived together simultaneously.

My parents bought the Woodlawn house in the late summer of 1954 for $17,000. They learned the basement was built during the Civil War and that two houses burned down to the basement between the war's end in 1865 and the 1896 construction of the structure they bought.

Our street was in a neighborhood where everyone watched everyone's children. We crossed people's yards when we played hide and seek. Nobody got mad. We played kickball in the street and moved aside for passing cars. Nobody cared. We played kick-the-can until dark. Nobody got in trouble. If anyone did something wrong, that child's mother knew before her child returned home. Children were safe on Woodlawn Avenue in the heart of Webster Groves, Missouri.

There were oak, maple, sycamores, birch, dogwood, and redbud trees on Woodlawn and throughout Webster Groves. On a rainy spring day, every street in town dripped with pastel colors; each yard was a Monet painting. Falls were fiery fairylands of explosive oranges, reds, and golden yellows, the season, a virtual kaleidoscope of colors. People burned their leaves in the streets then, and the smoldering sweet smell of mixed woods and foliage cast an autumnal spell over children. We raked large piles of leaves on our front lawns and jumped into them repeatedly. We made wax paper-stained glass by pressing the colorful leaves between two sheets of wax paper, ironing them together, and hanging them in our home windows. We built leaf forts and castles on weekends and played in those until dusk. The early evening shadows helped us make beds where we nestled down into the cold, damp leaves with our friends and made-up stories, all the while fearing the inevitable call of "supper's ready!" and the homework that awaited us for school the next day. It felt like a bazillion hours before we could play together the next day.

Magical glass-like ice storms settled over Webster during the winter. Hilly yards around the houses became tiers of crystal bushes and trees that glistened and sparkled from the frozen droplets that clung to them like diamonds. Woodlawn had the best sledding for miles when it snowed enough that school was canceled. Rick, Jimmy, and I played in the snow till we were soaked, and Mother made us come inside. We stripped off our ice-covered mittens, leggings, and socks and put them on our large steam radiators throughout our house to sizzle until the smell of hot wool announced they were dry. Sometimes it took until both *Howdy Doody*, and *Wranglers Club* were over on television before our faces and hands lost their chapped, frozen redness.

Our house on Woodlawn was a small, square gray house. The front of it looked like a face with two windows for eyes above the front door of a mouth. The house felt huge compared to our little yellow house on Grant Road. Our "new" house had two stories and a screened-in porch with a deck on top of it that was hooked to Mother and Daddy's bedroom. The scary basement had thick, rough walls and skinny gray wooden stairs wound up to the speck of a hall landing on the first floor. There was an outside entrance with medieval-looking stone stairs that led down to the exterior door of the basement. Beside the door to the left were a shower and a toilet that jutted rudely from the wall. There were no enclosures for these; they were added as soon as indoor facilities became available. The realtors explained to my parents that they were there for the "hired help."

The basement was petrifying to me as a little girl. The twisty wooden stairs descended into the basement's cold darkness and increased my fear of it. We had no dryer, so Mother had to go down to the basement to hang wet clothes on the makeshift cords that curled around and through the wooden rafters when it was too cold to hang clothes on the outside clothesline. One afternoon while Mother was slinging towels over the cords in the basement, she heard enormous wings flapping, not tiny wings like those of an insect. She saw a large shadow fly through the rafters and circle around her head.

Mother ran screaming up the rickety stairs to the tiny hall and slammed the door. Jimmy and I were watching television in the living room and ran to the closed hall door to be with Mother. "Ricky, Ricky," she yelled. "Rick, come here right now!" The second Rick arrived, Mother opened the basement door, pushed him onto the landing, handed him a broom, slammed the door behind him, and locked it. "There is something down there! Don't even think about coming back up here until you kill it!" Mother bellowed. I had never heard my mother call my older brother Rick before that moment. Next, we heard Rick thrashing and cursing in the basement and then knocking on his side of the door.

"Here it is!" he said proudly, showing Mother, the dead bat on a dirty dustpan.

"Jesus, Mary, and Joseph! Take that filthy thing outside and throw it in the garbage!" Mother said. No thanks were awarded to our family's shaking pubescent hero, but once again, he came through for us and was never called Ricky again.

Our house had large side and back yards dotted with dogwood and redbud trees. I loved looking at them in the spring out the windows over the kitchen sink. Our even larger front yard had oak trees with trunks so thick it took four children to hold hands and stretch our arms around them. An old horse trough sat on the front porch where Mother planted bright red geraniums in the summer, her only gardening effort each year. One Halloween, we went to visit Daddy in the hospital because he was having unstoppable nose bleeds, and Mother put a sterling silver tray filled with candy on the horse trough. Though one greedy trick-or-treater might have taken off with all the candy, nobody took the sterling silver tray. On the left side of the front porch was a single set of stairs and a raised rock flower bed full of juniper bushes that made me break out with crimson blisters if I got anywhere near them.

We had a mysterious front door made of heavy dark brown wood. It had a rectangular medieval-looking smaller door that served as a window built in the middle of it. We opened it when someone rang the doorbell. We could see the entire person, head to toe, standing on the porch. Two flights of cement stairs on the right side of the front porch crisscrossed down to a long, narrow cement sidewalk that twisted and turned down to the street. My father loved slapstick humor and liked to look out the front door window in the winter and watch Rick's guy friends slip and slide down the icy sidewalk to the street when they left our house to go home. Daddy laughed even harder if they slid the whole way on their "behinds."

Our house was small, but on the day we moved to Woodlawn, I saw our home through the rainbow eyes of a child; it was my protective castle, where I was safe with my family and not yet afraid of a single tomorrow.

CHAPTER SIX

WHERE IS GOD THE FATHER?

Mother enrolled Rick and me in Mary Queen of Peace Parochial School in the fall of 1954 before our moving boxes were unpacked in our house on Woodlawn. It was only a few blocks from our house, but Mother drove us to school because it was "too dangerous for you children to walk the sidewalk beside busy Lockwood Avenue." She did not want us to miss the first day of school. Mary Queen of Peace parish church and school contained three gray-white cement block buildings. The center circular building was the church, the small rectangular building to the left was the rectory and the larger rectangular building to the right was the school. Rick was in the second grade, and I was in morning kindergarten.

Sunday mass at Mary Queen of Peace intrigued me when I was five. First, I saw everyone cross themselves with holy water and genuflect before going into the pew to sit down. Once Father came out to say the mass, much movement began. We stood, kneeled, sat, stood, then sat again, etc. I grew tired, bored, and restless throughout the service.

"Mother, when will everybody make up their minds about what we are supposed to do?"

"Sssh," she warned, "no talking, Tatter, just do what I do, or we will have to sit in the cry room."

The cry room was for babies; I didn't like the thought of going there. I was a big girl; Jimmy was the baby, and he was at home. "The only reason you get to sit in church with me," Mother said, "is because you have to obey me." Rick was lucky; he was already in Catechism class. What I couldn't know was that I would spend the next thirteen years of my life in Catechism classes and church for mass every Sunday and all Holy Days of Obligation.

When I did get there, Catechism classes taught me about sin, a lot of it. Sin was everywhere. It was a sin to eat meat on Friday, so we ate tuna pot pies, fish sticks, salmon cakes, and macaroni and cheese. After confirmation, if I did not abstain from food for one hour before communion, that was a sin. According to the Catholic Register's rating system, it was a sin to see a movie rated B, or even worse, C, because those ratings meant the movies were sins for me or condemned sins for me if I saw even one second of them. Everything was "banned." The word terrified me; it was a word that conjured panic before I knew what it meant entirely. *Banned!* No other word was more horrifying.

I had to consult the seven deadly sins before going to confession to be sure I had not committed any of them. Confession was frequent and an absolute must before the Holy Days of Obligation, like Christmas and Easter. People who didn't go to communion had sins on their souls and were forbidden to go to communion on Sunday. They had to sit down while everyone else went to communion. To me, that felt like broadcasting that they were sinners who neglected confession or did something even worse.

Before I confessed, I thought hard about my sins and knew the exact number of days since my last one. I didn't want to bore the priest who heard my sins; I felt terrible for him sitting in his little closet to hear sin after sin from people. I rehearsed in my mind what I prepared to say whenever I entered my side of the blonde confessional with three doors. Once, I could not think of any sins, so I made some up, but when I came out of my closet, I knew I lied and that lying was a sin, so I was right back to square one and got right back in line to confess again. The one thing I knew for sure was that I did not want to be repetitive for Father, so the temptation to make up exciting sins was a constant problem for me. I wanted my sins to be unique and new for him.

It was stressful to wait in line to confess, but inside the confessional booth was no better. I knelt on the hard kneeling bench and waited for Father to finish hearing the sins of the person on the other side of him. I had to plug my ears because if I listened to a single word of talking or mumbling from the other sinner, that was also a sin. The second he slid open my window with the holes in it, I whispered, "Bless me, Father, for I have sinned! It has been two months, three weeks, and four days since my last confession. Father, since that time, I yelled at my younger brother three times, said the word, hell, once, and had angry thoughts toward a boy in our neighborhood two times. I am sorry for these sins and all the others I have committed." Then, whatever priest was behind the window spoke to me.

"Make a perfect *Act of Contrition*, my child.," he said. This was a severe part of confession. I had to mean every single word, or my whole prayer was canceled in the eyes of God. I didn't know how, but somehow, God told the priest if my sincerity was real or fake.

"Oh my God, I am heartily sorry for having offended thee. I detest all my sins because of thy just punishments, but most of all, because I offended thee, oh my God, who art all good and deserving of all my love. I firmly resolve with the help of thy grace to sin no more and to avoid the near occasion of sin." I got in trouble during my first confession for saying, "hardly sorry" instead of "heartily sorry."

I got lucky in some of my confessions over others. If, when the window slid back, and Father Cooper was behind it, that was proof that God had already answered one prayer for me. Father Cooper was my favorite priest. Father Cooper was our youth priest at Mary Queen of Peace; he was kind, young, and handsome with strawberry blonde hair and sparkling white teeth when he smiled. Even the smell of alcohol when he spoke didn't bother me; he still looked just like Richard Chamberlain on *Dr. Kildare* on television. My penance from Father Cooper was always three prayers, three times each: the *Hail Mary*, The *Our Father,* and the *Glory Be* prayers. Those were easy for me to memorize because they were like little poems.

"Go in peace, my child, and sin no more," Father Cooper whispered if my confession was successful. I always believed Father Cooper was rooting for me. But if Father O'Toole, the oldest priest in our parish, was behind the confessional window, that was a different story. His penance was five recitations of each prayer *and* the *Nicene Creed*, sometimes up to three. The *Nicene Creed* was so long that I never got through it once without having to look it up in my prayer book. I never could memorize it, even though we said it aloud in mass every Sunday. I mumbled fake words if I didn't have my prayer book when the congregation stood to recite it. At the end of confession with Father O'Toole, he said, "Go in peace," but I never thought he meant a word of it because he always left off the "my child" part.

The link between mother and child is an unconscious, mysterious connection. Like all children, the emotional, incessant energy I required as a child from my mother needed no questioning. It was obvious. There was only one person I called Mother. But the idea of calling priests "father" was on my mind even at five. I wondered why I had to call priests "father." They weren't my father; Daddy was my father. "Well, they stand in for God the Father on earth until we can be with Him in heaven," Mother said, "All the people in the pews are God the Father's congregation, Cathy, like a family, and the priests are the head of our congregation family, just like Daddy is the head of our family at home."

"But they don't take care of us like Daddy," I told her. "They don't buy us groceries, bring me surprises, sit on my bed and kiss me goodnight."

"They take care of our church needs, so we call priests 'fathers' out of appreciation and affection," Mother answered. "They are essential to us; priests baptize us when we are babies so we can go to heaven, and they say the last prayer we will ever say when we are old and are about to go live with God."

"How about all the time in between?" I asked.

"All that time, too," Mother said. "Children and grownups need fathers all our lives. They help us avoid bad things and remind us to say our prayers and love God."

"Well, okay," I said. "I will call them Father, but I will never call them Daddy, no matter what anybody tells me." I sat rigid and straight beside my mother at mass for thirteen years until I left for college in 1967. Prayer books and holy cards in hand, we sat side by side in the fourth pew on the left of the broad, green marble center aisle facing the altar. We wore white lace doilies bobby pinned to our heads, though sometimes Mother wore the Kelly-green velvet pillbox hat I bought from Lamberts Department Store for one of her birthdays. Mother and I heard Daddy's laughter boom across the church from the choir loft on Sundays when my Father did grace the Lord with his presence. He liked to goose Rick and Jimmy in front of him on their way up the staircase. Mother cringed each time she heard Rick yelp, "Quit it, Dad!" immediately followed by all three of them laughing.

"Your father!" she whispered to me and shook her head.

Daddy stayed in the Catholic Church after he converted and married Mother. Father Eihlers was his favorite priest. "I love Father Eihlers; he is a real man of God," Daddy said. "Father Eihlers is worth a hundred other clergymen in any faith." My father drove all over St. Louis to see him for confession when Father Eihlers was sent to other parishes. I wondered if Daddy did that because Father Eihlers understood all his reasons when my father didn't go to church. Once a week for 50 minutes, 52 weeks a year, Catholics sat, stood, knelt, and heard the same 52 parts of scripture, plus the ones used on the six Holy Days of Obligation. Absences from church for no good reason were a mortal sin if you weren't sick. "Father Eihlers understands I am mortal," Daddy told us.

Most Sunday mornings, just like the Norman Rockwell painting of the father cowering behind his newspaper as his family marches out for church, my father sat at home at our kitchen table in his pajamas and robe with the Sunday Post-Dispatch newspaper spread out in front of him. "I'll cook breakfast while you guys are gone," he said. "I'll heat the Straub's gooey butter coffee cake and make Jones sausage when you get back." We never left him there a single time without his adding, "and hey guys, say one for me!"

Daddy, Rick, and Jimmy left early during Holy Communion when my father went to church. They sneaked down the choir loft stairs and out the side door. Mother, devout in her post-communion prayers, never showed if she noticed. I noticed, though, because it was an eternity between communion and the benediction before we could leave.

I passed that time while Father cleaned his chalice and communion trays by studying the circular sanctuary and all fourteen-carat gold frames on the Madonna-blue walls. Each frame held photographs of the Pope in white and gold regalia or contained colorful, thick oil paintings of the Apostles and Jesus. I counted the beautiful, large stained-glass windows depicting the suffering of Jesus at each Station of the Cross. Outside on top of the green slate roof of our church stood a life-sized, gold Virgin Mary who greeted parishioners and our growling stomachs wanting breakfast upon our arrival, and she watched over us when we departed for home.

The Ecumenical Council in Rome during the 1960s told priests they could turn around and look at us; until then, we only saw their backs during mass. Father O'Toole's Latin was so hard to understand that I didn't try. I hypnotized myself with the rays of sunlight that streamed through the stained-glass windows and danced across the marble floor. I liked the beautiful gold and white Irish lace that draped the altar, but high above it was the life-size statue of Jesus. His face was full of pain as He hung from a massive marble cross. The sorrowful look on His face hurt me to look at it. The blood that dripped from the nails in His hands and feet upset me. That He went through all that agony for me made me feel guilty and sad.

At five years old, I understood why I could not see any images of the Holy Ghost. Except for Casper, I knew all other ghosts were invisible. I could not account for the whereabouts of God the Father; there were no material representations of Him. Where was He? I determined that God the Father was outside, that the colorful rays of light that streamed into the church and bounced curious patterns on the floor were His way of asking me to let Him inside. It was years later before I learned what God the Father was saying to me when I was five, but until then, I only sat in Mary Queen of Peace beside my mother and wished He would come inside and sit on the other side of me.

I was always cold in church. Summer, winter, spring, and fall, no matter the season or year, I wore a sweater in church and believed that if God the Father would come inside our church and sit beside me, I would always be warm.

♄

CHAPTER SEVEN
KINDERGARTEN

It was equally cold inside Mary Queen of Peace School during my kindergarten year. Sister Gertrude Marie was my teacher, demoted from teaching high school to the lower grades because she was getting too old to handle the older kids. Sister Gertrude Marie did not like children of any age. I lived for recess. The church parking lot was our playground. If time got away from Sister Gertrude Marie, we got to play with kids of all ages, but if it didn't, we were marched directly back to our little kindergarten classroom with the heavy metal door.

Sister Gertrude Marie stared at us with squinty, gray eyes behind the steel-rimmed frames of her glasses. The scowl on her face and the threatening edge to her cackling voice scared us. We stifled fears and sniffles on the backs of our prayer hands or the sleeves of our sweaters when Sister Gertrude Marie's heavy black shoes clumped down the aisles between our chairs. We knew when she was coming behind us because we could hear her swinging rosary beads clang together on the front of her habit.

One morning during snack and rest time, Sister Gertrude Marie placed our red and white checkered, oilcloth placemats on each desk. Patrick James Callahan got so eager for treat time that he pounded his fists on his desk. Patrick sat across the aisle from me and jittered in his chair until the graham crackers and milk reached him.

"Patrick James Callahan," Sister yelled, "sit still this second!"

"I can't, Sister, I try, but I can't," he said, "I'm hungry."

"Fine then. Today, you will not get any snacks at all! Put your head down on your desk, do it now!" she barked. Patrick had dirty blonde hair in a choppy haircut, and his uniform was always wrinkled. He was sweaty and smelled terrible when he came inside from recess, a combination of dust and sour milk.

"Sister, I gotta go potty," Patrick said, keeping his head down while the rest of the class ate our crackers and drank our milk. Sister Gertrude Marie ignored him. Then, squirming in his seat, he raised his hand and said, "Sister Gertrude Marie, please, I have to pee-pee." I put my head down on my placemat; I knew what would happen.

"Patrick James Callahan, you know this is not how you are supposed to ask to use the lavatory. You sit right there until you ask properly, and then I will tell you when you can leave," said Sister Gertrude Marie.

I heard the dripping sound and then smelled the yellow puddle under Patrick James Callahan's chair. He squeezed his crotch with both hands, squirmed, and cried. I cried too. A few boys in the class giggled and pointed when they saw what happened, and Sister Gertrude Marie became even angrier.

"Patrick James Callahan, you bad boy! Look, class; look at what Patrick James Callahan has done! Shame on you, Patrick James Callahan!" Sister Gertrude Marie jerked him out of his chair and said, "come with me right now! The rest of you put your heads down on your desks!"

After Sister Gertrude Marie yanked him from the classroom and the heavy metal door slammed, everyone was silent. I felt my heartbeat, my eyes stung, and I saw the tears drop beside my milk carton onto my placemat.

After a few moments, the door opened again, but a gentle voice spoke, "Children, you may sit up now." Sister Barbara Ellen was at the front of the room with a mop and a bucket. Her young, freckled face smiled, and her clear green eyes shone. "While Sister Gertrude Marie takes care of Patrick, why don't we take out our Baltimore Catechisms? Would this week's star helpers collect the placemats and pass the trash basket for the milk cartons, please?" We dutifully raised our desks and took out our green Catechisms as Sister Barbara Ellen mopped under Patrick's chair. "Now, Sister Gertrude Marie says you are on chapter two. Why don't we begin by reviewing chapter one? Books closed everyone. First question. Who can tell me who is God?" Every hand flew up in the air, but she called on me. "Yes, Catherine Claire Miller, will you tell us?"

"God is the supreme being who made all things," I said as I stood beside my chair and wiped the tears off my face.

"Good!" Sister Barbara Ellen said. "Word for word, what does that mean?" My head hurt from crying, and I was worried about Patrick, so it was challenging to think of an answer.

"I guess, does it mean God made you, Sister, and that God made me, and that God made all animals and well, that God made everything?"

"Correct. Well done. You may sit down, Catherine."

"But Sister," I asked before I sat down, "does that also mean God made Sister Gertrude Marie, too?" There was an inhaled silence.

"Yes, my dear," Sister Barbara Ellen said and walked to the metal door, peeked out of it, and closed it again. Then a miracle happened. Sister Barbara Ellen turned around and looked at the entire class. Her green eyes crinkled at the sides, and then she laughed. She laughed so hard that some of her red hair sneaked out from beneath the Cornette of her habit. Soon all of us looked at each other without knowing why we laughed long and hard along with Sister Barbara Ellen.

"Yes, Catherine Claire Miller," Sister said finally, "God made Sister Gertrude Marie, too!"

It was the only time our entire class laughed together all year.

ℒ

CHAPTER EIGHT
HEROES AND HEROINES

The Walling family lived in the house across the street from us on Woodlawn. Mr. Walling was in the worst battles of the Japanese theater in WWII. Mr. Walling was a quiet but cheerful man who waved to Rick and me if we were playing in our front yard when he came home from work. Mrs. Walling was beautiful and pregnant the whole time they lived in their house. Their oldest child was Lori, one year older than I was. Winnie was younger, followed by Kirk and, eventually, Evan. Lori and I played together outside whenever her parents worked in their yard. We became friends despite our different years in school.

Mrs. Walling liked to read like my mother. One afternoon I noticed she was reading *The Carpetbaggers*. She wanted to drink iced coffee in a freezing cold, turquoise metal glass while she read. I picked up the book one afternoon when she left the den to check on dinner cooking in the kitchen. I opened the book to a random page. It was nothing like the books I read or my mother read! This was my first time reading anything explicit about sex. I found it so titillating that I read more pages every time Mrs. Walling left the room. I paid more attention to all the books Mrs. Walling read after that.

Mr. Walling's job moved his family to Park Ridge, Illinois, when I was ten. I took the train to visit Lori for two weeks that summer. My father gave me a letter to read on the train for my first trip to go anywhere by myself; he knew I was scared to death.

Dear Tat,

I bet you are excited to visit Lori! You two girls will have so much fun, and you will get to swim in Lake Michigan. Don't be afraid. You are growing up and will be taking lots of trips in your life. We will all miss you while you are gone, especially me! Tell the Walling family hello from us. I will be here on the platform waiting for you when you come home.

Love, Daddy. XOXO

The visit could have gone better. Lori and I had lots of arguments. "Be silent." I learned from watching my mother that I needed to be silent when I was angry or if my feelings were hurt. "Your mouth can get you in trouble, Cathy, so hold your tongue when you get angry," she told me, "be silent."

I gave Lori Mother's silent treatment during our fights. I countered her smart Alec remarks with, "No comment!" Mrs. Walling sided with Lori every time; she told Lori to say mean things to me like "Cat got your tongue?" or "Are you deaf or just dumb?" I could not run across the street to my house like I did when problems happened with Lori on Woodlawn. Instead, I counted the endless fourteen days and repeatedly read Daddy's train letter until I took the train back home.

"Did you learn anything about Illinois when you were there?" Daddy asked. I told him about Abe Lincoln, how Springfield was the capital, and how I swam in Lake Michigan and went shopping on the Miracle Mile. I didn't tell him that I also learned to stop standing up for myself and hide my anger or hurt to keep everyone else happy.

I didn't tell Mother about our fights during my visit; I just told her I didn't want to visit the Wallings again.

"Cathy," Mother said, "Lori has a scar from a congenital disability that worries her mother. Lori had a disability when she was born called a cleft, but it was repaired at birth. However, the doctors could not fix the small scar between her nose and mouth. Mrs. Walling is sensitive to people who might be mean to Lori about it, so she tries to protect Lori's feelings from being hurt."

"Oh," I said, but I still did not understand why Mrs. Walling was mean to me. I never called Lori a name or called attention to her scar; she was my friend, and I never even noticed it. "Okay, Mother," I said, "but I still don't want to visit them anymore."

Bristol Grade School was a public school my father attended when he was young. Mother moved Rick and me from Mary Queen of Peace to Bristol after my kindergarten year. "Public schools teach children how to live in the real world, not like Catholic schools or boarding schools," Mother told us, though eventually, we learned public schools were free. Rick and I had many of the same teachers Daddy did at Bristol, even our principal, Mr. Nowlin, was the same principal Daddy had too.

Rick and I walked the twelve-plus blocks every day, not uphill both ways in the snow, but rain or shine, cold or hot, whatever the season, we walked. Rick usually ditched me for his friends, so I walked most of the way to Bristol alone. "See ya later, Claire," Rick said. He loved to tease me by calling me by my middle name, though oddly enough, I liked my middle name best. Most mornings, he went with Jake Fox, an odd-looking boy with dark curly hair and a large, flat mole on his neck. Mickey Zandermeister was one of Bristol's bad boys who joined them when they passed his house at the top of Woodlawn and Rockhill. Micky had blonde hair, snapping blue eyes, and a loose mouth. My older brother was chubby with strawberry red hair and more freckles than we could count, and we tried to count them on one arm once, but neither of us knew what number came after nine hundred and ninety-nine.

Rick, Jake, and Mickey were often in trouble at Bristol during Rick's first year there and continued to build their reputations during the others that followed. One day during our first year at Bristol, their antics occurred in the boys' bathroom. Mr. Nowlin called Daddy and told him to come to Bristol as soon as possible. The story went that Daddy arrived last, and Mr. Fox and Mr. Zandermeister were already waiting outside Mr. Nowlin's office.

"Are all the fathers here?" Mr. Nowlin asked his secretary from his office door.

"Yes sir, they are all here," she said.

"Then have them come in."

Inside the principal's office, the boys sat in a row against the wall and faced Mr. Nowlin at his desk. A growling Mr. Nowlin sat down and addressed the three fathers, "Gentleman, I am very unhappy with the behavior of your three boys. It was reported to me that these young men urinated over the dividers between the stalls in the boys' bathroom today. I have disciplined them, but I think you, fathers, must also pursue this matter at home." Mr. Fox and Mr. Zandermeister were embarrassed and glared at their sons, but Daddy just tried not to laugh.

"Yes sir, I will," Daddy said, forcing a stern face. "I am extremely disappointed in you, Rick Miller. You know better."

"Agreed," said Mr. Fox said to Mr. Nowlin. "Jay, this isn't over," he said to his son.

"Fine," said Mr. Zandermeister to the principal. Then with angry eyes flaring, he said to his son, "Mickey, you will not like what is going to happen to you at home, bud."

Rick and Jake fell silent and looked down at the floor. Mickey Zandermeister smirked.

"Boys," Mr. Nowlin said, "go outside and wait for your fathers." The boys filed out of the office, and Mr. Nowlin shook hands with each man before he left. "Mr. Miller," he said, "please wait a minute; I want to talk to you."

"Of course," Daddy said in absolute obedience.

Once Daddy and Mr. Nowlin were alone, Mr. Nowlin said, "Good Lord Hank, I haven't had that kind of bladder pressure for fifty years!"

"We had a good belly laugh over the whole mess," Daddy said each time he told this story, and each time I heard it, I thought, wow, boys love their penises. I also wondered which of the three boys thought up the brilliant idea of peeing over stall dividers and which two were dumb enough to be pressured into doing it. Boys baffled me in many ways.

I was a measly first grader at Bristol when Rick and his cohorts were big third graders. It was one of the last days of school in May when I learned that bad things and good things could happen simultaneously.

I did not mind walking to Bristol alone. I never needed to create an imaginary friend to walk with me because I relied on my romantic imagination to transform me into heroines, like Sheena, Queen of the Jungle, on her way to safari camp instead of school. I wandered through backyards with white stone walls, flowerbeds, and lavish green shrubbery beneath cathedrals of trees. My inner drama queen always took over. One of the many yards I walked through to shorten the distance to school belonged to the Collins family. I needed to squeeze between the side of their chipped gray garage and a splintery fence to access my passageway to cross their yard. Once through, my Sheena character conquered the rest of the jungle's treachery with long-legged ease.

The Collins had a special needs child, retarded was the word used in the 1950s. Her name was Lassie, and she was in the first grade with me. Lassie was the first child, or adult, whom I noticed differed from everyone else. I wondered why God didn't make her perfect like everyone else.

"Why is Lassie different?" I asked my mother. "What happened to her?"

"Lassie is perfect, just how she is," Mother answered. "Something just happened when her mother was pregnant with her when Lassie was inside her mother."

What? I thought. "You mean all the mothers who have babies inside their tummies could have a baby like Lassie?"

"Yes," Mother said, "but you don't have to worry about it." But I did worry about it.

Lassie's mother drove her to school, and one day, my jungle escapades came to an abrupt halt a block before reaching Bristol because I heard boys' voices laughing and calling her names.

"Here Lassie, here Lassie, here girl!" The voices yelled, mimicking how Timmy called his dog on the *Lassie* television show. In the distance, I saw the back of the Collins' wood-paneled station wagon pull in front of the school. Lassie left the car from the front passenger side and walked into the second-grade entrance as her mother drove away. Mrs. Collins was too far down the street to hear the boys' whistling and dog calling. I ran as fast as possible, hanging on to my jiggling book bag and red plaid lunch box, but I was too late. Lassie heard them and ran crying into school. She didn't understand their words, but she did understand their belittling tone; there is a specific sound to childhood cruelty that is impossible to miss. I turned to see whose voices they were. I saw Jake and Mickey and then Rick. It was as though I got punched in my stomach, and the wind was knocked right out of me. I felt my anger grow white hot on my face.

"You guys are all jerks, big fat, stupid jerks, and I hate you!" I screamed as the three cackling cronies disappeared all palsy-walsy inside the fourth-grade entrance. The bell rang just as I reached my classroom and slid into my seat.

"Saved by the bell, Cathy Miller, you were almost late!" Mrs. Palmer said. "Please try not to dawdle on your way to school."

"Yes, mam," I said from my back seat beside the row of old, peeling, painted windows. I looked over at Lassie across the room. She had no tears; there was no sadness on her face at all. She smiled, hummed even, and opened her pink Sky King pencil box. I sat for a moment and watched her. My heart was still beating hard, and I was still angry, but Lassie's mood was happy. I did not understand why she did not retain the pain and insult in her mind for more than a few moments. I decided she was blessed with the saintly virtue of forgiveness that I certainly did not possess that morning. Either way, the mean behavior of the boys was no longer harming her, only me.

I was still fuming as I walked home that afternoon. I thought about Rick and his friends. My brother was no hero to me that morning, and I wanted Daddy not to call him that anymore! I had as many thoughts as I had steps toward home and tried to sort out my emotions about the day's events. I was too young to know about the power of male peer pressure. I knew that girls could be mean to each other with words and that boys could be mean to each other with their fists, but it was the first time I discovered boys could use words to be mean to a girl.

That night I asked Daddy what he thought about the matter.

"Tatter, boys, are human and make mistakes just like girls," my father said.

"Can they still be heroes if they make mistakes?" I asked.

"Absolutely. All people make mistakes. The important thing is to apologize and not make the same mistake again," he added. "Boys need to learn to be kind just like girls do."

That settled it for me. Rick was my big brother. He helped our family every time he was asked to help. I loved Rick; he was a great brother to Jimmy and me. I decided I needed to forgive him just like Lassie did. I would not unmake our family's hero in my eyes or anyone else's. It was a good decision, and the many years ahead proved it.

Mother came into my room the night after the day's insults toward Lassie. I was in bed, and her arrival surprised me; it was something she seldom did, unlike Daddy, who never missed a night. Most nights, Mother went to bed before the rest of us, but that night she came in after she got home from Bristol's end-of-the-year parent/teacher conferences. I put down my book, sat up, and leaned against my brown metal headboard to look at her. She squeezed by the foot of my bed and sat on the cedar box under the window that faced the front of the house. She looked tired and unhappy, sitting there with her hands folded in her lap.

"I love going to see your teachers for conferences, Tat. You never give me a moment's worry. "Tonight, your teacher, Mrs. Palmer, said, 'I don't even have to ask who your child is, Mrs. Miller. You are Cathy's mother.' Tat, you never give me a minute's worry," Mother repeated, and then got up and left my room.

If Mrs. Palmer was saying I looked like my mother, I missed the compliment, but I understood my mother's message to me: I must never give my mother a reason to worry; her life was hard enough. She needed a heroine, and I needed to be perfect.

A new family of heroes and heroines moved next door to us in the late summer of 1955. Where the Harold Milton family lived on one side of our house, the Charlie Cordeal family moved into the house on the other. Milton's house heaved with sadness; it was a house absent joy and musicality and radiated dark forces that bounced between pain and punishment like a metronome. The Charlie Cordeal family's house was just the opposite. There were no five-foot walls around their property like the Milton's, just a chain-link fence surrounding a backyard full of children and a black Labrador named Pee Wee. Pee Wee dug holes under the fence to pay daily visits to my mother for treats, and the Cordeal family bubbled with laughter; their chatter and music spilled through their windows into ours.

There were four children in the Cordeal family, and Mrs. Cordeal was expecting a fifth baby when they moved to Woodlawn. Mary was the oldest, born in 1950, followed by Jane in 1951, Michael in 1953, and John in 1955. They were a good Catholic family. Mr. Cordeal was the organist at Mary Queen of Peace and taught piano and organ lessons in his studio inside their house. Over the years, the Cordeal family proved to be the type of neighbors people write about when praising the good old days.

I did not recognize that I was really a girl until I met Mary. She told her mother she wanted to play with "the little girl who lives next door and wears a white coat." Mary was a year younger than me and was my first loyal girlfriend. We never had fights as I had with Lori. Mary was a beautiful little girl, half my height, with thick dark brown hair, huge brown eyes, and pinker cheeks than any doll ever made. Mother said, "Mary is sugar, spice, and everything nice." One time Mother offered Mary a piece of lemon candy from Grandma Kelly's gold-trimmed Havilland candy jar that sat on our side table between two light brown brocade chairs in the living room. "Mary," Mother said, offering her the candy, "I swear you are wearing tons of rouge. You will never need a bit of rouge during your life, not even when you're older."

Mary loved my father. She could not keep from giggling around Daddy, and he knew how to keep her giggles going. Daddy and Mary were the last connection between our two houses during the year's warm months. Mary shared a room with her sister, Jane, on the second floor over their kitchen window. Their windows faced the doorway to the sun porch attached to my mother and father's bedroom. Mary stayed up late at night studying at her desk when school was in session. She was the last to go to sleep in her house. Her single desk light was visible to Daddy from the doorway. Daddy was always awake watching war movies on his portable television set while Mary was doing her homework. Daddy, a lover of fresh air, kept the door to the sun porch open until Mother said she could see her breath and demanded he shut the door for the winter. Sometimes, Mary was still slaving away when both Daddy's Late Show and the Late, Late Show were over.

"Goodnight, Abe," Daddy called to Mary out the screen door, "Now, Abe, don't burn that midnight oil all night. It would be best if you had your beauty sleep. And don't let those bed bugs bite!"

"Goodnight, Mr. Miller," she giggled back. "I won't."

Mary and I watched Shirley Temple movies together and played with our Shirley Temple dolls. We listened to Frank Sinatra's records in her bedroom and tried to learn the latest dances on American Bandstand when we were in our living room. We roller skated in her basement and played school together in my bedroom. Female relatives in her family gathered old dresses and jewelry and put them in a trunk for us to play dress-up. Mary and I became a variety of fascinating women. We walked to Velvet Freeze on Lockwood Avenue for ice cream, jumped rope, and played hopscotch with Jimmy and the other Cordeal kids on their blacktop driveway. Rick was seldom around, usually with his friends, but when he was around, Mary blushed from her crush on him. "I can't talk when I am around your older brother, Cathy," she confided. "He makes me so nervous!"

The Cordeals had a tire swing in their backyard; one afternoon, Rick was sitting on the tire and swinging. "Come sit up here with me, Mary, and swing with me," Rick said. When she saw him staring at her, Mary told me she froze.

"Oh Cathy, I nearly fainted," Mary said. "I climbed up on his lap but couldn't say a word while we were swinging; my heart was beating too hard in my throat!"

Charlotte Peters had a local television show and lived in a contemporary purple and pink house behind the Cordeals. The Peters had a rope they let the kids in the neighborhood used as a swing. It was a different kind of swinging experience from the tire swing. It was much more dangerous and much more fun. Two kids who lived on Belview Street broke their arms while riding on the rope swing. Rick loved Charlotte Peters' swing. He slid the rope over his head, put it under his arms, and then ran until his feet left the ground. He flew high over the Peters' creek bridge and circled in the air until his feet touched the ground again. "Rick is the best at the rope swing!" Mary said while we sat on the dusty ground to wait for our turns.

I loved Mary's father as much as she loved mine. Mr. Cordeal loaded his children, Jimmy, and me into their Country Squire station wagon and took us to either Katz Drug store or the Central Hardware store. Mr. Cordeal did something funny on every one of those trips. He did many silly things to make us squeal with laughter. He put a Playtex Bra on his head or a toilet seat around his neck.

On Saturdays or Sundays in the fall, the Cordeals invited Jimmy and me to their family gatherings at her grandparents' country home in nearby Eureka, Missouri. Mr. Cordeal loaded us into the Country Squire again for the short drive. We sang *we're all going to the country in the Country Squire with the bumpy tire!* Mr. Cordeal kept us singing merry songs until we arrived. Mrs. Cordeal and her parents, whom Mary called Pop-Pop and Ging-Ging, never failed to make Jimmy and me feel welcome.

Mrs. Cordeal's dinners at the country house were delicious. She made steaming pans of lasagna, spaghetti, and other Italian foods oozed with cheeses and spices. There were enormous bowls of ice-cold vegetable and fruit salads, stacks of buttery garlic bread, and always homemade fudge brownies, lemon cakes, or Boston cream pies. Jimmy and I were in heaven eating something different from the gag-worthy spaghetti our mother made with tomato juice, one pound of hamburger, ketchup, and a large can of Franco-American spaghetti.

Mary and I lived for the weekend to play together. Mary went to Mary Queen of Peace, and since I went to Bristol, we barely had an hour to see each other after school, but we made sure that every minute the two Woodlawn musketeers were together counted. The loneliness and hurt feelings I received from Mrs. Walling, Lori, and smart alec neighborhood boys disappeared when I was with Mary and the Cordeals. My previous sorrows got filed away somewhere in my young, tender psyche when they moved next door to us, and I hoped never to feel them again.

ø

CHAPTER NINE

NEIGHBORHOOD DETECTIVE

There were two windows in my tiny, pink-painted room. The one that faced the front of the house and the one that faced the side yard and the Milton house. Harold and Florence Milton had three children when we moved to Woodlawn. Marvin was a four-year-old special needs boy with thick dark blonde hair. His two-year-old sister, Betsy, had light blonde hair and was a cute baby. They were followed later by a chubby baby boy named Andy, born a year after Betsy. Florence Milton's parents, Mr. and Mrs. Otterman, lived in their house too.

I was only inside the Milton house once. I had to take my shoes off when I entered the kitchen door. The cement block walls made it cold inside, especially on the cement floors, and there was not a single rug anywhere. There were no curtains on the windows, and the overgrown bushes outside them made all the rooms dark. The smell in the kitchen was sour and pungent from foods I didn't recognize. All three children slept in the same room; it was so crowded that there was no place to play in their room. My closet of a bedroom at home felt spacious in comparison. I thanked Mrs. Milton for my visit when I left, and as I ran home, I suspected that visit was the only time I would be inside their house.

Our family knew Mr. Milton best because Monday through Friday nights were the same. The minute Mother, Rick, Jimmy, and I sat down for dinner, Mr. Milton came to our house "for his liquid courage," as Daddy called it. Mr. Milton never knocked; he just came up our backstairs and into the kitchen where the four of us ate on weeknights around our oval gray and white Formica table. Daddy ate later those nights because he was "doing business deals" with clients that I later found out were poker games or cocktail hours with his buddies at the Chatterbox Bar. My back was to our backdoor in our crowded kitchen whenever I was seated at the table. Each night I heard Mr. Milton's heavy feet clump up the stairs behind me.

"Good evening, Miller family," he said over the top of my head before he crossed between the refrigerator and Jimmy to my left. Next, he squeezed between the stove and Mother's chair across from me to the liquor cabinet behind her left shoulder. Mr. Milton's body odor, stale cigarettes, and earlier glasses of courage followed him like Peter Pan's shadow. The smell overpowered Mother's horrible Tuesday nights' bland and beige menu of boiled-to-death bay leaf chicken, celery, onions, and rice.

In front of the kitchen sink, Rick first said, "Hi, Mr. Milton," followed by me, Jimmy, and Mother. We greeted Mr. Milton clockwise. Mr. Milton was different shades of brown all over. Besides his dark expression and brunette hair, he wore a daily uniform of dark brown suit pants, a dingy-white wrinkled shirt, and a lighter brown, also wrinkled, paisley tie. He was a skinny man who snaked through our kitchen five nights a week to get to his brown bottle of bourbon. He got a glass from the shelf below the liquor bottles, shimmied again behind Jimmy, and swung the freezer door over Jimmy's head to get ice before squirming back to his liquor bottle again. Mr. Milton's bourbon bottle had the words *Harold's Bottle* written boldly in Daddy's printing on the adhesive tape Daddy made as a label.

"Hard day at work today, Harold?" Mother asked, not looking up, knowing Mr. Milton was directly behind her.

"Not as hard as going home," he answered over her head.

Then our dinner conversations got quiet. We all stared at our blue and white plates with the windmills of Holland beneath our food. The only sounds came from the silverware scraping our plates and the ice clinking in Mr. Milton's drink. After he drained his glass of every drop, Mr. Milton placed his glass in the sink and put his bottle back in the cabinet.

"Well, gotta face the music next door," he said and snaked back to the door. "Thanks, Mary. Night kids," he called over his shoulder as he clumped back down the stairs to walk across our yard to whatever unhappiness awaited him that evening.

"Poor Mr. Milton," I said.

"Yeah, poor Mr. Milton," Jimmy said.

"Poor Harold," Mother said.

"Yep," Rick said.

The outside of the Milton house was dirty-white stucco. It was a split two-story house about forty feet from the street. Their home was separated from their neighbors on the other side by an equally dirty-white stucco wall about five feet high with broken bricks that toppled off the top. The front access to their house was a crumbled stone walkway from the street to their front door. The Milton's garage in the back was a distance away from their house, like our garage was from ours, but theirs had an apartment built over it, which was where Mrs. Milton's younger brother, Maury, stayed from time to time. Maury was not there often. He was a bald man who wore a sad smile and had several black moles on his face. A gravel path from the garage led to Milton's back door past an open trash barrel that smoldered twenty-four hours a day and a dog pen for Cleo, their Basset Hound.

One Friday afternoon after school, when Mary was helping her mother, I got out my detective notebook and went around our neighborhood to see if there were any crimes I could investigate, like Nancy Drew. I poked and peeked into lives foreign to me, searching for plots and actions like those in my growing collection of her books. The Milton family and their house held great mystery for me. Except for Mr. Milton, the family members were like characters in a book or faceless silhouettes moving about their lives. But that Friday afternoon, not only did the members of the Milton family become very real to me but so did others.

I changed into my play clothes and celebrated the start of the weekend by eating two slices of cinnamon toast soaked in Land o' Lakes' butter. I put my dish in the sink and went outside to go sleuthing. I began at the Milton house. Their front yard was barely alive even during green and grassy Missouri spring weather, but on that late fall afternoon, it was worse; there was no way to sneak up on their house with the crackling and snapping of the yard beneath my feet.

In my detective notebook, I wrote that *Milton's yard is creepy evidence, probably like what goes on inside their house. It is a battle between what has already died and what needs to die.* The dead Juniper bushes did not scratch me that day and give me red welts. I made sure not to have any physical signs of sleuthing for Mother to see when I got home. That day I was protected from her wrath by high-water blue corduroy pants and Rick's hand-me-down long sleeve yellow flannel shirt. Mother's words of discipline from one of my summer detective days echoed in my mind. "Look at your arms and legs! You are not sleuthing, Cathy; you are snooping! Stay OUT of Milton's yard. Their children are too young to play with you anyway," she said.

The falling leaves on the knotty branches of the half-dead Elm tree forbid my access to the rusty doorbell, but I gathered my courage and ran to the porch. A shadow moved to the window and opened it a crack just before I rang the bell.

"What do you want, Cathy Miller?" the voice cackled.

"Oh, hi, Mrs. Milton," I whispered. "May the kids come out and play?"

"No! Not now! Get back in your own yard," she said and slammed my plan and her window shut.

I sat on the curb for a few minutes before I went down to the end of our street by Lockwood Avenue to look for another mystery. The corner house on the same side of Woodlawn as our house was where Richard Johnson lived. "Richard, like Lassie, is a special child," Mother told me. "He goes to a special school, and when he is at home, he stays inside his house where his mother and father take care of him. There are many special people in our neighborhood, and the church tells us to be nice to everyone, especially those less fortunate than we are." My father told me that my mother learned to be friendly to those in need from Grandma Kelly, who fed hungry hobos and bums during the depression when they got off the trains behind her house on Lockwood and knocked on the family's back door.

"Your Grandma Kelly served them anything she was cooking in the kitchen when that happened. She handed them plates of food through the door, and they ate on the steps of the Kelly back porch."

I looked at Richard Johnson's house and admired the bright green shutters against the clean white house paint. Yellow is my favorite color, but I would settle for any color, though green ones are probably the best. I wrote, *wish we had shutters.*

I crossed the street and stood in front of the house on the opposite corner. This house was hidden behind a gray cement wall with little window holes. I was sure there was a crime lurking behind that wall, but before I investigated further, I heard more summer words from Mother in my ear.

"Don't go in their yard, Cathy; they are a retired couple who don't like other people very much."

"Why don't they like people?" I asked. "Aren't people nice to them?"

"Some people are, like you and me, but others are not as understanding. The couple who live there is Japanese. The Japanese were one of America's enemies during World War II. Though the war was over before you were born, some people cannot forgive, so they are often cruel. It's not right, but it happens in real life."

Not, right? It was downright mean. I knew little about World War II, but I knew my heart would hurt if people were mean to them; I learned that from Lassie. My mother always talked to me like I was thirty, no matter how old I was. Daddy said she did that because I was the only other female in our house, "Your mother gets lonesome, and women need to talk to each other a lot," he said.

I heard a swishing sound from the shiny red and yellow leaves that peeked over the wall. I pulled on the branch and hoisted myself up to the top. To my delight, there was a garden with more colors than my giant-sized crayon box. A waterfall sprayed sparkling water droplets onto mossy rocks around a small pond. The garden was ablaze with gold, bronze, and purple chrysanthemums blooming between copper-colored trees and crimson bushes. I wrote, *this yard is more beautiful than any garden in Mother's magazines, maybe more than any book I ever read, except for The Secret Garden.* A large stone sculpture of a happy little fat man sat in the middle of the pond. I deduced I was not on Woodlawn but in an enchanted, faraway land.

"What are you doing, little girl?" an angry voice said.

I looked down into flashing eyes behind round metal glasses. The man wore a short green jacket, cropped, baggy, tan pants, and a straw hat with a string pulled tight under his chin. "I was just looking at your pretty garden," I told him and hopped down from the wall onto my side.

"Yes, well, you've seen it now, so go home. Go home, little girl," he said.

"Yes sir, I will," I said through one of the window holes. I wanted him to know I was one of the nice people. "But sir, I love your beautiful garden; thank you for letting me look at it!"

I ran up the street and stopped in front of Mr. Grant's abandoned house across and down a bit from our house. Rick and his friends called Mr. Grant's "the haunted house." I sat down on what was left of the rock wall around his front porch to catch my breath. I wondered what mysteries Mr. Grant's house would tell me if it could talk. I noted in my detective notebook that *Mr. Grant's house is falling apart, and I don't think it can be fixed up again.* I walked onto the slanted porch and peered through one of the dirty windows. The thick, rippled glass was broken in several places. I wrote that *Mickey Z probably broke all these windows with rocks.* The inside of the living room was visible from the dim rays of what was left of the day's sunlight. The dirty, dusty house was empty, yet it wasn't. The wallpaper was shredded from multicolored glass bottles thrown in rage against the walls. I had goosebumps and sensed why all the boys thought it was haunted. The carpet bled red, spotted all over from jagged hobnail tumblers crushed beneath bare feet. "The guy was a murderer," the boys told me, but I did not believe them. I saw lightning bugs dance in Mr. Grant's front yard on summer nights.

I remembered that Daddy told me one night when he sat on my bed, "Mr. Grant did not live long after World War II." I turned around and looked across the street at the happy face in front of our gray house. I was glad it smiled at Mr. Grant's old, converted barn that once housed what Daddy called "a broken man."

"Mr. Grant was an alcoholic, Tat; he drank too much. He was severely wounded in the war, pierced not just by weapons but by the sharp shards of his memories," Daddy said. "In many ways, the inside of Mr. Grant was more damaged than the inside of his house."

I looked down and saw my shadow had grown longer while I was on the front porch of Mr. Grant's house. It was time to go home. I crossed the street and ran up our driveway to my backyard. I looked at Milton's house again and determined I might still have a little more time for detective work. The Milton family had no backyard, just a pile of large, chunky, and chalky rocks surrounded by a chain-link fence with sharp, pointed places that jutted out from where links were cut or rusted. Cleo moaned inside her too-short doghouse on top of the rocks. The acidic stench of Cleo's yellow existence floated across the driveway and reached me. At night in my bedroom, if my window was open, I heard the sad, frequent flapping of her ears from the bottle flies that continually buzzed around her head and bit her. I wrote, *why would anyone have a dog only to keep it on a chain outside all day and all night, even in the winter? Why do they even have Cleo? They never let her in their house! This is a crime; I know that for sure!*

I watched Cleo drag her long chain, clang her empty feeding dish, and try to flip it against the fence, just when Mrs. Otterman banged through their dented metal back door. I jumped and ran to the corner of our garage to hide. I watched her dump table scraps and curse words over the fence. "There you go, you damn filthy dog," she said and went back inside the house. Mr. Otterman passed her on his way out of the house with the trash.

Mr. and Mrs. Otterman were not dwarfs but seemed like them next to my family members. I was already several inches taller than both. Mr. Otterman had big brown spots on top of his bald head that matched the smaller ones all over his broad hands and strong arms that poked out of his gray work shirts when his sleeves were rolled up. Mrs. Otterman wore a tight bun on the back of her head, like a cluster of Brillo pads with loose wiry hairs that kinked around her sallow face. Mrs. Otterman's huge swollen breasts swung over her doll-size waist, and when she walked, she had balloons for hips that bobbed up and down beneath her dark flowered dresses.

The metal door slammed again. Mrs. Otterman came back outside, holding a tiny pink trash can. "Stop! Stop, old man!" she yelled. "You forgot the bathroom can!" She had a fingernail-down-a-blackboard sound to her voice that sent shivers through me.

"Yes, old woman, I see that," Mr. Otterman said. Mr. Otterman's thick Jewish-German accent made it hard to understand him. He threw the contents of the can into the trash and lit a fire. Both stood and stared into the blaze. I was close enough to see Mr. Otterman's ice-blue eyes squint from the heat of the burning trash. The fire grew so intense that it became intolerable for me to stay hidden; the fire crackled and popped, and the heavy smoke and ash blew toward me. I ran from behind the corner of our garage and made a B-Line toward our back porch, but Mrs. Otterman saw me.

"You! Come here. Come over here right now, Cathy Miller!" she screeched.

"Come here, Fraulein," Mr. Otterman said. His much kinder tone gave me the confidence to walk back to them. "Now, were you spying on us?" he asked.

"No sir, I wasn't," I lied.

"You want to snoop and stare at people, do you?" Mrs. Otterman said, her beady eyes fixated on me. "Then, Cathy Miller, you stare at this!" She yanked up her sleeve and thrust her left forearm toward me. "Now go home, you rude girl, and ask your mother to explain what these black numbers on my arm mean! Go on! Leave us be!"

I started to cry, turned, and walked toward our house. I had no idea what I was looking at on her arm. I climbed the stairs, went into the kitchen, and hid my tears from my mother, who was taking a casserole out of the oven. She set it down on the top of the stove and turned around to look at me. "Cathy," she said, "what have you been doing?"

"Nothing. I was playing outside," I mumbled, washing my hands at the sink.

"Well, set the table for dinner." I did as I was told.

"Tat, did something happen while you were outside?" Mother said, still watching me.

"No, mam, I'm just tired from the week at school," I answered, hoping that would end the interrogation. I was saved by Jimmy and Rick, who thundered down the stairs and plopped into their chairs at the table.

"I hate tuna casserole," Jimmy said.

"No meat on Fridays," Mother said.

"Phew! What is that horrible smell outside? Jimmy asked.

"Dad says it is Mrs. Otterman burning her old brassieres," Rick volunteered and made Jimmy laugh.

"That's enough, Rick," Mother ordered. "You say the grace."

"Yes, mam," Rick said. "In the name of the Father, the Son, and the Holy Ghost. Bless us, oh Lord, for these thy gifts which we are about to receive, from thy bounty, through Christ our Lord. Let's eat. Amen."

Daddy came in and sat on my bed that night as usual. "Anything you want to talk about tonight, Tatter?" I didn't know why, but I felt shame about what I did after school and what Mrs. Otterman showed me on her arm. I couldn't talk about it, not even with my father.

"No, Daddy, I'm tired; I'm not even going to read tonight," I said and looked at my new Nancy Drew book beside me.

"Okay honey, sleep well; tomorrow's Saturday. No school! Let's crack open your windows a little, Tatter. I can smell winter coming. There won't be many nights left that are warm enough for us to sleep with fresh air," he said and opened my window facing Milton's house.

We didn't play our Chicago game that night. Daddy made a funny face in my doorway, sucked in his tummy, and made his pants fall past his boxer shorts to his slippers.

"I love you, Daddy," I said as he pulled up his pants, blew me a kiss, and went back to his room to put on his pajamas and watch another war movie.

I heard Cleo wailing next door and wondered if she was still hungry. I was glad we didn't treat Candy, our Beagle like the Miltons treated Cleo. I rolled over on my stomach, propped my chin on my windowsill, and peered through the window at the Milton house. Mrs. Milton banged through the back door and started yelling. Mrs. Milton loved to yell, especially at six-year-old Marvin.

"Did you wet your pants again, Marvin, you bad boy? Did you? Did you?" she screamed.

"You are such a bad boy! You stay outside like Cleo. You stay out here all night until you learn not to wet your pants. That's what you get until you learn!" I heard the back door bang again.

"No, Mommy, no," Marvin sobbed. "Mommy, please, please, no!" he begged and pounded on the door with his fists, arms, and head. I watched him cry and didn't even notice the tear that dropped on my windowsill. This was one of only three times I remember calling for my mother after I was in bed.

"Okay, Tat," she said. She closed my window and clicked on my reading light. "I want you to read the new Nancy Drew book I brought you. It looks like a good one. Goodnight."

Marvin's cries were muffled, but I still heard them; his door banging softened, but I still felt them. I hurt all over when I heard Mrs. Milton spank him and Marvin bang on their back door again and again. The noises grew louder as though they were coming through my wall, and Marvin was crying in my room. The front of my nightie and the cover of the Nancy Drew book also grew wet. I looked up at my doorway and saw Mother dialing the phone on the hall table just outside my door.

"Hello. Yes. This is Mary Miller on Woodlawn Avenue. I want to report my neighbor, Florence Milton. She has locked her young mongoloid child outside for the second time; the last time, I am afraid he was out there all night. Please come and check on him. His name is Marvin. We live on your right side at about the middle of the street if you come from Rock Hill Road. You will hear him crying and banging on his back door. Yes, please come right away." She put down the receiver and leaned against the door frame.

"Mother, what is a mongoloid child?" I asked.

"Well," she answered, "it is a child who never ages in his mind. Marvin will always be a little boy; his brain, in some ways, may never grow past five years old," she said. "But, like Lassie and Richard, Marvin will be happy most of his life because their brains don't hold on to bad things that happen for very long. It is hard to understand, but Marvin is probably the happiest person in that house; he is one of God's sweetest children. Now Tat, read your new book; everything will be fine in a few minutes."

I stared at my ceiling through blurry eyes, hoping to find the answers to all my questions that day. I stared until the flashing red light in front of the Milton house flashed through my windows and moved across my pink walls. When the red light disappeared and Marvin was inside their home, I got out of bed and cracked my window open again. The air was cooler; I smelled winter coming, too, just like Daddy said.

Back under my covers, I picked up my book and looked at the cover, *The Clue of the Velvet Mask*. I slid the book under my bed, where I kept my detective notebook. I no longer wanted to read Nancy Drew books anymore; I was not cut out for detective work.

I clicked off my light, rolled onto my side, and let the wall-to-wall quiet of our Miller house comfort me. It would be five years before I learned what the black tattoo numbers were on the arm of Mrs. Otterman. But that night, I learned to stop snooping into other people's lives. More important, though, I realized I was proud of my mother. I closed my eyes, and in my prayers, I promised God I would spend the rest of my life making my mother proud of me.

⌀

CHAPTER TEN

GOLDEN SUMMER OF CHAOS

In the early summer of 1960, we got Max, our dachshund, after Bill the Milkman ran over Candy, our beagle, in May. Candy got off her chain in our backyard. "Bill the Milkman and I cried this morning over coffee," Mother told me when I got home from school. "Bill cried and cried; he couldn't stop saying he was sorry. He said that Candy just raced out of nowhere and ran beside his truck, that she jumped in front of it before he could stop." Mother's eyes were bright red from crying. "I never got Candy to stop chasing cars, no matter how hard I tried to keep her in our yard. It was my fault, not Bill's."

My mother loved animals "more than she loves people," Daddy said. "Your mother would hit a tree and kill us all if it meant she could avoid harming a squirrel in the street." My mother and Bill the Milkman sat at our kitchen table and had coffee twice a week when he came to deliver our milk. He was a cheerful, kind, older man, and I thought he brightened Mother's mornings when we were at school. I was glad I didn't see him cry the day he ran over Candy. It was hard enough to see the tears in my mother's eyes and choke back my own when I got home. I was sure Bill the Milkman's sorrow would have broken my heart completely. Our whole family loved him.

Our Miller war with the bugs happened in late June. I discovered the invasion one night after midnight. I had finished another Happy Hollister book and hid it with my flashlight under Grandma Kelly's pink chenille bedspread. The World War II movies in Mother and Daddy's bedroom were over for the night, and everyone in the house was asleep, even Max, who slept on an old towel at the foot of Mother's bed.

I discovered the bug invasion happened because I couldn't sleep. I knew I would be in trouble for being awake because I was always in trouble for being awake. I closed my eyes to say my prayers but was too hungry to pray. I sneaked downstairs to the kitchen. I flicked on the light in the kitchen, and the entire linoleum floor moved; the floor was alive with giant, black water bugs that clicked and collided together. They raced for cover under the stove, refrigerator, and sink. I stifled a scream on the back of my hand like Fay Wray in *King Kong* and then slapped off the light. I ran up the stairs, afraid to arrive in my bedroom with bloody stumps of legs and missing feet. I ran for my life and was identical to the scrambling, terrified people in the nuclear horror movie, *Them!*

No matter how tired I got, I forced myself to stay awake all night. I tried to distract my fear with another book, but I felt *them* down there, in the kitchen, growing to giant sizes, gathering their army together, ready to crawl all over me; their babies wanting to tickle my skin and twitch inside my ears. I was positive that if I dozed off for a second, at least one of those ugly bugs would climb into my mouth and wiggle down my throat. They knew I was an open-mouth drooler and snorer from adenoids and tonsil problems. I prayed aloud, "God, please save me!"

The next morning Mother came to my doorway to wake me. I sat up and looked at her. I was no longer sitting straight up in bed but lying on my side, face on my pillow, book and flashlight beside me. I failed in my decision to stay on watch.

Mother did not believe my detailed report about the water bug onslaught in the kitchen. "Really Cathy, such an exaggeration! You see far too many movies and read much too late at night." Right then, something tickled my face. I thought it was the ties of my Moulin Rouge scarf to cover the orange juice cans I used for hair rollers and brushed it away. But it wasn't! I jumped out of bed and flicked my cheek. Two water bugs flipped onto my bed and scampered under Grandma Kelly's bedspread.

"I told you!" I said, crying. Mother started the screaming.

"Hank! Dear Lord, call the bug man!" she yelled.

"Bugs? Where?" Daddy called from downstairs in the kitchen.

"Everywhere! They are everywhere! They are in Cathy's bed!" Mother continued to scream, "Call the bug man! Call the bug man! God knows we can't afford it but call him Hank right now!"

"Jesus H. Christ!" Daddy yelled up the stairs, "I'll call them! I'll call them!"

"Rick, Cathy, Jimmy, all of you come here right now!" Mother ordered us into the hall that connected our bedroom doors like the center of the legs of an octopus. We just stared, mouths open; Mother's usual creamy face was bright red, and her hazel eyes were on fire. "You will not, under any circumstances, ever eat anywhere but in the kitchen! Do you hear me? Do you?" Rick and Jimmy nodded obediently, but I still cried; I felt the water bugs crawling across my face.

The bug man arrived that afternoon. I immediately thought he was far too handsome to be a bug man. He was more handsome than the photographs of movie stars I sent away to Hollywood for the previous winter. He was more handsome than Dr. Ben Casey or Dr. Kildare on television or even Charlton Heston in his short purple and gold *Ben-Hur* tunic. The bug man smelled like the best parts of summer, fresh lemonade and homemade ice cream. He was friendly, too; he let me follow him while spraying "zap juice" inside and outside our house. I read his name stitched in red on his gray workman's shirt. Mother taught me always to say people's names whenever possible. "It is a way to validate people," she said.

"Jack," I said in the kitchen, "why do we have so many bugs?"

"Well," he said to help an eleven-year-old understand, "we had so much rain in St. Louis this spring, the Missouri and Mississippi Rivers overflowed their banks. The ground remained so moist that the bugs kept laying eggs and made more bugs." On our second floor, I asked the bug man two more questions.

"Can you kill them? All of them? "

"I sure will," he promised. Jack was so handsome that I believed in his promise. "Is this your room?" he asked.

"Yes, it is the smallest room except for the bathroom off the kitchen, but there were bugs in my bed."

"Really? It is a terrific room. I like your big desk," he said to steer me away from the memory while he sprayed behind the secondhand desk that took up half my room. "Your desk looks like the one the president has in the White House, only his is brown wood, and yours is blonde. I bet you do lots of important things at your desk, too," Jack said and then stopped to smile at me for a moment.

I felt my face redden. Something happened inside of me. It was my first time to feel that girl-tingle from a real man, not just when the movie cameras faded to the fireplace when men and women kissed on television. "Wow! Look at all these books," Jack said; "who reads all these books?"

"I do," I whispered.

"Good for you," he said and winked at me. "You know, you never have to be lonely if you can read. There's always a friend waiting inside the cover." Mother might have been the one who told me that, but I wanted it to be Jack.

Jack was my first real man crush. I liked Jack, the bug man who talked to me while he sprayed "zap juice" into the corners and baseboards of my room. I was suddenly happy we had so many water bugs that Daddy needed to call him.

We went back downstairs after he finished upstairs. Daddy was waiting with his checkbook. Mother, Rick, and Jimmy were at Lambert's Department Store buying new sneakers that Mother said would be "another horrible expense."

"Guess that will do it, Mr. Miller," Jack said and handed Daddy the bill. Daddy bulged his eyes, slapped his hand to his forehead, and pretended to be in shock.

It was a good thing Jack's name really was Jack because Daddy called every man Jack when he had to pay for something. "Good God, Jack! Thirty-five dollars?" Daddy asked, moving his hand over his heart. "Is that even with my coupon, Jack?"

"Yes, Mr. Miller, you see, that coupon expired," Jack answered.

My father loved coupons almost as much as S & H green stamps. He clipped them out of the Globe-Democrat and the St. Louis Post Dispatch, morning and evening editions. Mother said, "Your father would buy one shoe if he had a coupon."

"I'm sorry, sir; I just can't accept that coupon anymore," Jack said. This was the part of all transactions when Daddy talked about the army.

"Well, Jack, I'm fighting a goddamn war against those goddamn bugs right here in this house, a war just as bad as WWII! Do you guarantee your work, Jack, for thirty-five dollars?"

"Yes, sir, we stand by our work. Just call the number on the bill, and I'll come back if you have more trouble."

"How often can I call?" Daddy asked and flashed his best smile. Mother said Daddy had perfect white teeth like Gregory Peck. Jack flashed his best smile back at Daddy, and I felt that tingle again.

"Okay, Mr. Miller, Ollie the Barber warned me about you. Thirty dollars. I'll give you the coupon deal but don't tell anyone else in Webster that I did."

"Good man. You gotta deal, Jack," Daddy said. He gave Jack the check, clapped him on the back, and exchanged the coupon for a receipt. We walked the handsome lemonade-smelling bug man out the backdoor, down our crooked back porch steps, and across the yard to our gravel driveway, where his truck was parked with a gigantic green plastic bug on the roof. Daddy and I waved to Jack, the bug man, as he rolled down our long driveway, turned right, and disappeared down Woodlawn toward Lockwood.

"See that, Tatter, no more reason to be afraid; we have no more bugs," Daddy said and grabbed my hand. "We've got a thirty-dollar guarantee that all we will see now are dead soldiers." I hoped dead soldier bugs might not scare me as much as live bugs.

That night Daddy sat on my bed and told me one of his war stories, how a huge hairy tarantula crawled up his leg in a cave in France while they were laying pipe. It was a good try to temper the horrors of my bug experience, but it did not work. That night I kept looking under my sheet and a's bedspread for the ones that didn't die. I don't remember if I did that out of fear or more out of hope that we might need Jack to come back again.

Daddy was right; each day of June, Mother found fewer and fewer dead soldiers. She made Rick sweep them up and carry them in a dustpan to the big trash barrel behind our garage or dump their bodies into the black wrought iron garbage can buried in the ground at the bottom of the back porch stairs. "I hated that job almost as much as when Mother locked me in the basement with that bat," Rick told me. "It was another sickening job having to carry all the dead soldiers to their mass graves."

Jimmy hid a few more enormous corpses in a wooden matchbox and buried them in his sandbox inside the pen Daddy built because sometimes Jimmy bit other children in the neighborhood. Mother made him bite on a bar of soap, but when that did not cure the problem, Mother had Daddy put up the pen. "Whenever I hear a child cry somewhere in the neighborhood, I run to the window to see if Jimmy is still in his pen!" Mother said. Jimmy's matchbox friends were safe in the sandbox inside Jimmy's pen, but when he took them into the house one night, Mother found them the next day when she used her dust mop under his bed.

The thermometer on our back porch climbed higher than ever by the first of July that summer. The intensity of the heat created a constant argument between my parents about the living room air conditioner, the only air conditioner we had in our house. "Good God, Mary, we need to eat in the dining room where we can at least get the overflow of cool air," Daddy said.

"You only have dinner with us on the weekends anyway, Hank; it saves us money on the electrical bill for the kids and me to eat in the kitchen!" Mother said.

The hot, steamy 1960 St. Louis summer imprisoned all of us within the close quarters of our house, and though Mother would not admit it, the weather made her edgier than usual. The sweltering heat felt like God threw a heavy wet army blanket over us. Typical family irritations multiplied; everything became an argument.

Daddy never told Mother what he spent on anything; it was his fruitless strategy to reduce their tension. He sometimes told Mother he won things, like the new television set he never won in their bedroom. Other times Daddy used his "bought one and got one free approach." Those secrets he sealed with me with a wink.

"Why in heaven's name do we need sixteen bottles of mouthwash, Hank?" Mother asked one blistering day in the kitchen as she took four bottles of Lavoris, four bottles of Listerine, and four bottles of Scope out of the Kegel Drugstore bags. "We don't have enough money for groceries, but we sure have the cleanest breath in Webster!" Mother's sarcasm toward all of us could ooze under closed doors, but it upset me most when directed at my father.

"Judas Priest, Mary, Kegel's had a buy one, get one free deal this weekend on dental products; these bottles will save us money in the long run!" Daddy said before he escaped through the kitchen's swinging door into the semi-air-conditioned dining room.

On the Fourth of July that summer, Daddy found coupons in the newspapers for free wall-sized American flags with every fill-up at the Mobile Oil station in Webster. "I come here all the time, Bobby," he told the attendant while Jimmy and I watched from the back seat of whatever car Daddy drove home from whichever car dealer he was working at the time. "The Millers are patriots, Bobby. I need three flags with this fill-up, one for each of my kids."

"But Mr. Miller, these are enormous flags; one flag per fill-up is the rule."

"Oh Bob, give them to him, will you," said Bobby's boss coming out of the office. "Hank Miller will wear you down until you do."

"Thanks, Jerry," Daddy called out the window and turned the car around with Jimmy and me holding onto the three giant American flags. Daddy put them across our laps with their poles sticking out of our windows on both sides of the backseat. Bobby tied oily yellow cloths to the ends so my father wouldn't get arrested.

"Go straight home, Hank," Jerry yelled. "Don't drive far like that; it's dangerous!"

"Okay!" Daddy called out his window. We drove out of the station and headed in the opposite direction from our house. Daddy turned around in his seat to check on Jimmy, and I draped in red, white, and blue in the back seat, and then called out his window, "God bless America, Jerry! Happy Fourth!"

"Now, kids, what we need are some greasy burgers and fries from White Castle!" Daddy told us. White Castle was miles away from Webster, off the highway. "I am counting on you guys to hold on to those flags!" We went from thirty miles per hour to sixty-five in an instant.

All three of us filled up on the tiny White Castle burgers, stringy fries, and milkshakes in their parking lot while Jimmy and I clutched the huge flags the whole time we ate. We held on to them for over an hour and a half by the time we drove up our driveway. "Now, kids," Daddy said as he parked, "let's not tell your mother, we went to White Castle; it will only make her mad this close to dinner." He looked directly at Jimmy, "This means you, NBC; you broadcast every move anyone makes in this family. Your sister knows how to keep secrets."

It took all three of us fighting them, but Daddy, Jimmy, and I got the cumbersome flags onto the back porch, but their size and length overflowed into the kitchen and kept the screened back door open. "Damnit, we've got to move these fast, or we will let every fly in St. Louis into this house!" Daddy yelled. "Where's Rick?"

It was never a good sign when Mother called Daddy Henry Miller. "He's upstairs playing his pinball game in his room!" Mother challenged Daddy's patriotism the moment we set the flags down. "Where on God's green earth do you plan to fly flags that big, Henry Miller?"

"Rick, come down here and help carry these flags upstairs to our room!" Daddy yelled.

"We are going to fly them off the sun porch, Mother," Jimmy announced, "so everyone in Webster can see them."

"You mean everyone in Missouri," Mother said, glaring at my father. "Just where do you plan to store these, Hank?"

"Yes, well, we'll fly them from the sun porch off our bedroom, as Jimmy said, so it is only logical to store them in our room. Rick, lean them against the wall beside your mother's bed," Daddy said as Rick walked into the kitchen.

"What?" Mother seethed with her hands on her hips and every drop of her Irish blood blazing. And then came the silence.

"It'll be great, Mom," Rick said when he came back to the kitchen, breathing hard from his first two trips up the stairs.

"Yeah, it'll be great, Mommy," Jimmy said to mimic Rick. With still one flag to go, I ran upstairs to read.

"Jimmy, help Rick take the third flag up," I heard Daddy say. A noisy battle ensued when thirteen-year-old Rick and seven-year-old Jimmy fought each other as they took the giant flag up the stairs to the landing, turned it around on the last four steps, and somehow propped it up with the others in the corner beside Mother's bed.

Mother and Daddy were still in the kitchen, not speaking to one another, when I came downstairs an hour later to set the table for dinner. My problem was how on God's green earth I would eat Mother's roast after consuming a bag of hamburgers, fries, and a chocolate milkshake.

Jack, the bug man, cured our water bug problem in June, but in August, we fought the attack of the ants one night, the night Mr. Cordeal and my father became actual neighbors to one another, rather than just two busy dads who waved out the windows of their cars when they passed on Woodlawn. At least two of our American flags flew from my parents' sun porch daily. Part of Daddy's nightly ritual was to furl them up and lean them against the wall beside Mother while she read in bed. The St. Louis heat index in the suburbs climbed well over one hundred degrees with over eighty-five percent humidity when Mother finally decided we could eat our meals in the dining room.

"Just leave them out there, Daddy," Jimmy said.

"Jimmy, we can't fly old glory at night unless there is a light on her," Daddy told him.

"Don't you dare, Hank," Mother threatened when she saw my father light up at the thought.

It was a suffocating night, a stick-to-your-sheet night. Daddy opened the screen door to the sun porch, and we each opened one window in our bedrooms so the window fan on the stairway could draw slightly cooler air into the house and move it around a little. I was in my room reading, wearing my favorite baby doll pajamas I received from Aunt Marylene for my birthday, baby blue ones with yellow daisies embroidered across the front. Jimmy and Rick were wearing only underwear and were sprawled out on their twin beds watching *Have Gun Will Travel* on Daddy's old small black and white portable television he gave them when he "won" the bigger one. Daddy told Mother he also won a transistor radio for me in Mr. Lemcke's Appliance, Television, and Hi-Fi store contest. Daddy told me not to tell Mother but told me there was no contest, and he dickered with Mr. Lemcke to throw it in for free when he purchased the new TV.

Daddy was sitting in his brown recliner the night of the ant attack. He was wearing his nightly summer uniform, paper thin, faded blue boxer shorts and sleeveless tank top undershirt that made him look like a six-foot, seven-inch tropical bird, crane-like figure, all long stick legs, and round belly. Gangsters were having a shootout instead of cowboys or soldiers on his television. Mother was deep into one of her murder mysteries, munching on the Cheez-its she hid in the bottom drawer of their shared nightstand between their beds. Max growled and jerked in his dream of chasing rabbits and squirrels at the foot of Mother's bed as I stood in their doorway. "That dog is more in your mother's bed than I am!" Daddy said to me. Mother had one semi-see-through nightgown, most likely left over from her bridal trousseau from when she married Daddy. It was a pale celery green, and she only wore it on the hottest summer nights. All of Mother's other nightgowns were floral cotton.

Mother's stomach gurgled when she was lying on her back. Almost every night, Rick, Jimmy, and I heard the gurgling sounds in Mother's stomach that were not only loud enough to hear in our bedrooms but were high-pitched ones that led to longer-lasting lower tones before they started all over again. Mother liked to interrupt Daddy's movies each night to ask Daddy questions when she looked up from her books.

"Who is that actor, Hank?"

"James Cagney," Daddy answered and rolled his eyes toward me in the doorway.

"That's James Cagney? I never heard of him," Mother said.

"Holy Mary, Mother of God, of course, you have heard of James Cagney. We've seen a million of his movies. Go to sleep; you need sleep." Whenever someone in our family annoyed Daddy enough, he accused them of needing sleep.

"Are you sure it is James Cagney? Maybe his name is Robert Cagney or Cary Cagney?" she insisted.

"Cary Cagney? Good God Almighty, Mary, you've got to go to sleep. Trust me; it is James Cagney!" Daddy turned around to end their conversation and saw an army of ants crawling in a thick line from the porch door, into the American flags, down the wall, over Mother's walnut headboard, and into the nightstand between their beds. "Jesus God!" Daddy said, loud enough to bring Max to all fours and Jimmy and Rick to their doorway. The three of us were never scared when my father cursed; he loved to curse.

"It is all for show," Mother told us, "Much ado about nothing," Daddy said he needed to curse for emphasis, but nobody else in the family was allowed to swear. "It is a sin to use the name of the Lord in vain!" Mother said. I never understood why Daddy's cursing didn't bother us or anybody else; mostly, it made people laugh. I figured God let Daddy off the hook for that sin since people were not offended.

"What's going on, Dad?" Rick asked.

"A million goddamn ants, that's what," Daddy said.

"Oh Lord," Mother said, jumping up.

Daddy unlatched the screen door and looked at all of us. "You see, everybody. I need to make an example of your mother. This is exactly why she doesn't want us to eat anywhere but the goddamn kitchen! The Cheez-Its your mother keeps in our nightstand have drawn every lousy ant in St. Louis to our bedroom." The army sergeant's tone told us it was every man for himself. "Rick, you and Cathy each take a drawer out to the sun porch. Jimmy, hold the door open for your mother and me to get the rest of the damn nightstand outside. Watch it, Jimmy! Don't let the damn dog out! He'll fall off the porch!" The porch was fifteen feet above the lawn and had only a sparse, white, waist-high railing.

"Daddy, the ants are *in* your American flags, too!" I told him.

"Jesus God," he said, "Rick, get the goddamned flags!" Rick grabbed two and dragged them outside, and I dragged one. We were careful about leaning them against the rickety railing. Once we were all out on the sun porch, Jimmy came out with us. Unbeknownst to all of us, the too-short spring slammed the screen door shut and swung the locking hook inside the door into the locked position. I couldn't balance my heavy flag, which slid onto the porch floor. "Cathy, pick up that flag! Don't let the son of a bitch flag touch the gravel on this black tar paper crap!" Daddy hollered. He took my flag from me and one of Rick's from him. "Rick, bring your other flag over here where I am. Cathy, you and your mother, take everything out of the nightstand drawers and get all the damn ants out of them. Rick, unfurl your flag and shake the shit out of the thing like I am."

My father was a sight to behold in his underwear bird outfit shaking and waving the American flags like gigantic red, white and blue wings. Jimmy went wild, laughing, clapping, and jumping all around us, having a rip-roaring good time getting underfoot. "Damnit, Jimmy, calm the hell down before you fly off the porch and fall nine thousand feet and break your silly neck," Daddy said, sweating profusely and still waving and shaking his flags.

"Dang it, I am missing *Have Gun Will Travel*, Rick moaned while he shook his flag and tried to swat mosquitoes at the same time.

We looked down and across the side yard between the oak trees to Cordeal's kitchen window facing our house. We could see Mr. and Mrs. Cordeal washing dishes after a family party. Mother and I contributed to our cartoon antics by madly scraping and pounding the ants out of the drawers with her hairbrushes until familiar voices penetrated through the hot, humid air.

According to Mrs. Cordeal, she said, "Look, Charlie, look at that, the Millers are conducting some ceremony! They're swinging American flags and beating furniture!"

"Don't stare at them, Mary Ruth; they may be having some sort of family ritual!" Charlie reportedly told her.

"Oh, dear Lord," Mother said, hearing them, "Hank, we need to go in and do this tomorrow. The Cordeals are watching us and think we are crazy acting like this out here at this hour!"

"We are damn crazy," Daddy said. "At least I am going goddamn crazy! All right, damn it, let's go in. Jimmy, get the door, and we'll haul all this stuff back the hell inside." Jimmy pulled on the door handle, but it was locked tight.

"Daddy, the door is locked," Jimmy said with legitimate fear.

"What?" Daddy yelled. "Who locked the goddamn door?" he demanded, testing it for himself. "Jesus God, we can't stay out here all damn night; we'll be eaten alive by these mosquitoes."

"Dad, Mr. and Mrs. Cordeal are in their kitchen," Rick said. "Maybe they can help us."

"Oh Lord, Hank, no," Mother protested, "I am in my nightgown and curlers!"

"Hell yes," Daddy told Rick. "Hey!" he called to the Cordeal's window. "We sure could use a little help up here!"

"See, they're ignoring us," Mother said and cringed behind the branches of one of the oak trees.

"Hey, you! Mr. and Mrs. Cordeal!" Daddy yelled louder.

"Lord help us," Mother prayed into the leaves.

"Yes?" Mr. Cordeal called out his window.

"We seem to be locked out of our house. Do you think you could come over and come inside and let us in?" They must have whispered because we couldn't hear them.

"Of course, Charlie will," said Mrs. Cordeal with a degree of caution.

"How do I get in?" Mr. Cordeal asked.

"You'll have to take the dining room screen off the window below us and to your right, then open it and crawl through the window; that would be the best way," Daddy said. All the doors are locked, so be careful you don't bust your behind falling over the chair under that window in the dark. Also, a wiener dog is in the bedroom, but Max is harmless."

"I'll do my best, Mr. Miller," Mr. Cordeal said.

"I may as well be naked," Mother said, "and look at you! Oh lord, what's worse, you've never even met Mr. Cordeal!"

"Forget that, Mary!" Daddy said. "Let's just get the hell back inside the house so we can all go to bed!"

Mr. Cordeal did just as Daddy asked. We fell in line behind Daddy when we heard Mr. Cordeal unlock the screen door. My father extended his hand toward Mr. Cordeal's and said, "I'm Hank

Miller. Don't ask how this happened; believe me, you don't want to know."

"Charlie Cordeal, I won't ask then." They shook hands and laughed.

"Hell of a way for us to finally meet," Daddy said. "Thank you for helping us. You already know my wife, Mary."

Mother cowered behind Daddy, reached up, and waved over his shoulder. "Thank you, Charlie," she said, followed by the three of us shouting, "Thank you, Mr. Cordeal."

"Looks like it has been quite a night, Mary. Well, goodnight, Millers. Let me know anytime I can help."

"Well, let's hope to hell you never have to do this again," Daddy said. "I hope I can return the favor one day."

Neither man knew how much help they would be to each other in the future. They couldn't know that my father would help Mr. Cordeal carry Mrs. Cordeal to their car when she had a miscarriage or that my father would clean up under her chair in their family room where it happened. They couldn't know that Mr. Cordeal would bring my father lunch upstairs on a tray, day after day, while my mother was at work and my father convalesced from heart attacks. None of us that night could know that we would never see the likes of such loving, generous neighbors again.

We returned everything to its proper place in my parents' room after the last ant met its fate. Finally, we all went to bed. Mother was silent, not over her embarrassment at what she called "being almost naked in front of Mr. Cordeal." Daddy fumed over the Cheez-Its, ants, and being locked out.

"Hero," Daddy called from his recliner to Rick, "shut off your damn TV. You and the kid go to sleep! And Tatter, no reading tonight, lights out!" he ordered and hoped to get control of his household. It was quiet, parental angry quiet. I only heard the soft whirring of the window fan, and I only saw the flickering light from Daddy's television bounce off the hall floor. I turned on my side, curled into my fetal position, and prayed, *In the name of the Father, the Son, and the Holy Ghost, thank you, God, for the Cordeals. Amen.*

I closed my eyes but kept visualizing our crazy family and our Keystone Cops' nuttiness out on the porch. I saw it from the Cordeal's perspective, and it attacked my funny bone. I could not hold back my laughter. I started singing, too loud and too strong not to get in trouble, *the ants go marching one by one/ hurrah, hurrah/ the ants go marching one by one/hurrah, hurrah/ the ants go marching one by one, the little one stops to suck his thumb/ and they all go marching down, to the earth, to get out, of the rain/ boom, boom, boom.* I stopped singing and listened. I heard no applause or acknowledgment of my hilarious vocal performance meant to lighten the heavy silence in the house.

Well, I thought, I refuse to let everyone else's bad mood ruin my good one. I turned my face into my pillow and let my laughter go. I soon heard Rick muffling his laughter, followed by Jimmy's squeals and then the celebration of Daddy's full belly laughter and Mother's cry-coughing-laughter complete with nose-blowing.

"Well, if that wasn't the god-damndest- thing ever!" Daddy said. This made us all laugh even harder, a long, symphonic family kind of laughter, each contributing our happy part of the whole that was the Millers. "Okay, everybody, knock it the hell off now! Settle down!" Daddy said, standing in the hall. "Get to sleep, you guys," he said to my brothers. He poked his head into my room and sang in a whisper, and *we all went marching out, to the porch, with the flags to get rid of the ants, boom, boom, boom.* Night, Tatter," he said and chuckled his way back to his movie.

My eleventh summer ended, and amid all its chaos, it was a summer of identification as profitable to my growth as discovering gold. I wasn't *as* afraid of bugs; I gained a new appreciation for the American flag and learned that laughter eased our Miller problems and sometimes calmed us, even at one hundred-plus degrees. With all its bedlam, the summer gave me an unwitting premonition I needed later when my romanticism collapsed under the weight of realities that frightened me more than any bug ever did.

ℬ

CHAPTER ELEVEN

GRANDMA MILLER

Grandma Miller was the only grandparent I was old enough to know since Grandma Kelly died when I was an infant, and both my grandfathers passed away before I was born. Grandma Miller was wrinkled all over her body – arms, face, legs, even fingers. She wore thin, dark, flowered dresses that hiked up in the back and revealed a dingy pink or beige slip that hung at least two inches below the hemline. Grandma Miller's skin smelled like medicine, lilac water, and perspiration. She had white hair that turned bright yellow if Mother didn't wash it with bluing. The widow's hump on her back made Grandma walk bent over, and she had to use a cane for balance. Mother often poked me in the middle of my back and said, "Stand up straight, Cathy; you don't want to end up stooped over like Grandma Miller."

Every Sunday, we had family dinners in our dining room on Woodlawn. Mother set the table on Sundays with Grandma Kelly's gold-trimmed Haviland china and her gold-trimmed Haviland crystal glasses. Mother had only a few things left from her Kelly family, so our Sunday dinner table settings were special and unique from every other day of the week.

Our dining room table was too big for the size of the room. Grandma Miller sat beside Rick with Daddy to his right; Jimmy sat across the table from Rick, and I sat across from Grandma Miller with Jimmy on my left. Mother sat to my right, and Daddy was at the head of the table across from Mother with the only chair with arms. Mother was closest to the swinging kitchen door for obvious reasons. Jimmy's chair was only inches from the HiFi that rested on an old, cracked marble-topped table. We were never told whose family most of our furniture came from, but I thought most came from Mother's side since information about them was so sparse and secretive.

The backs of Rick's and Grandma Miller's chairs were so close to the buffet that they had to be careful not to scratch them when they sat down or got up from the table. Our pet water turtle, Clyde, resided on the buffet behind Grandma in his plastic bowl with a palm tree. Mother sat in front of the radiator that was painted to match the moss green walls so it "disappeared." Burgundy and dark green flowered drapes on the window to Mother's left. I sat next to the bird cage for my lime green parakeet, Petey, in front of the window. Sometimes during dinners, Petey scratched the gravel at the bottom of his cage, and some fell into my lap. Daddy had the most room since the archway to the living room was directly behind him. Max was on the floor under the radiator that made grill marks on his wiener stomach and singed off his red hair in the winter.

Our dining quarters were so tight that Mother had to stand up to get enough leverage to scoop the ice cream we always had for Grandma's favorite dessert. We never had dessert any other time except for birthday cakes because Mother said we were all "fat enough." One Sunday, Mother forgot to take the ice cream out of the deep freeze early enough to soften. It was so frozen that Mother lost control of the scooper and threw vanilla ice cream over Petey's cage and into the drapes. "Jesus, God, Mary!" Daddy said. Grandma Miller laughed so hard she cried.

Rick, Jimmy, and I loved being with the adults at the Sunday dining room table. Our most animated family conversations took place over the week's best meal of either roast beef or barbecued steaks. There was lots of laughter because Daddy got us all going with his stories of when he grew up. Occasionally, the conversations grew critical of one another, and I would cry. "Uh oh, Cathy's overly tired," someone always said. This hurt my feelings and made me cry harder. I wondered if that was said on purpose to hurt my feelings. I was teased at school for being tall and thought I was safe not to be teased at home. On those nights, I looked around the table at my family's faces and wished I was adopted. I didn't feel part of my family then and believed my *real* family could never have been so mean. I just sat in silence and watched my roast beef surface from beneath the pool of gravy on my plate and continued to wonder why I was nothing like anyone else at the table.

Every Grandma Miller Sunday, I watched her put some of her ice cream in her coffee, no matter what flavor the ice cream, peppermint, chocolate, strawberry, or even peach, all went into her coffee. We loved to make Grandma Miller tell her favorite joke, not because it was funny, but because she could not get the whole thing out before collapsing into laughter.

"Did you hear the story about the woman who backed into the airplane propeller?" she said. "Well, well, it dis-assed her!" She never got "dis-assed her" out of her mouth in her convulsion of laughter. Daddy always had to finish the joke for her. I loved watching her laugh so hard. It was the only time I remember she was happy.

I rode with Daddy to take Grandma Miller home after Sunday dinners throughout my elementary school years until my sophomore year in high school when she died. Rick saw Grandma weekly and brought her the weekend newspapers on Saturday nights.

"Goodnight, Kate," Daddy said when we parked in front of her apartment house. He leaned across the front seat and kissed the smudged red rouge mark on her left cheek. I never heard my father call Grandma Miller, Mother, or Mom, only Kate. Daddy waited in the car while I helped Grandma inside. I thought her small apartment saddened my father since he could not afford to provide a nicer place for her, like their family home on Sherwood Drive, where he grew up before the Millers lost all their money in the depression. The apartment house was on the corner of Lockwood Avenue and Rockhill Road, directly across Lockwood from the house where Mother grew up. The apartment house looked charming on the outside. It was a large brick building with a beautiful yard full of trees on the Rockhill side.

The small apartment elevator inside held up to four people at a time. The woodwork in the apartment house was dark brown, and the wallpaper was off-white with a slight floral pattern in assorted colors. The carpeting in the hallways was deep maroon with images of swirling tan feathers woven into it. The heavy elevator doors rattled when they opened, and it took Grandma Miller and I both to pull back the solid brass cage. Grandma's apartment was on the third floor. The long hallway smelled of sick, old people to me when

I was in grade school; it made my eyes sting. Once Grandma and I got out of the elevator, we turned left, and I held my breath while I walked to her door, the last door on the right side. We had to walk very slowly, which challenged me to keep hold of my breath and not smell anything until she unlocked her door.

Grandma Miller had a tiny, efficiency apartment with only two small windows, one in the living room and one in the bedroom. The drapes on the windows were never closed, but there were crooked Venetian blinds that cast shadows like horizontal prison bars across the wall when the sun shined through them. Grandma had solid walnut furniture too big for the limited space. If Grandma Miller went behind her tall wingback chair and bent over to turn on her reading light, she disappeared. I sat on her loveseat amid many needlepoint pillows. There were no sounds in Grandma Miller's apartment, no traffic noises on Lockwood or Rockhill, no sounds of trees blowing or neighborhood children laughing outside. There were no sounds of a radio or phonograph playing, not even a clock ticking. The only sound was a low hum in the summer that came from her small window air conditioner. Grandma had no photographs of anyone except her parents, Great Grandfather and Grandmother Blackmer, framed in large, dark oil paintings that hung over her maroon velvet loveseat. Neither of them was smiling, and their eyes followed me around the room whenever I got up from the loveseat.

Grandma Miller's kitchenette was somehow part of the living room. It was no bigger than a Betty Crocker toy kitchen. Her refrigerator was a white waist-high box with a small white counter. Beside that was a two-burner cooktop with another small counter where a toaster oven sat. There was no oven like we had at home, not even an EZ Bake

Oven like my toy one when we lived on Grant Road. The kitchenette did not have cabinets, just open shelves for dishes and canned goods. Grandma Miller didn't have a table; she ate her meals on a metal TV tray with pink hummingbirds painted on it that sat beside her wingback chair.

Grandma Miller's bedroom contained a small single bed missing a spread. One side of the bed was tight against the wall, so there was no way to get around it to place a bedspread on it. A pretty, handmade navy blue and white quilt with tiny rosebud embroidery was folded neatly at the bottom of her bed. Grandma Miller didn't have a closet, only a wooden clothing rack on the wall that held her flowered dresses, a soft blue robe, and two pink flannel nightgowns.

The apartment's bathroom mainly was a bathtub. The toilet and sink looked forced into the room. Everything in there was white; the tile floor, the walls, the towels, and Grandma's stacked sheets and pillowcases were all white. Sometimes I sat on her bed and held her sterling silver hand mirror with her monogram *KMB* engraved on the front. It was shiny, slightly dented, but always polished, even if Grandma Miller was sick.

On Sunday nights, after we entered Grandma's apartment together, she hung up her coat and put away the care package meal Mother packed for her after dinner. "Goodnight, Grandma," I said. She opened her arms and hugged me until I knew it was time for Mother to shampoo her hair again. It was hard to pull away from her boney grip when she grasped my wrists tight after our hug.

I felt sorry for Grandma Miller. I knew since kindergarten that she was lonely, but her tight grip scared me; I thought she was stealing my youth. "Come by after school this week, Cathy, and we will watch the Lone Ranger," she said. "I have a new pint of Borden's coffee ice cream from Straub's." Grandma Miller waited for a pint of ice cream to almost totally melt before she poured it into ice cube trays and put it in her tiny freezer.

"Okay, Grandma, I will be here," I promised her. I kept those promises until I left Bristol and went to Hixson Junior High, too far across town in the opposite direction. Daddy liked that I visited Grandma Miller at least once a week. Every Sunday night, when Grandma closed her apartment door, I said, "Did you lock it, Grandma?"

"I sure did, Missy!" she said on her side of the door.

"I didn't hear the click," I said from my side. Then, when I heard the lock click, I ran down the hall as fast as I could, past the elevator, and bounded down the three flights of stairs two at a time.

"Did you hear the click, Missy?" Daddy said when I was in the front seat beside him. I nodded, and we laughed. Every Grandma Sunday night, without fail, my father said, "Thank you, Tatter, for spending time with your grandmother. I am proud of you." The loneliness of Grandma Miller followed me out of the apartment and into the car as we drove home. I knew Daddy felt it too, and I wished my father and Grandma were more affectionate with one another.

On the day of Grandma Miller's funeral, Mother, Rick, and Jimmy all hurried to our car in the rain. Daddy and I shared an umbrella and arrived at the car together. He held the door for me, closed the umbrella, and looked up into the rain. "Look, Tat," he said, "the heavens are crying for her."

❧

CHAPTER TWELVE
JOLLY GREEN GIANT

All the girls talked about this kind of "date" in the fall of my fifth-grade year at Bristol. It was a date when parents dropped their daughters off at the movies and didn't know they would sit with boys. Kathie Grayson and I met Jimmy Hardwick and Billy Brownley for such a date. The boy-crazy years for the girls of my generation and the peer pressure for having a boyfriend were beginning.

"Did you tell Hardwick and Brownley to meet us inside the lobby by the candy counter?" I asked Kathie in front of the ticket booth at the Ozark Theater. Kathie was a good friend at school. The kids at school called us Grayson and Miller because it was cool to call everyone by their last names. It was incredibly cool because there were duplicate first names like mine. There were lots of Cathys when I was young. There were songs on the radio; *I'm So Close to Cathy*, *Cathy's Clown*, and a doll in toy stores too, Chatty Cathy. She had a cord at the back of her neck that, when you pulled it, she said happy things like "Hi! My name is Cathy; let's be friends!" Just in my fifth grade alone, there were three Kathys, one Kathie, one Cathie, and me. When the teachers called the role in music, library, or art, at least three of us answered, "Here!"

I liked being a duplicate, though I never felt I belonged to the duplicate group because the others were all popular, and I was too tall a girl to be popular. I stuck out of the crowd like the little boy with no hair in the movie *Hans Christian Anderson*. I cried every time I watched Danny Kaye sing *The Ugly Duckling* to him because I knew just how ostracized the little boy felt. Age eleven was the start of the years in my life when it became impossible for me to turn my frowns upside down. The kids at school called me the Jolly Green Giant if I wore green to school.

"No, I know our parents don't want us to have boyfriends yet," Kathie said as she waved to her father in front of the Ozark as he drove away.

Mother never failed to tell me that Kathie's parents were luckier than she was because they got to take us to the movies while my parents had to pick us up afterward. I never knew why Mother complained about driving us home because she only did it once; Daddy always did it, and he never complained. He just waited in front of the Ozark in his blue striped pajamas, tan leather slippers, brown overcoat to hide his pajamas, and gray business hat. Mother was home in her nightgown reading in bed by 8:30 p.m.

Kathie loved to get in our car after the movies because every time Daddy drove, the car was a different company car that he drove home from work every day. Mother and I often had to find a phone booth and call home from the parking lot of the A&P grocery store because we forgot the color and make of the car we drove there. Kathie loved my father because he told her jokes, usually the same ones, repeatedly on the way home. He looked at her in the back seat in his rear-view mirror when we passed the Webster Cemetery and said, "Do you know how many people are dead there, Kathie?"

"No, Mr. Miller, how many people are dead there?" Kathie always said to play along.

"All of them!" he said. Then they both laughed for two blocks.

Fifth-grade date nights included Mrs. Reynolds, who sold the movie tickets behind the glass window of her ticket booth and stared at us over her glasses on the end of her nose. "Mrs. Reynolds, what time will the movies be over tonight?" I asked. Mrs. Reynolds had blue hair, wore a red jacket, and was always crabby.

"Eleven-thirty. Cathy Miller, you tell Henry Miller eleven-thirty sharp! You call him right when you get inside and tell him eleven-thirty. Do you hear me?" Mrs. Reynolds worked at the Ozark when my father was my age. She remembered my father because he got in trouble throwing Jujubes at the screen. Daddy said, "I only did it once."

"Yes, mam," I told her and held up the dime Mother gave me for the call. Inside I forgot to call home because Hardwick and Brownley were waiting. I was almost sick to my stomach; I was so nervous. I never sat in the movies with a boy. Kathie was not worried, though; she had sat with boys before.

"Hi, Hardwick," Grayson said, tossing her long blond hair with her hand. The boys were waiting inside the small lobby where posters of the following week's coming attraction were mounted on the wall.

"Hi, Grayson," Hardwick said, pulling at the neck of his green-striped tee shirt. I was impressed because he only wore that shirt on special assembly days at school. Grayson and Hardwick looked cute together, I thought.

Brownley was even shorter than Hardwick, just a pinch taller than Kathie and only half as tall as me. "Hi, Miller," Brownley said, grinning and holding out his popcorn. "Want some? It's buttered." He looked cute in his blue shirt, jeans, and high-top tennis shoes; Brownley was never without a sweet smile. He never called me the Jolly Green Giant once that I knew.

"No thanks," I told him, and I loved buttered popcorn more than anything next to ice cream if Daddy smashed it up and stirred it in my bowl until it was creamy like Dairy Queen ice cream. Nothing smelled better than Ozark popcorn when you came in the door; the smell was better than turkey in the oven on Thanksgiving. I knew I wouldn't eat anything that night even though Mother gave me enough money to buy two treats, one for each feature.

Brownley and I followed Kathie and Hardwick down the aisle. I felt funny walking beside Brownley, like everyone was staring at us.

"Hey, Hardwick, don't pick your seat," Brownley said and laughed at his joke.

"That's disgusting, Brownley," Grayson told him, and I silently thought so too. Mother taught me to hate bathroom humor.

Grayson and Hardwick found four seats on the aisle on the right side of the theater facing the screen. Brownley was on the aisle next to me, then Hardwick, then Grayson. Brownley and I were almost the same height when we sat down. This was the moment when I knew I hated my legs; it was their fault I was the Jolly Green Giant. I sat between the two boys and not beside Grayson. It was almost more than my nerves could bear. "Oh gosh, I forgot to call my parents, Kathie," I said.

"Oh, that's right. We'll be right back," she told the boys. I slid past Brownley to the aisle with Kathie behind me. I felt so free walking up the aisle with just a girl, so much better than walking down the aisle with a boy.

I called home and told Daddy what time to pick us up; Kathie and I went to the Ladies' room to look at ourselves and talk in the mirror. Kathie brushed her hair hard to make it shine and put on a pale layer of Ponytail Pink lipstick. "You have lipstick?" I asked and looked at my short dirty dishwasher hair and how crooked Mother cut my bangs the day before.

"Try it," Kathie said.

My mother didn't let me wear lipstick. "No lipstick until you're sixteen, and no patent leather shoes ever!" she said. "The nuns at Sacred Heart boarding school taught us that ladies never wear patent leather shoes because it is how the boys look up girls' dresses."

I was much more like my father than my mother in almost every way, so I took the risk and used Kathie's lipstick. I did my best to get it in the right places on my lips. I didn't look pretty like Kathie wearing it, but at least I showed up a little more in the mirror. Besides, if my lips were stained after the movie, Mother wouldn't see them anyway because she would already be asleep, so if my lips were still stained in the morning, I would tell her they were chapped.

My feeling free drained out of me by the time we sat back down with the boys, and the lights dimmed. I thought the movie was a comedy because many people were laughing in the audience when Doris Day was on the screen. The movie was in Technicolor and something about not eating daisies. I did not know what was happening in the movie because he held my left hand after Brownley finished his popcorn. I was sure Kathie and Hardwick didn't watch much of the movie because when the intermission lights came up, Hardwick wore more Ponytail Pink than Kathie.

"Meet you back at the seats, Miller," Brownley said. All four of us filed up the aisle; I was still ten inches taller than Brownley; I did not get any shorter during the first feature, nor did he get taller. At the top of the aisle, the boys turned toward the men's room.

"Yeah, at the seats," Hardwick added.

I followed Kathie to the ladies' room like a Great Dane behind a Chihuahua. Kathie brushed the shine back into her hair, and I washed the popcorn butter off my left hand. "Did anything, you know, happen?" she asked me.

"Brownley held my hand," I told her.

"Well, that's something! Maybe something else will happen during the second feature. Want more lipstick?"

"No thanks," I said; "mine is still good." I was hoping that something might happen during the next movie, but I had no idea what I wanted that to be.

Something did. When John Wayne punched Maureen O'Hara's brother in the nose, Brownley put his right arm around me. I was glad that he was eating Dots this time instead of popcorn. Maureen O'Hara's face flushed when John Wayne talked to her, which was hard to do in a black-and-white movie. I felt my face flush, too, and was glad Brownley couldn't see it in the dark. His arm was still around me when John Wayne dragged Maureen O'Hara up and down the Irish hills and across the fields toward their little cottage.

My heart was beating extra hard when John Wayne threw Maureen O'Hara down on the bed, and the bed broke. I could feel Brownley looking at me then, all the way to the part in the movie where John Wayne chased Maureen O'Hara from the little crooked stream and over the rock wall to *THE END* sign.

The lights came up, and everything looked brighter than before the movie started. All the people in the theater squinted as they filed out to the aisle from their seats. I didn't look at Brownley, and Brownley didn't look at me. We acted like we didn't even know each other. I hurried past him and looked for tall people hoping to get lost among them in the crowd. I heard Kathie's voice, "Wait up, Miller, wait for me." I didn't wait until I got inside the lobby and could lean on a wall.

The cool fall air hit my hot face as the theatre entrance doors flung open, and people went to their cars. I tried not to get squashed while I waited for Kathie and kept looking outside for Daddy. I tried hard to remember what company car was in the driveway when Mr. Grayson picked me up. It was a blue something or other. Kathie tugged on my sleeve and said, "Were you going to a fire or what?"

"No," I said and then lied about not wanting Daddy to wait.

"Did something happen during the second movie?" she asked as we jumped into the crowd and went down the stairs in front of the marque.

"Yes," I told her, "Brownley put his arm around me."

"Hooray! Way to go!" she said, and for a second, I felt like I was *in* our duplicate group.

"Hi, Mr. Miller," Grayson said, crawling into the backseat behind me.

"Hi, Kathie," he said. "How were the movies? Was it a great girls' night out?"

"They were both good!" Kathie and I said in unison to hide the part about our secret dates. Doing that felt strange to me; I had never kept a secret from my father.

"It was a great *girls'* night out," Grayson said, emphasizing *girls.*

We turned onto Berry Road, the dark block just before the street where Kathie lived, and Daddy said, "Kathie, do you know why it is so dark right here?"

"No, Mr. Miller, why is it so dark right here?"

"Because there are no streetlights!" Daddy said, and they both laughed until we were parked in front of Grayson's fancy contemporary house. Daddy had practiced that joke on Mary two weeks before and got the same hysterical results. "Blink your porch lights when you are safe, Miss Grayson," Daddy said.

"I will, Mr. Miller; thank you for doing the pickup. Call me tomorrow, Cath, right after you get home from mass! *We've got to talk!*" Kathie yelled from her porch.

The porch light flickered, and Daddy patted my knee when we drove away. "Homeward bound, Tat," he said; "I will get back in time to see our troops storm Normandy on the *Late, Late Show.* That was a great day for America. We lost thousands of brave men, and World War II was over soon after that day, at least in the European theater. It cost our boys their lives, and they were just boys, but they saved the loss of many more lives by their courage and sacrifice."

We mainly rode from Kathie's house to ours in silence. "Tatter, you are pretty quiet. Are you okay? Do you feel all right tonight?" Daddy asked me.

"I'm fine," I said and tried to hide my flushed face by looking out my passenger side window. I said something ridiculous like, "That's neat about World War II; I just think I'm sleepy." I looked at my reflection in my window and wondered if Daddy could tell I had a secret. I sensed he missed our laughing game, which we usually played alone in the car. I didn't feel like playing it. I felt different, a Chatty Cathy who wanted to be quiet. "Daddy," I asked, "is it okay if I'm quiet?"

"It is just fine to be quiet, Tat," he said and patted my knee again. I loved being quiet with my father as much as I loved laughing with him; I just loved to be with him, period.

At home, Daddy hung his overcoat in the closet and put his hat on the shelf. "May I, Miss Miller?" he said and helped me out of my red car coat to hang it next to his. "This coat won't fit you much longer, Tat; you will be a teenager soon. Now, off you go to bed. Your mother is asleep, so be quiet when you get upstairs. Also, when you brush your teeth, be sure to wash your lips too." He knew my secret! I prayed he would forget it while doing the nightly household chores he always listed for me. "Tat, I have to lock the doors, put food in Maxie's bowl, put down a can of orange juice from the freezer into the icebox, empty the trash, put coffee in the coffee pot for breakfast in the morning and turn off the lights, then I'll be upstairs to kiss you goodnight."

I sat in bed against my headboard wearing my rainbow-colored baby doll pajamas and wrote in my diary. *I hate my legs. I had my first date tonight with Bill Brownley. He is not as handsome as Paul Newman, and his eyes are brown. I'll look on Monday in Mrs. Thornsberry's class to be sure.* There was more I wanted to write, but Daddy came in and kissed me goodnight. He never said another word about my lips.

"Oh, Marsha," Daddy called me with great passion from his bedroom. He loved for us to play like some silly couple on an old radio program he remembered.

"Oh, John," I passioned back.

"Oh, Marsha, Marsha, Marsha," he called out again.

"Oh, John, John, John," I called back. It was our laughing game, the one we didn't play on the way home earlier.

"Good night, Tat, I love you, don't go to Chicago!"

"Good night, Daddy; I won't, and I love you, too." I curled with my knees up under my chin and rolled to my side. I played my first date over in my head like a third feature. *God,* I prayed; *Brownley didn't act like it mattered at all that I was taller than he is, or did he hide it?"*

That night I couldn't know that my fifth-grade seedling of womanhood was to be stomped out two weeks later when Brownley sat with a different girl at the Ozark in the same two seats where he sat with me. When I found out, all I wrote was that *I knew he hated that I am so tall.*

Years later, at our fiftieth high school reunion in 2017, I discovered something else about that first date night. Jimmy Hardwick leaned over from the table next to mine, touched my left hand, and said, "Miller, you are still tall, slim, and beautiful. By any chance, do you remember sitting between Brownley and me at the Ozark Theater in the fifth grade?"

I wondered, sitting at the reunion holding hands with my handsome husband, that if I had known that it was Kathie's date at the movies who saw the real me, maybe the Jolly Green Giant might have felt a little less green during all the ego-shattering years that followed.

✄

CHAPTER THIRTEEN
JELLY ROLL BLUES

Thursdays were Lucille days, one Thursday each of the four seasons. Lucille was an African American woman who helped my mother "deep clean" our house those four times a year. Deep cleaning was the most challenging part of housework; it involved moving furniture, cleaning baseboards, washing windows, etc. Many of the Caucasian families in Webster in the sixties were still wealthy; they had someone clean their homes twice a month or more. Those families were not like our family or those like us who dealt with collapsed finances and were no longer members of the social register. We tried to appear as though we still had money while money disappeared into thin air. We lived like inept magicians.

When I was twelve years old, Lucille's summer Thursday was the first time I noticed Lucille's skin was black, and mine was white. That morning I smelled coffee first and then bacon frying. I heard the shower running and Daddy singing in the bathroom; *I'll be down to getcha in a Taxi, honey; better be ready about half-past eight.* Downstairs I heard the familiar sounds of breakfast dishes clinking and my brothers' chatter.

"Cathy, time to get up!" Mother called from the bottom of the stairs. "You must watch Jimmy while I get Lucille at the bus; Rick has baseball practice."

"Okay, I'm just making my bed," I said.

"One day, Tat, you are going to make your bed with one of your legs still in it," Daddy said in my doorway. I hugged him good morning and smelled that he was fresh from his shower and his daily promise that this day would be his lucky day. "Feel my hair," he joked when he pulled the towel off his head. "Wouldn't you just love to run barefoot through it?"

"Oh, my goodness, Daddy, it is so soft!" I responded as I ran my fingers through it. I sat on my bed and waited for him to give me his morning weather report.

"Gonna be over a hundred today, Tat," he said and then left to get dressed. I listened to him finish his song in his bedroom while I threw my pajamas in the hamper and pulled on my white shorts and crop top with the red cherries. *I'm gonna dance off all my shoes when they play those jelly roll blues tomorrow night at the Dark Town Strutters' Ball.*

"I am barely going to make it in time for Lucille's bus! Mother was on a dead run in the kitchen when I arrived. Cathy, please clean up the kitchen so Lucille and I can get right to work when we get back. Keep an eye on Jimmy, so he doesn't bother anyone if he goes outside."

Mother was obsessed with everyone's weight in our family; she had a mortal fear of one of us becoming fat. Daddy came through the kitchen and kissed me on top of my head while I ate my egg on top of shredded toast in a coffee cup. "Hey, look at this!" he said, then sucked in his stomach and made his pants fall to the floor. "I've lost some weight! That will make your mother happy!"

"Make it a good day, Daddy," I said.

"It is gonna be a great day!" he said and went out to his car, most likely on his way to see a loan shark in St. Louis, find a poker game, or go to the horse races at Cahokia Downs across the river before going to work at the car dealership. My mother would have been much better at managing money than my father. Still, she was a Post WWII woman who hid her intelligence and disappointment when marital finances disproved the happily ever after fairy tale. Many women of her age still lived captured in the pre-Rosie the Riveter philosophy that the man of the family handled the finances, even if he didn't handle them well.

I checked on Jimmy as soon as I finished the dishes and was happy that he was watching cartoons in the living room and not bothering anyone. I heard the back screen door slam and ran back to the kitchen to greet Lucille. "Hi, Lucille," I said, hugging her. I felt the warm dampness from her long bus ride that released her familiar scent of Lysol and lilac talcum powder.

"Miz Cathy, let Lucille take a good look at you! You is growin' up! You growed a foot since I saw you in March!"

Lucille and Mother were total opposites but only physically. Lucille was round and cushiony, a woman whose age was impossible to tell. She had lovely full lips, not skinny ones like mine, and broken teeth that looked like chips of white popcorn when she smiled, something she did almost all the time. Her skin was a dusty black, and her hair was a bit wiry with just a slight touch of gray in the front. Mother was Audrey Hepburn-boney, with blonde wavy hair, creamy white skin, and high cheekbones. She smelled of Jergens hand lotion and Camay soap. Both Lucille and my mother wore wrap-around cotton cleaning dresses. Lucille's was homemade, a faded blue with cheerful yellow flowers printed on it. Mother's cleaning dress was from Rudolph's Dry Goods. It was light green with dark green leaves embroidered across the front. Mother was happiest on Lucille's days, more content than on her other stay-at-home days when she wondered whether my father went to work or elsewhere.

Mary was helping her mother with something that day and would only be free to play after dinner. This was fine because my job that day was to keep Jimmy busy and move him from room to room so Mother and Lucille could clean. I liked to listen to them chatter while they worked. "My Walter drinks too much, and most of the time, he doesn't have no job, but he makes me laugh," Lucille said when they stopped for lunch. "Mr. Miller is funny, too, isn't he, Miz Miller?

"Hank is funny, Lucille, yes; it is his best character trait," Mother said.

The big event on Lucille's days was her fried chicken dinner. She made glorious, hot, crispy, juicy, and tender chicken with lots of pepper. Mother had to put newspapers all around the stove on the floor when Lucille cooked because the grease popped everywhere from the two sizzling black iron frying pans. Lucille's cooking was our quarterly feast.

The thermometer on the porch hit one hundred around 5:00 p.m., and Mother turned the window air conditioner on in the living room to cool down the dining room so we could eat there.

Jimmy was safe outside in his pen, so I peeled potatoes and washed Daddy's tomatoes from his garden that evening instead of watching him. Lucille made fresh fried okra, baking powder biscuits, and cream gravy.

"We need to set a place for Lucille," Mother said while the two of us set the table. "Cathy, call Rick and Jimmy to wash up for dinner." Rick never had dinner at any of his friends' houses on Lucille's days; I was jealous of how often he managed to get invitations away from home on other nights.

Lucille put the last bowl of our banquet on the table and disappeared behind the swinging door to the kitchen. The four of us sat down at our places, but Lucille did not come in and sit at the place we set for her. "Lucille, we are waiting for you," Mother called.

"Oh no, Miz Miller, I gonna eat right here in the kitchen," said Lucille from her side of the swinging door.

"Please, Lucille, it is too hot in the kitchen; it is much cooler here; please join us."

"No, mam. Now, Miz Miller, please don't make no fuss; I'm just gonna eat here where I am at."

"That's it!" Mother declared, looking at us. "Kids, pick up your plates and take your food into the kitchen. If Lucille is not going to eat with us, we will eat with her." We got up and carried every dish, bowl, plate, and spoon back to the hot oven kitchen, doing our best not to knock each other down going in and out of the swinging door.

We sat down, held hands, and Mother said grace; it was a spectacular meal. We five laughed and talked between every bite, relishing every morsel of our feast. Lucille told us stories about Walter and her seven cats. Mother laughed until tears ran down her cheeks, and she had to blow her nose five times during dinner. I watched and listened as Mother and Lucille traded observations about husbands loved and tolerated while Rick and Jimmy crunched on second and third helpings of fried chicken. Our laughter continued through the meal until the last bites of Lucille's fresh peach cobbler. Not one of us ever mentioned the heat, not one time.

After dinner, Rick and Jimmy disappeared as usual, but I didn't mind helping with the dishes; I wanted to be with Mother and Lucille; I wanted to be one of them somehow. My eyes were fixed on their genuine friendship as they made separate plates for their husbands. Mother put Daddy's dinner on Grandma Kelly's china, each course in its separate dish, and then covered each with foil; Daddy hated his foods to touch each other. Lucille put Walter's dinner in plastic containers with Snap-On lids she had brought from home. The last step of their post-dinner ritual was to roll the chicken bones, necks, and gizzards in newspapers for Lucille's cats.

"Miz Miller, I'm goin' change my dress now," Lucille said and went into our tiny half bath off the kitchen.

"Mother," I asked, "may I ride with you to take Lucille to the bus?" I never wanted to go before, especially on Lucille's summer visits, because kickball began right after dinner at the Cordeals, followed by Eskimo pies and catching lightning bugs.

"Really? I'd love that, Tat," she said. Lucille returned to the kitchen wearing a clean dress with bright red flowers and bright red lipstick on her lips. The loose, damp, wiry wisps of her hair from hard work all day were tucked neatly into a braid.

"Boy Lucille, you look so pretty!" I told her.

"Well, thank you, Miz Cathy," she said. "Walter likes me to look nice when I comes home from work."

I carried Lucille's ragbag with all the day's dirty cleaning cloths. Mother and I each took a bundle, and Lucille took the bag with Walter's dinner as we trooped out to Mother's old Pontiac. "You sit in the back, Tat," Mother said; "you sit up front with me, Lucille." But Lucille would not have that arrangement; she plopped into the back seat before I could sit there.

"You belongs up front with your mother," Lucille said. It felt strange riding next to Mother in the place where Rick usually sat, but it was lovely.

Mother got out of the car at the bus stop in front of Lamberts and helped Lucille with her things. She sat beside her on the chipped, gray-painted bus stop bench. I waited in the car on the street in front of them and watched. They were two women, side by side, so opposite, yet so the same. Then I saw the others.

There were lots of Lucilles dragging their blistered feet to the bus, three, maybe four Lucilles walking toward the bus stop from four different directions: all bone-tired, weary Black women carrying ragbags and tattered purses, but each welcoming another with a smile. I was happy Mother parked close enough for me to hear all the women greet each other; I felt blessed somehow.

"Evenin' Miz Lucille, woo whee it be hot," said a tiny woman in a beige flowered cotton dress. It was clear that she was the oldest of all the women.

"Well, I be, Miz Luanne; you weren't on the bus this mornin'," Lucille said to her, "I thought you mighta been still sick or somethin', but you look right as rain now."

"No, mam, I ain't sick no more," said the little woman. "Jonesie made me go to the Doc, and he fixed me up real good, so I rode the late bus."

"Miz Luanne, I wants you to meet Miz Miller. I works for her four times a year. Miz Miller this here is Miz Luanne Jones." Mother stood and let Mrs. Jones have her seat. "I been ridin' on the bus to work with Miz Luanne for near twenty years now," Lucille said.

"Miz Miller, you shore lucky to have Lucille as your cleanin' lady," Mrs. Jones said.

"I'm even luckier to have Lucille as my friend," Mother answered.

"Well, don't I know it, because Lucille is my friend too, the goodest friend I have!"

Mother smiled and patted the old woman's hand. I was struck by how lovely Mother looked in the yellow glow of the bus stop as she smiled at the oldest woman. Why hadn't I noticed how beautiful my mother's smile was before?

The sun sank low behind the layers of thick green leaves of the large, numerous trees that lined every street in Webster. The streetlights flickered on, making small circular halos of light around them. Mother looked her most movie star beautiful standing in her whiteness, laughing with them in the pale-yellow glow. Goodness, I thought as I peered from my pubescent peanut gallery in the car. Maybe Mother really is Grace Kelly.

"Here she comes," Mrs. Jones said, motioning to the big green and white city bus roaring down Lockwood with the *East St. Louis* sign in its front window. I jumped out of the car and ran to Lucille.

"Bye, Lucille!" I said and hugged her, "say hello to all your cats for me." Mother handed all her things up to her. Lucille waited until all the other ladies climbed aboard the bus before she got found a seat.

"Night, Miz Miller, see you Thursday 'fore Thanksgivin' and bye Miz Cathy; I sees you then, too," Lucille said, giving Mother and me her best popcorn teeth smile.

"I will be right here to pick you up," Mother said, "and Lucille, you take care of yourself once in a while, too, will you?"

The bus doors closed, and the interior lights shone, spotlighting its precious cargo of exhausted but talkative cleaning ladies. It was a social club I never knew existed and never forgot. The old bus revved up and sent thick black smoke and diesel fumes into the air. I stood beside my mother as we watched and waved until the old bus rattled and disappeared over the hill on Lockwood Avenue.

Mother yawned and sighed when we got in the car to go home. "It was a good day," she said. I felt inexplicably shy. I wanted to hold my mother's hand and hold it all the way home, but touching my mother was not easy; our family had to wait for her to touch us first.

"Mother, I love Lucille," I said when she parked the old Pontiac in our garage.

"I do, too, Cathy," she said.

The whole day felt like a shared secret with Lucille and Mother, the best kind of secret. The day had been relaxed and serene as Mother and I walked up our skinny, cracked sidewalk to the back porch. I turned and heard all the kids playing in the Cordeals' yard. "Mother, do I still have time to play?" I asked.

She looked at me awhile and patted my arm, "just a very brief time, Tat," she said and went into the house.

I skipped across the grass toward the kids' excited sounds and sang, *"I'm going to dance off all my shoes when they play those jelly roll blues tomorrow night at the Dark Town Strutters Ball.* I was twelve years old, and there were still a few more lightning bugs to catch.

⌀

CHAPTER FOURTEEN

THE THIRD MUSKETEER

I touched my future during the summer of 1961, all because of Mary and our new friend, Pam, who became the third Woodlawn musketeer. Mary and I opened a vacation school for the kids in our neighborhood. I was the twelve-year-old teacher, and Mary was the eleven-year-old one. Our classroom was on our gray screened porch beneath my parents' sun porch. Mr. and Mrs. Cordeal had added Ann and Ellen, and Tommy was on his way. Our porch school was big enough for an enrollment of ten. Our parents found an old chalkboard and wooden desks from the 1800s that were used in one-room schoolhouses. One student sat on the front seat of the student's desk behind him. The desks had ink wells and slots for pencils, and their tops lifted. It was in the best interest of our parents to equip the porch classroom so that Mary and I could successfully keep all the kids busy for two hours each morning and two hours each afternoon.

Mary and I learned classroom management skills that summer. We charged a dime, a kid, a day. Our four through seven-year-old charges taught us much more than we taught them as they colored in their coloring books, listened to the stories we read, and played organized games during recess. We learned about sibling rivalry: "Michael, don't take John's glasses, or he can't see his book!" Hyperactivity: "Jimmy, you must sit down in school; you can't run up and down the aisles." Separation anxiety: "Annie, your Daddy has to teach piano today; he can't help you color your tree." The needs of special needs children: "Stop crying, Marvin; don't be upset, I'll tie your shoes, and everything will be fine." Mary was the older sister to most of our students, and I came with a matching built-in bossiness that helped run our school.

I could never have managed our little school without Mary. I needed her goodness and patience. It was a defining time for me; I discovered teaching, and I found I loved it. I was magnetized by the flashes of light that appeared in the wide-open eyes of our younger peers. Their fiery cerebral light bulbs sparked and exploded with new knowledge that was addictive, even if it was only produced from a limited curriculum and the impromptu teaching styles of two little girls. Teaching in our one-room schoolhouse under rustling Missouri oak trees with my first loyal girlfriend by my side, a rush of joy was unleashed inside me, a thrill and delight I never lost in all thirty-five years I spent as a teacher.

When we held our classes, Mary and I did not know that a new family had moved across the street to the Wallings' house. Mrs. Milton made herself known to them immediately. She told Mrs. Shontz, on their first meeting, "Now Jeanne, I understand your son Tommy had Scarlatina. Well, you know, after a case of that disease, your son's eyes may be crossed forever!" Mrs. Shontz was a pretty, freckled, redheaded Irish woman who wasn't sure how to take that remark.

Mr. Cordeal, upon hearing of the encounter, introduced himself to Mrs. Shontz this way, "Welcome to our neighborhood. I heard you met our lovely Flor-ass Milton already!" Forever after that day, Mrs. Florence Milton was known as Flor-ass by almost every adult on Woodlawn.

Mary and I were so busy with our school that we overlooked Pam, the Shontz's daughter, who sat across the street reading books on her front porch. We didn't know she felt left out of our endeavors. Her brother, Tommy, was Jimmy's age, and Pam was my age and would be in the sixth grade at Bristol that fall. The sixth grade would be my second year without Rick at the same school I was in. Mary would still attend Mary Queen of Peace. I don't remember the moment Mary and I first met Pam. I only remember that the arrival of a new girlfriend would help me face my last Jolly Green Giant year in Bristol. I believed God sent her to me.

Pam was a lively, cute girl between Mary and me in height. She had curly light brown hair from the Toni home permanents her mother gave her. She had large, beaming brown eyes and talked faster than anyone I knew. "Pam is bubbling over with enthusiasm," Daddy said; "she has a lot to tell us." At first, it was hard for Mary and me to keep up with what Pam was saying, but soon, we caught up with her and talked just as fast. "If the Webster Power and Light Company tied electric motors to the mouths of you three," Daddy said, "they could light all of Webster Groves!"

Pam talked faster and became a woman more quickly than Mary and me. She had the beginnings of breasts when we met her, more than just pokey little nipples like we had. In truth, Mary and I never caught up with Pam that way. She started her periods at twelve. I was fourteen before "my aunt came to visit," and Mary was almost fourteen when hers arrived.

Summer was nearing its end when we met, but we were determined to make the most of what was left of it before school started. We held theatrical productions in my garage and forced the kids and our parents to watch us lip sync and "dance" to songs from *Oklahoma, Wildcat, South Pacific, Gigi,* and every musical the three of us owned. We tortured our audiences with not even a shred of talent. One of the shows we three hams performed was on the large slab of concrete attached to the Cordeals' house that was the beginning of a studio enlargement for Mr. Cordeal. This production also featured dramatic reenactments from famous movie scenes. An hour into the performance, the gathering clouds sprinkled rain on our show and audience. The humidity had to have climbed to 100%, and our lack of talent and musicality drove the pregnant Mrs. Cordeal to her breaking point. In the middle of what I considered my brilliant reenactment of Vivian Leigh's pre-intermission speech in *Gone with the Wind,* Mrs. Cordeal melted down.

"As God is my witness, I'll never be hungry again," I said in total drama on my knees, holding a carrot high above my head. Mrs. Cordeal jumped up from her lawn chair and let out one long scream!

"I can't stand it! I can't sit here another minute!" she said. "Adults, Charlie and I will serve cold drinks inside in five minutes. Please join us!"

Pam, Mary, and I were devastated. The adults fled and were going to miss the best part of the show when the three of us sang *I'm Gonna Wash that Man Right Outta My Hair* over the top of Mitzi Gaynor. We looked out at who was left in our audience. Rick was not there; he was off with his friends and missed every second. Rain or no rain, Jimmy, Michael, John, and Pam's brother, Tommy, ran away to play kickball. All we had left in our audience was Jane, Ann, and Ellen, and they got up and ran to the Cordeal's swing set.

Though the invisible curtain came crashing down on that show, our audience prisoners were forced to return to our living room before Christmas for our Holiday Extravaganza. Daddy ran the record player in the dining room where we performed, and Mr. Shontz held a blanket over the oval entrance to it so we had a curtain. Mary, Pam, and I subjected our families to every single cut on the *Bing Crosby Christmas Album*. We did okay with nobody leaving until Mary was on the fifth day of *the Twelve Days of Christmas*. Pam and I tied little pink ribbons to Mary's ankles for this; it was her most significant number. She pirouetted and leaped into the air over and over on each new day. This time it was my mother who had the breakdown. Just as Mary held up her hand to place five golden rings on each finger, Mother exclaimed, "Dear lord in heaven, help us! There are still seven more days! Hank, fix everyone a drink now!" Thus, that production ended before the curtain call as well. It was our last production in front of a live audience.

Nothing quite combined the imaginations of the three musketeers like our trips to Webster's Bird Park, especially the last trip that summer. The bird sanctuary was a gift to Webster Groves many years before we were born. The land was deeded to the city in the estate of one of its earliest citizens. Located at 262 West Swon Avenue, the Bird Park was within walking distance from Woodlawn. It was a unique place tucked in among Webster's largest and oldest homes. It was a small, wooded park with trails and rolling hills.

I was convinced the Bird Park was created specifically for us to provide space to rehearse our theatrical aspirations.

The trees had dual importance. They served as audiences that did not run away and created green walls circling the flagstone stage floor under an arbor. The trellises overhead made the top of our "stage," with roses that grew if it rained enough until mid-September. The Bird Park was the perfect fairy tale theater for all our once upon a times. It was our own Midwestern Greek amphitheater. Though it was only blocks from our homes, the Kingdom of Bird Park felt like galaxies away to three little girls searching for Neverland and towing thermos bottles of milk and brown paper bags with peanut butter sandwiches and smashed potato chips.

The sun and clouds collaborated with the trees to contribute to our theatrical art. They supplied powerful shadow images of monsters, wizards, and knights that lay in wait for us. My two best friends took turns being Snow White and would decorate her home and boss around her two dwarves on their knees. Both Snow Whites overacted but were consistently exuberant that someday their princes would come.

Pam's Sleeping Beauty pricked her finger on a sweetheart rose and caused a tragic collapse into a spell of scene-stealing sleepiness that lasted an eternity before my gallant, noble prince finally entered the scene to save her. Mary's Cinderella was beautiful, and her pink cheeks glowed as she scrubbed her stepmother's floors; she never once complained or begged for rest.

The characters in our created worlds also held log-rolling contests. They rolled down the long green sloping hill and laughed as their pubescent bodies banged into each other at the bottom.

When the late afternoon sunlight revealed enough grass stains on our summer shorts and our willing suspensions of disbelief became less willing and wearier, it was time to turn our dirty, laughter-tear-streaked faces toward home. We hurried through denouements of glass slipper-fittings, nap-waking kisses, and evil witch-shrinkings. We helped each other pick up our trash before we began our journey homeward. Arms around each other's waists and shoulders, we mourned the end of our summer vacation and bid solemn farewells to the Bird Park, making hopeful promises to return the second school was out the next year.

"I never see one bird," Mary said as we began climbing Swon Avenue.

"Me neither," said Pam.

"Well, maybe they are just well-behaved audience members," I concluded.

The trek back to Woodlawn was slower and more silent on that last playday before school. The walk home was uphill primarily and steeper than our walk down to the Bird Park. The minute we rounded Woodlawn's corner from Rock Hill Road, we ran down the street to our houses. Mary reached her first.

"Next summer, I want to be Sleeping Beauty," she yelled before disappearing around the corner of her house and going in her back door.

"Then I get to be Cinderella!" Pam hollered from across the street on her front porch before entering her front door.

I sat down on the front steps of my house before I went inside. Why do I always have to be the prince? I wondered. I didn't want to always have the male roles, and the longer I sat and thought about it, the more depressed I got. I hated being tall! I finally stood up, turned my most dramatic posture toward the spotlight from a beam of sunlight peeking around the Milton house, and declared out loud, "God, if you didn't make me an actress, then I will be a director!"

It was the second time I touched my future that summer, but I could not envision how different my thirteenth summer would be from my twelfth one and how much harder my life journey would get.

∅

PART THREE
JUNIOR HIGH SCHOOL

In the valley of the Jolly

Ho, ho, ho,

Green Giant

- Television Commercial

CHAPTER FIFTEEN
FIVE FOOT, TWELVE INCHES

The hypersensitive reactions I experienced in childhood from my mother's repeated warnings of "don't wear your feelings on your sleeve!" paled in comparison to the more severe reactions I had in adolescence. Sensitivity to lights and sounds heightened, along with side effects of some medications. I was startled easily by almost any kind of change or family problem. Anxiety and fear ruled me. My need to hide my emotions grew more intense. Children don't come with directions, and I certainly didn't. What is said and what children hear varies from child to child. What our parents told us and what my brothers and I heard them say had three different interpretations for Rick, Jimmy, and me.

I wasn't supposed to hear my mother talking to my father the Monday after my thirteenth birthday in 1961, but I did. Her words traveled through the screen door, across the back porch, and down the four scuffed gray stairs where I was sitting and taking off my dirty Keds tennis shoes after walking home in the spring rain from after-school volleyball. Daddy was never home before dinner on Mondays, but he was that day.

"She's so tall, Hank," Mother said to Daddy, "and she's still growing! Dr. Blyer says she won't stop growing until she starts menstruating. She shows no signs of that yet and is already almost six feet tall!"

"What do you want to do, Mary?" Daddy said. "What can we do?"

"Dr. Blyer said we can force her periods to start, that the thyroid gland will signal the pituitary gland, and she'll stop growing and start her periods, but we have to see an endocrinologist."

"Just how in the hell do we do that to a thirteen-year-old girl, Mary? It sounds horrible, like a goddamn science experiment or something," Daddy said.

"They give her a pill, something new. Dr. Blyer says it is a form of the new birth control pill, but it works for cases like this, too," Mother explained.

"Cases like this? She isn't a freak! I'm six foot, seven goddamn inches tall, and you are five foot, seven inches tall, for Christ's sake. Cathy comes by her height normally."

Mother started to cry. "It's nobody's fault, Hank, but she's getting too tall for a girl, and she's getting hippy and gaining weight. She weighs one hundred and fifty pounds."

"Well, I don't like this," Daddy said as his voice grew louder, "not one damn bit, Mary!"

"Too tall for a girl" and "freak!" I stopped breathing. Hearing those words from my parents was worse than being called the "Jolly Green Giant" by some kids at school. Was there truth in their words? There was a sudden drop in my stomach and a distortive click in my brain. I already hated my body. I walked slowly up the stairs in my socks and opened the screen door. Mother's face was cradled in her hands, and she had her elbows on the kitchen table.

Daddy was behind her, pouring whiskey over ice in a glass. I didn't say hello; I didn't say anything. I just stood there, all five feet, almost twelve inches of me.

"There's my Tatter," Daddy said with an overabundance of enthusiasm. "How was volleyball?"

"Fine," I said. Mother snapped up straight, stood, and turned away from me. She went to the pot of vegetable beef soup on the stove and stirred it. I walked between the icebox and the kitchen table and prayed my broadening hips wouldn't brush against anything. I walked through the hall to the living room and climbed the narrow oak stairs to my room.

I stared at myself in the mirror over my dresser. I wanted to shrink, become invisible like the incredible shrinking man. I wanted more than just my physical body to disappear; I wanted no trace of my existence left. My reflection revealed a pitiful creature who committed an unspeakable crime, one from which she could never absolve herself, the crime of being a girl who never felt a cramp or produced a drop of menstrual blood.

That night I wrote full disclosure of my sorrows between the lines of *I am fat! I am a freak!* And *I am too tall for a girl!* I was wounded in a war of words, fatally wounded, I believed. How would I overcome my injuries and scale the mountains of my teenage tomorrow? I prayed, *Lord God, please help me. Tell me in the morning what to do with this pain. I am so scared.*

The next day, before breakfast in the morning and again before bed at night, I began compulsive physical exercise and worried about every mouthful of food, obsessions that lasted thirty years.

Not quite a month after I overheard my parents talk about my mother's concerns about my height, I came home after school to find my mother opening a large can of peaches in the sink. I studied her lean and lithe body while I set the table. When did I get so much taller than she was? The gentle May breeze blew through our yellow and white gingham curtains over the sink, and I looked at my mother. She shed more lovely light than the halo over the Madonna on the holy card she used as her bookmark. I watched her model-perfect, one-hundred-and-fifteen-pound frame maneuver gracefully around our crowded kitchen. My mother, as an example of the female of our species, was physically a tough act to follow.

Mother opened two glass Ball jars of whole succulent peaches and poured their syrupy deliciousness into the imitation cut-glass bowl I bought at Lambert's with my allowance for Mother and Daddy's wedding anniversary. I stood behind her and marveled at her smooth, creamy hands as she cut each peach in half and spun them around in their juices until they floated in the bowl. It startled me when she captured two halves in our dented metal cullender and ran cold water over them until they lost their glimmer.

"Whose peaches are those, Mother?" I asked.

"These are yours, Cathy," she said. "It is time you went on a diet. I don't want you to start smoking to lose weight like I did when I was a teenager."

What? I was not about to start smoking. I knew that ever since I was ten and cleared away the breakfast plates from a family smoke-choking Easter brunch with relatives. One plate had a cigarette stubbed out in an egg yolk. Eggs were my favorite food; it was not only disgusting but sacrilege. At that moment, my lifetime gag reflex deterrent from smoking was created.

"Mother, are you saying I need to lose weight because I am fat?" I asked. "I mean, am I that fat?"

"Not yet, but you favor your father's side of the family. This was my mother's too much information answer. Besides Tat, after we go to a new doctor next week, you will start menstruating, and girls always get fat around the time they start their periods."

Oh God, please help me, I thought and sank hard and heavy on my contact-papered chair at the table. I just stared at the small bowl of peaches at my place.

Mother called Rick and Jimmy to the table. The three of them chatted awhile; I just watched my brothers as they ate their sugary peaches and thought about how fat I was. I could barely manage my devastation when Mother, using her fork as a pointer, said, "Kids, I want to talk to you about masturbation." Her waving fork meant a maternal lecture was about to commence.

"Masturbation is as wrong as wetting your pants."

"What?" Rick said in shock; his fifteen-year-old freckled face went beet red up to his carrot-colored crew cut.

"Who is wetting their pants?" seven-year-old Jimmy demanded, "and what is masturbation?"

What is going on? I thought as I became increasingly confused over everything Mother had said since I walked into the kitchen. My mother had been full of odd observations during the last part of the school year ever since Miss Beck, our sixth-grade gym teacher, took the girls to a room by ourselves and taught us about sex and reproduction. The boys talked briefly about the same with Mr.

Roach, our science teacher, but then got to play basketball for the rest of the hour. Miss Beck gave us girls a booklet I put on my desk when I got home. It was called *Very Personally Yours* and had a woman's graceful, manicured hand with long, red polished fingernails on the cover. The booklet was supposed to tell the girls everything about sex, and it was frightening. All I got out of Miss Beck's hour-long sex education speech to the girls was that I might have syphilis or, at the very least, gonorrhea.

Daddy explained to me the night of Mother's lecture that I couldn't have those diseases since I never had sexual intercourse. I was relieved; it had been a scary day to look at my body and feel symptoms. Daddy explained everything well.

"Masturbation is nothing you need to worry about now, Jimmy,' Mother said, looking at Rick, whose potential guilt did not go unnoticed by me.

"Well then, why are we talking about it?" Jimmy said, "None of us have wet our pants since we were babies!"

"Yeah," Rick whispered like a prayer. "Let's just drop it, okay?"

"Okay," Mother said, "what do you want to talk about?"

"Anything else," he begged.

What happened during the rest of dinner that night escaped my memory, except that my peaches were dry and tasteless.

Mother and I went to the new doctor the week after her masturbation talk. I was terrified of doctors, even though Dr. Blyer was the only one I ever knew. He lived a few blocks from our house and gave us all our childhood shots in his home office. "My God, Cathy," Mother said on the day of each appointment with Dr. Blyer, "you go to the doctor a hundred times in your mind before you go!" Mother never understood my medical terrors.

I didn't have a shot the day of the new doctor. Instead, I was hooked to a breathing machine for an hour. The new doctor was an endocrinologist whose office was forty minutes away in Clayton. I had trouble controlling my shaking when we walked into his office; I tried hard to maintain it because Mother kept looking at me with irritation. The nurse was nice enough; she explained that nothing would happen during the appointment that would cause me pain. She was right, nothing hurt, but I froze to death, lying on the cold metal table hooked to the breathing machine with only a thin white sheet on top of me. I thought about the movie *Frankenstein* while I was lying there. The engine in the machine sounded just like the one attached to Boris Karloff. I stared at the ceiling and visualized myself as the Monster. I saw myself going to Hixson Junior High School in the fall and all the other kids pointing at me before they screamed and ran down the halls.

Mother sat on a chair and read her latest mystery behind me. The hour felt like days. My thoughts eventually turned to prayer for God to speed up time. Mother and I waited in the lobby afterward for the doctor to call us back to his office. I looked at the floor with shame as Mother, and the doctor talked about me.

"Mrs. Miller, Cathy has hypothyroidism. It is a condition in which the thyroid gland doesn't produce enough thyroid hormone. This affects her heart rate, body temperature, and all the aspects of her metabolism. Though it is most prevalent in older women, Cathy requires medication now. After we find the correct dose for her, if she still doesn't start her period, she will qualify for a combining estrogen and progestogen, forcing her periods to begin.

"Will she keep growing until she menstruates?" Mother asked.

"Yes, but the thyroid medication may do the trick for us, and maybe we won't need the other medication." Us? I thought. I heard no "us" in what either of them said.

I didn't talk on the way home in the car; I sat and listened to Mother talk about how today was "the best thing for you, Cathy." But I realized I was going to hit 72 inches and be five foot, twelve inches tall, at the very least.

ℒ

CHAPTER SIXTEEN
HORMONES AND CALORIES

There were two groups of teenage girls when I was an adolescent. There were boy-crazy good girls and sex-crazy bad girls. The good girls grew up to be nurses, teachers, or secretaries before they got married. Bad girls were so sex-crazy that they either got pregnant before they got married and had to be shipped off to their "aunts' houses" until their babies were born, or they married right out of high school after having trapped some dumb guy.

Pam and I were boy-crazy good girls. During our thirteenth summer, the one that followed Mother's masturbation talk, Pam and I began to practice kissing each other. We were going to be seventh graders and noticed that the boys and girls that we knew from Bristol were pairing off, and we wanted to be good at kissing in case we got boyfriends at James T. Hixson Junior High. Pam already had a no-kissing sixth-grade boyfriend named Chuck Black, who said, "Hi ya, Toots!" to her whenever they passed in the halls. He gave her his ID bracelet to wear, but her mother made her give it back to him when school was out for summer.

The three musketeers took turns spending the night at either Pam's house or my house; there were not enough beds at Mary's house. At first, Pam and I tried kissing our pillows when we spent the night together, and Mary was not with us. Mary was only going to be in the sixth grade at Mary Queen of Peace, so Pam and I thought she was too young to practice kissing. Pam and I scheduled those overnights when we knew Mary was busy and couldn't join us. Pillow kissing did not work, so we changed tactics and practiced by kissing each other, taking turns as to who the boy was. Next, we explored our bodies until Pam's mother shared her thoughts about what good girls did and did not do together, so after that, Pam and I restricted our sexual explorations to verbal discussions only.

Pam was into a B-size bra, and I was still flat as a tack, especially on the left side, after Quinton Lindsey's brutal dodgeball throw hit my breast when I was twelve, the first month of the sixth grade. The pain was excruciating, and the sting of embarrassment was even worse. Many sixth-grade boys were fixated on breasts and ran their hands down our backs to see who was wearing a bra and who wasn't. They snapped the bra straps across girls' backs and said, "Turtle snap, snap!"

I knew Quinton Lindsey in gym class aimed his small red dodgeball directly at my left breast. The tears streamed down my face, and I clutched my little flat breast and ran to the girls' restroom as fast as I could. Miss Beck came in and made me show it to her. Horrified, I raised my shirt. I never let anyone see my body, not even my family. I felt humiliated as the tears ran down my face, and I showed my nipple to my masculine gym teacher. I forced myself to look at it in the mirror. Dark purple bruising and swelling encircled my nipple, and I covered it immediately. "You're just fine," Miss Beck said. "Now Cathy, wash your face and come back to class."

By the end of the summer before the seventh grade, it was evident that Quinton's precise aim stunted the left side of my womanhood, even though the new medication from the endocrinologist seemed to help my right breast bud a tiny bit. "It will catch up, Cath," Pam assured me, but I still added a plea to my prayers at night. I asked God to help my breasts match each other like the other girls in gym class. Mother got me a training bra, which was exciting, though only my right breast needed one, and the little stretchy thing did nothing for my flat leftie. This was when I started putting a tiny bit of folded toilet paper on the left side of my bra to fill out the wrinkles. It was also when I began to wear baggy shirts.

Every Sunday night on the phone during the summer, Pam and I read the TV Guide cover to cover to map out the movies we planned to watch all week. Monday through Thursday, we watched the Early Show together at 4:00 p.m., either on the black and white Magnavox in my living room or on the Shontz's new Sylvania color television in their much larger living room. We saw Paul Newman stare at Joanne Woodward in the closing scene of *The Long Hot Summer* and did our best to memorize the dialogue.

"You don't scare me, Mr. Quick," Joanne told him while she fidgeted with her blonde schoolteacher bun to avoid looking at his baby blue eyes.

"Oh, but I do, little lady," Paul said. He did, too; he just stood there with his blue denim shirt slung over his shoulder while his chest glistened from the scorching heat of the southern sun and the fires of Tennessee Williams' screenplay. "You can move away. You can run for miles, but I'll find you, little lady. I will hunt you down. You can count on it."

"I'm counting on you to hunt me down," Pam said to Paul on the screen as we panted.

"Let's set a goal, Cath, to have boyfriends by the end of the seventh grade." Still breathless from the sexual tension at the end of the movie, we made the pact and were dead serious about it.

That night I tossed and turned with fantasies I played and replayed in my head of being kissed like Paul kissed Joanne. "Can't sleep, Tat?" Daddy said, his tall shadow towering over my bed.

"No, Daddy, I told him, grateful for the darkness that camouflaged my blush.

"You are a lot like me, Tat. Just remember that dreams or nightmares are your mind taking out the garbage." That remark made me burst out laughing. My father never failed to make me laugh whenever I needed relief from any problem. Daddy's choice of words that night, contrasting to the romance and poetry I was creating in my mind, was just too much for me to hold on to my fantasy kiss.

"Okay, Daddy," I said and continued laughing, "I'll remember."

"Night, honey," he said and kissed my forehead. "Don't go to Chicago; I would miss you way too much."

"I won't, Daddy," I told him and then thought, I will never leave my father.

On Friday nights when Pam, Mary, and I had sleepovers on our screened porch, Mother's diet and my calorie counting went out the window. The three musketeers ate a box of Kraft's macaroni and cheese made with milk, salt, and heaps of butter, followed by a large bag of potato chips with the California dip that Mrs. Cordeal taught us how to make from a large container of sour cream and two packages of dried Lipton onion soup during the Late Show at 10:00 p.m. After polishing all of that off, during the Late, Late Show, we made bowls and bowls of buttered popcorn and ate all of that to the last kernel. Finally, before we went to sleep around 2:00 A.M., we ate a Sara Lee frozen coconut cream pie divided three ways. We dared each other to sleep naked under our sheets. We took off our nighties, and one of us said, "Is everyone naked?" As soon as there were three yes answers, one of us said, 'I can't do it!" Then all of us put our pajamas back on.

Every Sunday night after one of our porch sleepovers, I got furious with myself for ruining a week of my self-inflicted starvation and verbally flogged myself in my diary; I *am fat! I am an idiot! I am ugly! I will never get a boyfriend in seventh grade! I ruined everything.*

All summer, I prayed I would get a boyfriend in the seventh grade and fulfill my pact with Pam. I needed it to happen; I needed to be ready, and vacation time before school started was ticking away. I dreamt about *it*, read about *it*, watched movies, listened to songs about *it*, and talked to Pam about *it*. I craved *it*.

"You know *it's* bigger than both of us," Bogart told Ingrid Bergman in *Casablanca.*

"You want *it*, Scarlett. You need kissing badly," Rhett told her, pages before he carried her in her flowing red velvet robe up the massive staircase to their bedroom in *Gone with the Wind.*

"Always pick the man who kicks the door down," said the unhappily married Barbara Stanwyck to Marilyn Monroe in *Clash by Night.*

I picked up the phone on the first ring whenever I knew Pam was calling. "I'm not supposed to be on the phone, Cath, but *Home from the Hill* is tomorrow at 4:00 p.m.! My house! George Peppard, baby, George-the-hunk Peppard!

Pam and I were in front of her television at 3:55 p.m. At 4:45 p.m., George Peppard, playing Robert Mitchem's illegitimate son, was wearing loosely tied pajama bottoms and no shirt when he walked into the bedroom of sultry Ina Balin, the girlfriend of his half but legitimate brother, George Hamilton. George Peppard was there to soothe Ina from a nightmare. He held her close to his bare chest to calm her down, then laid her on the bed and covered her with a blanket. Ina whispered to him as he turned to leave the room, "Don't go," she said and folded her cover back, and as her nightgown strap fell from her shoulder onto her arm, she reached out and tugged his hand.

George Peppard stayed, and Pam and I squirmed. We continued to squirm right through July. We said, "Don't go!" to each other before we hung up our phones at night, and each time we convulsed into squeals of laughter. We were the 1962 versions of thirteen-year-old sex-starved sisters with a pact.

Pam was up a bra size to a 34C by August. My height threatened to exceed five twelve; I was still in a training bra and gained another five pounds. "Cathy, you've got nothing to put in a regular bra," Mother said when I asked for a padded bra. "Don't worry; we will see about other bras when you start your periods."

"I thought you said I was built like Daddy's side of the family," I moaned. "Aunt EB and Aunt Jeanette both have big breasts."

"Yes, that's true," Mother answered, looking up at me, "but unfortunately, I think this is the one part of your body you inherited from flat-chested me."

That night I wrote in my diary, *I'm doomed. There will be no big breasts for me, not even one decent-sized breast.*

Two weeks before school started, Pam called. "Cath, we're moving. My Dad got a promotion, and we bought a house across the golf course on Algonquin Wood. We can cross the golf course between us, meet halfway and walk together to each other's houses. The bad thing is that I need to go to Steger Junior High instead of Hixson." Mary and I hated that news and feared that Pam's move would end Woodlawn's three musketeers.

Pam's family was busy packing and planning for the next two weeks. Our Early Show movie afternoons were over, so I hid in the Webster library and read *Peyton Place.* I didn't know what to do with my libido without Pam to watch movies with me. Though I didn't understand it, the energy of my sexual drive as a component in my life was intense then and never left me afterward. At home, I tried to find naughty parts in Mother's mystery books but found none. I did find some magazines Rick hid in his hideout down the basement and looked at those when he was at football practice. I remember a black-and-white picture of a naked Anita Eckberg that almost made me drop the magazine. I coveted her breasts and promised myself that somehow when I got older, I would find a way to buy them!

Our three musketeer Friday food-frenzied overnights ended too. I missed Pam, but fortunately, my cousin Diane visited. Diane was older, and I asked her to tell me about the movies, *Where the Boys Are, A Summer Place,* and *Parrish.* They were B-rated movies by the church, and I was forbidden to see them. Diane saved me those last weeks. We sat on my bed, and she described every second of every movie she got to see. Diane was a vivid movie describer. She was out of high school and dating a living doll named Johnny, who wore brown Bermuda shorts and drove a brown UPS truck. Diane was part of the boy-crazy good-girl group in school, while her older sister, Caroline, was part of the sex-crazy bad-girl group. I found it interesting later that their mother, my Aunt Catherine became a nun after her girls grew up and were on their own.

As summer ended, all I could see was tragedy ahead for me. I was positive Pam would have a boyfriend and be kissed on her first day at Steger, while at Hixon, I still would not have started my periods or have worn a real bra.

ℒ

CHAPTER SEVENTEEN

FEAR, WORRY, AND TWO GIRDLES

There were three grades in junior high: seventh, eighth, and ninth. It was a challenge to go from the sixth-grade top of the totem pole at Bristol to the bottom of it at Hixson, especially since ninth-graders were freshmen in high school. The freshmen boys and girls thought of themselves as Hixson men and women because seventh and eighth graders were technically still in grade school. I may have been with everyone at the bottom of the totem pole, but I towered over every girl and many boys in school, no matter their grades. This observation started me on a path of finding a way to make myself smaller.

I decided to wear two girdles to school. I couldn't do anything about my height, but maybe, if I packed my hippiness tight enough into a girdle, I might look thinner and smaller like the freshmen cheerleaders, and if I wore *two* girdles, I would look even smaller! The girls' fashion at Hixson in the early sixties was blouses or mohair sweaters, plain or plaid pleated skirts, stockings, white tennis shoes, and bucket bag purses. My choice of wearing two girdles caused a massive hassle for me time-wise. It meant getting up earlier than usual to attach my nylons to four garter fasteners on each leg instead of two. The first girdle was a problem; squeezing my one hundred and fifty-five pounds into it and hooking the fasteners to my nylons was no easy feat. I got a slight hormonal rush from how fast the second girdle slid easily over the first. I thought this was how clothes fit all the time for cheerleaders. The gym class presented the biggest problem. I didn't want the girls to laugh at me, so I hid my second girdle in my bucket bag and then had to hide in a stall in the girls' restroom just outside the gym to pull the second one in place. The extra time it took for this usually made me late for my next class.

All day I lived in terror that someone might bump into me and bounce off hard enough to know I was wearing two girdles. I tortured myself with this two-girdle practice for an entire month until Lawrence Gregg slapped my bottom in Mr. Tompkins' math class. Mr. T. resembled the actor Wally Cox. He had slicked-down brown hair, thick black glasses, and double-starched white shirts. I got A grades in his class because he was a good teacher, but I thought he was a knight in shining armor that day.

I was walking past Lawrence Gregg's desk to turn in a test when Lawrence slapped me on my two-girdled-rear. It was a hard slap and a loud one! I was mortified and turned fifty shades of red when Mr. T. said, "Lawrence Gregg, never touch a woman in that way again! Gentlemen, never do anything like that, ever! Am I clear?"

"Yes, sir," Lawrence said. "I won't, sir."

"Apologize to Miss Miller right now," Mr. T. ordered.

"I'm sorry, Cathy," Lawrence said.

"Okay," I mumbled. The mortification on my face did not come from the sexual insult of the slap but from the knowledge that

Lawrence Gregg discovered I wore two girdles and the fear that Lawrence might have broken a bone in his hand.

The incident ended my girdled attempt at shrinking my fat hips and having a cheerleader's body. Ironically, Lawrence and I became good friends in junior high. He was my first male telephone caller, the first of many boys who later called to talk to me but never dated me. I became Dear Cathy instead of Dear Abby. I spoke to Lawrence for hours on my new turquoise desk phone. We talked about all the girls with whom he was madly in love. We even said through the Beatles' first appearance on the Ed Sullivan Show, and I confessed I liked George best.

"I thought sure you would be in love with Paul like all the other girls," Lawrence said.

"Nope," I told him, "I'm not like other girls."

The only thing that helped me stop focusing on myself in the seventh grade was when Daddy had a heart attack. "Get up, Cathy," Mother called from the bottom of the stairs. "You are going to be late for school. Rick already left, and Jimmy's eating breakfast now."

I jumped up, made my bed, ran across the hall to the bathroom, washed my face, and ran back to my room; I had to make it fast so Daddy could get in the bathroom for his shower. I slid between my bed and my dresser and tore the brush rollers out of my hair, slid back to my closet less than a foot away from the end of my bed, grabbed the outfit I picked out the night before to wear, dressed, and slid back to my mirror. I was on my first application of spraying Aqua Net on my perfect flip hairstyle when I heard a loud thud in the bathroom. I knew it was Daddy. Mother was already with him from the kitchen before I slid back out, got around my bed, and crossed the hall to the bathroom.

"Hank? Hank?" she yelled on the other side of the closed bathroom door. All I could do was stand outside and stare at it. When the door opened, Mother gently pushed me out of her way and went to the phone. "Don't go into the bathroom, Cathy," she said and began to cry. She dialed the phone and said, "Dr. Jones, this is Mary Miller. Hank just fell in the bathroom; I can't move him."

"The hell you can't," Daddy said and staggered past me to their bedroom to lie on his bed. His face and body were devoid of all color; I could almost see through his skin. His appearance scared me so much that I was unaware I was crying too.

"Dr. Jones, please call an ambulance." Mother said and hung up the phone. "Cathy, finish getting ready. I am going to ask Charlie to take you to school." Mother closed the bathroom door and went into the bedroom to be with Daddy. Again, I just stood and looked at a closed door.

"Mother, please, please let me in to help you," I begged and shook their doorknob.

"No, Cathy," she answered. "Now go, finish getting dressed and go over to the Cordeals."

I was told later that when my father had this heart attack, his bowels were evacuated when he collapsed on the floor, and Mother didn't want me to see the mess. "I didn't want to embarrass your father or scare you any more than you already were," she told me. I have no memory of the rest of that day.

My mother went to the hospital and spent the day beside my father's bed. Rick and Jimmy didn't know of Daddy's attack until they got home from school. The phone rang off the wall with relatives, Mrs. Shontz, and other friends calling; Rick and I took turns repeating Mother's message, "Daddy had a heart attack; he is in the hospital. Mother is with him."

I do remember a few events of that night. Jimmy was watching television in the living room when Mrs. Cordeal brought steaming homemade lasagna over to us. Mary stood behind her mother with garlic bread and Jane with a salad behind her. "I'm so sorry about Mr. Miller," Mary said.

"Rick, call us if you need anything," Mrs. Cordeal said. "We are right next door. We have Hank in our prayers."

Mother came home from the hospital, still wearing her apron from breakfast. She looked so tired. "Good kids, I'm so glad you are eating," she said. "God bless the Cordeals; they are such wonderful neighbors." I got up to get a plate, but Mother stopped me. "No, Tat, I am just too tired to eat." Jimmy was excused from the table and went back to his television shows. Mother sank in her chair and wept. I had never seen my mother cry so hard.

"Jimmy is too young to know this," she told Rick and me, "but your father's heart attack was serious. Dr. Jones said that if your father makes it through the next three days and nights, he has a good chance to live many more years, but only if he stops smoking and drinking alcohol. Daddy will have to live upstairs for about two months when he comes home. Your father cannot climb up and down the stairs; it will be too hard on his heart." Rick and I didn't cry; we knew we didn't have the luxury.

People must have dropped off food for us the next week because I don't remember cooking dinner once. It was like none of us took a full breath, much less did anything normal during those three days and nights. Mother was at the hospital most of the time and insisted that Rick, Jimmy, and I go to school like always. I didn't hear a single word from the teachers or anyone else. I was deaf and numb with fear. I prayed on my knees each of the three nights, just like my father always prayed. I didn't care if I fell asleep on them; I couldn't feel anything, anyway. *Dear God, please let Daddy live. He's just got to be all right;* I prayed before I wrote in my diary that *Daddy had a horrible heart attack, and I am so scared, the most scared I have ever been. I don't have anyone to talk to about anything. Is it because we are Catholic that God is punishing us, or whatever the heck He is doing? I mean, geez, Pam is Catholic too, but she's got her dad, probably a boyfriend, and a new house. All I want is Daddy.*

✄

CHAPTER EIGHTEEN

DRAMA AND TRAUMA

They say a father is a girl's first boyfriend; it is the natural order of life for his daughter. A father is a protector, the first man to tell her, "I love you." It's why the future husband asks the father's permission to marry the daughter. It's why her father is the one on her wedding day to walk her down the aisle and give her away. The three days that determined whether my father would be alive to walk me down the aisle if I got married were panic-stricken; my brain did not stop bouncing between the drama that felt out of control at home and the trauma I felt inside me.

Nothing in our house was normal when Daddy was still in the hospital. Uncle Lou took Rick aside and told him, "You have to be the head of this family now." This pressure on my older brother at the age of sixteen forced him to say goodbye to his childhood years before he should have; it thrust him into the adult world to carry the weight of Mother, Jimmy, and me on his tenth-grade shoulders.

I tried to be strong when Daddy didn't come to my room and kiss me goodnight those three nights. My body ached all over from missing him. I felt alone and cast out of the adult conversations and concerns about my father. I felt like an oddity, someone like the creatures in the illegal freak shows Rick told me about, the ones that came through St. Louis in the early sixties. All I had was my diary as a confidante for my fears. *I am an amazon, a fat and flat-chested girl who may have no father and only one good nipple. How can such a creature ever find out if love is really a many-splendored thing? And why should I care about anything if Daddy dies? I am just selfish to worry about myself. I need Daddy.*

Jimmy was in the fourth grade and mainly oblivious to the severity of Daddy's hospitalization. He dealt with the tense atmosphere at home by escalating his hyperactivity, which made Mother, Rick, and me more anxious and nervous than ever. Jimmy's hyperactivity collided with my hypersensitivity and firing hormones on one of the three days we waited. Jimmy hid in my closet and waited for me to come into my room so he could scare me. Everything I was holding inside exploded. He popped out and screamed, "Boo!" I started screaming at him in my fury. Life was Boo enough already!

"There is something wrong with you," I yelled; "Mother said there was!" The minute I said it, I hated myself. I wanted to reel in every word, but it was too late. I saw the hurt on Jimmy's face, and before I could say I was sorry, he ran downstairs to Mother in the kitchen for comfort.

"Is that true?" he asked her. "Is there something wrong with me?"

I raced into the kitchen behind him. "I'm so sorry, Jimmy," I said. "I didn't mean it. You just scared me."

"What did she mean, Mother?" he asked.

"All she was talking about, Jimmy, is that sometimes you need help with your homework."

"Well, who doesn't?" he said, satisfied with her answer. "I'm going over to Mike's."

Out the door, he went, happily whistling toward Cordeals, but I felt no relief. I had hurt him, and I had to own it.

"You have a mean mouth, Cathy," Mother said, shaking her finger at me. "You use words like knives to cut people. You went too far with your mouth today. Someday, when you go too far, there will be no way to repair the damage. You must do your best with Jimmy and make up for your cruelty to him.

Back in my room, I did not think I could hate myself more. Was that the way my mother saw me? Was she speaking the truth? Her comment scared me far more than Jimmy's, "Boo!" It was not how I wanted to be perceived by anyone, much less by family members. At thirteen, I was exhausted trying to figure out who I was. I could not stop my brain from its constant search for identity. I tried so hard to be the glue in our family, to be the happy one and hide my feelings, but that day, I couldn't hide them, and they came out as rage.

It was a deep wound to learn that my words were swords, not armor. I failed at protecting my thoughts; I got weak and used them for defense. I needed a mask, a false self to project to others. So began my coping skill of saying "yes," when I meant "no." I learned to choke back emotions for fear of them overflowing. I could check and recheck my thoughts so that every word out of my mouth was part of my disguise. I became nearly perfect at it, but it wasn't easy. I was never a fan of silliness, shallow conversations, or fake politeness, even at my youngest. I thought people wanted the truth, but I was wrong. I needed to tell them what they wanted to hear, even if I wished sometimes to scream, "If you hate what I say, you ought to hear what I don't say!" Camouflaging my authentic self became more painful as I got older. Secretly, I was proud of my ability to connect with people, and I never feared but *craved* intimacy with them. I never liked cartoons, but the day I hurt Jimmy, I learned to make a cartoon version of myself and work harder to keep everyone laughing.

Daddy came home from the hospital on the Monday of my second week of school. He lived through his three days, and so had all of us. Our house was extra quiet that night. I was hunkered down in my bed with my Girl Scout flashlight finishing *To Kill a Mockingbird.* There were fresh sheets on my bed. I loved the smell of Tide and Clorox that Mother baked into them all weekend while they hung on the clothesline in the backyard. "Sheets must hang outside at least two days before their freshness is perfect," she said.

On Daddy's first night at home, I was still awake reading and thinking about how brilliant Harper Lee was as a writer. I remember thinking that Atticus might be the second-best father ever right before I heard Daddy's fingers tapping on my headboard. I was so happy to have him home; I needed him home.

"Hey, Tatter, you are in junior high now," he said.

"I guess," I sighed. "Daddy, how long do you have to stay upstairs to recover?"

"Two months," he said. "Tonight, you and I look like that tragedy mask hanging over there on your wall. Boy, we're a couple of sad sacks, aren't we?"

"Yep," I agreed and pulled at a loose thread on the front of my nightie.

"Tat," he said and snapped off the thread. "I know you miss Pam, but you'll make new girlfriends at Hixson, and you can still talk to her on the phone and see her on the weekends. And hey, don't forget, Mary is still right next door. Never forget about Mary.

"I could never forget about Mary, but I'm afraid Pam won't have time for us anymore," I said. "She will have boyfriends and activities at her new school. Daddy, did you know Steger is right across the street from the Chatterbox Bar; you'll probably see her more than I will."

"Well, honey, it looks like we both must make some changes. The doctor says no more Chatterbox Bar for me, so I guess we are both losing our chatterboxes." The laugh wrinkles around his eyes made a slow comeback and made me laugh.

"I'm so glad you are home, Daddy," I said as I hugged him, a hug I hoped would breathe more life back into him.

"I love you, Tat, no matter what, don't ever forget that. You have so many boyfriends ahead of you, don't rush things."

"I could never, ever forget you, Daddy," I promised, wiping the tears off his cheeks and then off my own. I smiled my first smile since Pam moved and Daddy got sick. My face felt as though it cracked. But something else, besides my dramatic teenage behavior, made my father sad that night.

"What's wrong, Daddy?" I asked.

"I just can't sleep, Tat," he said and sat down on my bed. "Can we talk a little more?"

"Yes, let's talk," I said. I scooted over to make room for him. I snapped off my flashlight, propped my pillows behind my head, and leaned against my headboard. I pulled my long legs up so he could lean against my headboard and run his Daddy extra-long legs at a diagonal across my narrow bed. A thin light shone from the bathroom night light, just bright enough for me to see his weary face. "Are you okay, Daddy? Do you feel all right?"

"I'm fine, Tat," he said, but that heart attack really scared me."

"It scared me too, and Mother, Rick, and Jimmy. "Those days and nights when we didn't know if you would live, or die, were the worst days of my life."

My father sighed a heavy sigh. "You know, honey, sometimes I think you, your mother, and your brothers would be better off if I did die."

I couldn't breathe. "What did you say? What?" I said loud enough to scare my father as well as myself. I heard Max jump down from Mother's bed and click across the hall's bare wood. He poked his red dachshund face around the corner of my room to check and see if we were all right.

"Sssh, Tatter, you'll wake everyone in the house. Come here, Maxie," Daddy said, scooping up Max's long body and putting him on the bed with us. "Honey, I didn't mean to scare you. I only meant that if I did die, you guys would get my life insurance, and then all of you would be better off. My insurance money could pay many bills and get this family back on track again."

"Daddy, just stop it; that's stupid, the dumbest thing I ever heard," I said, crying. I choked on the tears running down my face. "I hate what you said! I don't understand what it was, but whatever it was, I hate it!" I slid under my covers and stretched out my legs, almost pushing him off the bed. I started singing; I wanted to sing away what he said; I wanted him to sing with me like we always did. *Give me some men who are stouthearted men who will fight for the right they adore.* He didn't sing, though it was one of his favorite Nelson Eddy songs. I sang even louder, *shoulder to shoulder, bolder and bolder . . ..* It didn't work; the tears kept coming. "Take it back, Daddy, please," I begged, "say you didn't mean it."

I felt his chest cave in with a long exhale. "I didn't mean it, Tat. I'm so sorry. Oh, Tat, I'm so sorry I scared you; let's keep this a secret between us."

I didn't answer him. I wasn't going to answer him until I believed he was sorry. Why would he ever want to leave me or leave our family? I felt him sit up and sigh again. Max burrowed under my covers to be close to me, and there was an unbearable silence until my father spoke again.

"Where's Cathy? Does anybody know? Oh no! She must have gone to Chicago!"

I could still see his tired face and sadness through my covers. I was never to forget what he said. The mere suggestion of his death was a form of abandonment that permanently penetrated my heart and mind.

No matter how sorry my father was for what he said, no matter what reasons he had f it, all I heard and felt was his desire to leave me. The shock of his words caused me to go deep inside myself to my most secret place, where I learned to bury my worst fears, a deep-down secret place where once I arrived there, it was impossible to emerge from it unharmed. I became as sick as the secret. I trapped it inside me and buried it deep into my subconscious, where it manifested itself into lifelong recurring, anxiety-ridden dreams.

Daddy leaned and pretended to put all his weight on top of me. It was our Chicago game, the perfect way to hide my emotions from him. I yanked back my covers and tried to be the best actress ever.

"Ta-da! Here I am!" I said, but it was only a whispered pronouncement from a me no longer present, but a good enough performance to convince my father I forgave him.

"Oh, thank goodness," he said and squeezed me hard to his pajamaed chest; "I would be so sad if my Tatter ever really went to Chicago."

"I'm not gone, Daddy. I am right here," I assured him and then kissed him on his cheek.

"Forget I said anything, honey, please. Will you do that? It is just your old dad feeling blue, probably from the heart attack. I am still your Nelson Eddy, and you are still my Jeannette MacDonald. Right, honey?" He kissed me on my forehead and stood up, his thinning frame towering above me, just not quite as high. "Now go ahead and finish your book, then lights out. Okay?"

"Okay," I said and watched him disappear into the darkness in the hall. Max pulled free from my covers, jumped down from my bed, and turned to look at me. "It's okay, Maxie," I told him; "You go back to your bed now. Go on." He clicked away and disappeared after Daddy. I disappeared too, back under my covers to my secret place. I clicked on my flashlight and stared at Harper Lee's blurring words when I heard Daddy singing *Indian Love Call* from his bed.

"When I'm calling you, hoo, hoo, hoo, hoo, hoo, hoo. Will you answer too, hoo, hoo, hoo, hoo, hoo hoo?"

"Good night, Nelson," I called loud enough from underneath it all.

"Good night, Jeannette. I love you," he called from above.

Somehow in my secret place, I could escape back to Harper Lee. Each sentence I read from Scout became clearer to me.

"Atticus," [she told her father talking about Boo], *he was real nice."*

"...Most people are, Scout when you finally see them."

He turned out the light and went into Jem's room. He would be there all night, and he would be there when Jem waked up in the morning.

For the next two months, Mother, Rick, and I took turns taking my father's food trays upstairs to him. Most days, the guys from the Webster Groves Fire Department brought him lunch, or Mr. Cordeal brought lunch over to him. The men from the fire department loved my father. Each year, Daddy took over all the Christmas toys he promised Mother he wouldn't buy, and the firemen assembled them at the fire station between calls. Daddy paid them with beer and cigarettes. I never saw them at lunchtime because I was at school, but when the firemen came by, they sneaked him Playboy magazines to "read." My father read nothing but newspapers.

Many members of the Greatest Generation were smokers. A yellow outline showed on our walls if a picture was removed. Mother got thinner and thinner from her mounting worry over money; she smoked more than ever during Daddy's recovery. I was angry at her for smoking when Daddy was supposed to quit. I knew Rick was smoking, too, because he also smelled like tobacco.

Rick worked at Boyd's Men's Store (Boyd's) most nights to help with money, and we borrowed more money from my father's financially successful war buddy who lived in Texas. It was difficult for Mother to have her son work to cover household expenses before he was even out of high school. It was humiliating for my mother when my father borrowed money to pay a gambling debt, especially when she took phone calls from people who wanted to collect. Mother wore her sadness and embarrassment like a shroud for the two months my father lived upstairs. I was happy to have both my parents and thanked God they were both alive, but our home felt different after Daddy got sick, and I wondered if it would ever feel the way it used to feel again.

⌀

CHAPTER NINETEEN
THE BARE TRUTH

I didn't fit in with any specific crowd at school in the eighth grade, either. I relied on humor to protect myself from criticisms from all the cliques. I hoped I could be funny enough that nobody would sing about the Jolly Green Giant when I walked the halls of Hixson alone, but when I felt my most vulnerable, I still heard Bristol's old teasing echo i*n the valley of the Jolly, ho, ho, ho, Green Giant!* I made sure I never wore green in junior high.

I made good grades and busied myself by going from crush to crush on boys who would never be my boyfriends; it gave me something interesting to talk to Pam and Mary about on the phone at night. I was still looking for a boyfriend but was discouraged since I failed the seventh-grade pact with Pam. The bare truth was that I hated my body and lacked the confidence to be comfortable in my skin. It was easier to make fun of it myself before someone else did.

"I would wear clothes in the bathtub if I could still get clean!" I told Pam and Mary. The model Twiggy's less than one hundred pounds held psychological power enough to kill other girls in the sixties and me. There were no media to defend us and say, "Body shaming is wrong!" Nobody spoke out for us; we just stayed ashamed of our bodies. "Being naked is *unbearable,*" I said to make people laugh. My self-deprecating jokes worked; they always delivered the laughter needed to drown out criticism and ridicule.

I thought about babies' bodies when I babysat. They loved being naked and toddling around freshly powdered, squeaky clean after a bath. I was jealous that they were such liberated little creatures, with only Baby Magic covering their perfect skin. My father and brothers loved to be naked, too. I hid my eyes when all three took turns in the bathroom and walked down the hall without worrying about the world. Mother was taught in Catholic boarding schools that a woman's naked body was a carnal sin if she shared it with anyone except her husband. She instilled that fear in me. "Good girls only allow their husbands to see them naked," she preached.

I loved my robe. Even if it was a hundred degrees, I covered myself in my nightgowns with a sheet at night, though I had nothing to hide except my one developing breast. Hiding my emotions was difficult enough, but in the eighth grade, my life was run by the uncontrollable urge to hide everything about me that people could see as well. I never looked in a mirror at myself naked; I avoided eye contact, even with myself. It was safer to stay in my romantic imagination than to see my realistic flaws. One entry in my diary said *I hope sex feels better than it looks; maybe if I ever get married, my husband and I can make our babies in the dark.*

Rick was a sophomore at CBC, the private Catholic military school our cousin EB made possible after Rick got in trouble by joyriding in a car with his friends. We didn't have the money to pay for a private school. Mother sold magazines on the telephone to pay for my braces. It was hard work. Sometimes, I overheard people slamming down their phones or being verbally rude to her. Mother panicked anytime I used my mouth to pull on a pillowcase or ate a Slow Poke sucker. "My God, Cathy, don't use your teeth; they cost a fortune!" I committed the mortal sin of leaving my retainer on my lunch tray one day and had to go down to the cafeteria, put on plastic gloves, and go through the garbage cans to find it. "Thank God you found it!" Mother said. "It cost me thirty-five dollars in magazine sales!"

Rick was busy with sports and dating at CBC. I went home right after school every day to take care of Jimmy when Mother went back to work at Doubleday after Daddy's recovery. I knew Mother didn't like why she had to return to work, but I knew she loved working there. She had two good friends at Doubleday, Toppy Couzier and Lib Wright. "We have such fun working together," Mother said, and she smiled more often after returning to Doubleday.

Life at fourteen amounted to getting up, walking to school, walking home after school, watching Jimmy, calling Mother to help me make dinner over the phone, helping Mother with the dishes after dinner, folding clothes, doing two hours of homework, writing in my diary, reading in bed, going to sleep, and repeat. There were no clubs, no sports, no boys, and still no menstrual periods. If it hadn't been for Miss Martin, my drama teacher, I might have considered going into the convent like Audrey Hepburn in *The Nun's Story;* only I didn't want to shave my head; I thought I looked bad enough already.

Boys were more straightforward friendships to make than girls. I think they saw me as one of them because they still called me by my last name; some girls did, too, except for one girl, Sue Lance, who befriended me in October. We called each other Stanley and

Livingston. We could have named ourselves Mutt and Jeff because she was so petite and I was so tall, but we liked the idea of using Stanley (Sue) and Livingston (me) when we passed notes to each other in the halls. Sue was a fabulous dancer; she could shake her tail feather and tried hard to teach me how to dance in her basement recreation room on Saturdays when Mother was home with Jimmy.

"How can someone who sings like you, Cathy, have absolutely no rhythm in her body?" she asked, but the good friend she was kept trying.

"I think it is because I am always the boy in everything," I told her.

"That ends, now!" she said. Sue was the sweetest girl in school.

The Thursday President John F. Kennedy was shot in November; Jeff A. Davis met me at my locker after lunch before my gym class. We had two boys named Jeff Davis in our grade; the other was Jeff B. Davis. Jeff A. was a loveable prankster who played practical jokes, and Jeff B. was the huggable teddy bear type.

"Hey Miller," Jeff A. said, "did you hear? President Kennedy was shot in Texas!"

"Jeff," I said, "sometimes you are not funny, not funny at all!" But it was true. I was about to serve the volleyball in gym class when the principal came on the sound system and said, "Boys and girls, I am sorry to report that our President, John F. Kennedy, was shot in Texas this afternoon, and unfortunately, he did not survive. The staff is calling your parents now to arrange for you to go home."

Mother was working, so I went to Sue's house with her. Mrs. Lance picked us up and took us to their house until Mother came and picked me up after work. Jimmy went home from school with his friend Tony whose mother picked them up from Bristol and took them to her house. Rick had his own car and came home from CBC on his own. Mrs. Lance was sobbing when she arrived for Sue and me; she cried all the way to their house and for the rest of the afternoon. "This cannot be happening," she said over and over; "this is not America."

Mother and Daddy did not go to work on Friday. I watched television in my room with Daddy sitting beside me on my bed. We watched Jack Ruby shoot Oswald on live television. My father said, "Oh my God, oh my God! There it is, Tat, living and dying proof that there is nothing more corrupt or deplorable on earth than politics. It is a filthy, rotten to the core business." I did not know what he was talking about; all I knew was how sad we all were. Daddy and I cried when little John-John saluted his father's casket while standing beside his mother and sister at the President's funeral. I knew John-John didn't understand why he did that, but I knew his heart would break someday when he did know.

The only political argument between my parents that I was aware of occurred during the Nixon and Kennedy presidential election. My mother and father consistently voted the same. "Don't cancel my vote," they said to one another. Mother was a Democrat at heart, though she never admitted it; somehow, in the Nixon/ Kennedy election, she was determined to vote for Nixon. My father was a Republican and was going to vote for Nixon until he went downtown St. Louis and saw John F. Kennedy in a motorcade. "Tat, I yelled 'Good luck, Senator!' and Senator Kennedy called back to me, 'Yes sir, thank you, sir!' Guess what? He even shook my hand! Listen, Tat, that man wants to change politics in America if his own party doesn't kill him first! They don't like his plans for the country." Nobody in America knew what would happen, how the music would die, not even Arlo Guthrie.

The worst days of discomfort in my skin happened on gym class days when all the girls showered together or lost points if they didn't. It was no surprise that the day I finally started my period was a gym day. The thyroid pills did not work alone, so I took the estrogen/progestogen pill for three months. I was elated and embarrassed when I saw the blood between the legs of my white gym suit. I went to our gym teacher and told her what had happened. She gave me a Kotex pad and the belt with the two metal clips that cut into your skin in front and back. She handed me a small bag to take home my no longer white gym clothes. "Here you go, Miller," she said, tossing them to me.

My stomach hurt, and I felt like I had a mattress between my legs for the rest of the school day. I couldn't wait to go home. Hixson was a long way from Woodlawn, and the walk was torture. With each step, I was terrified the pad would fall between my legs and onto the ground.

I called Pam when I got home, but she wasn't home yet because she had Pep Club after school. I tried to change the pad with the extra one in the bag with my gym clothes, but I was so clumsy that it took me forever, especially with Jimmy banging on the door. "Claire, what are you doing? Claire, hurry up!" The rest of the afternoon felt endless until Mother got home.

"I started my period in gym class today," I whispered to her in the kitchen while we were putting away groceries.

"Did your gym teacher give you what you needed?" she asked, smiling. "That is good news!" I knew Mother would be happy.

"Yes," I said, "but I can't stand wearing this thing; it's like wearing a mattress between my legs, and the metal tab thing hurts my skin in the back!"

"It's okay, Tat, there is something better; I will show you how to use tampons. Let's go upstairs to the bathroom.

I was embarrassed to be naked in front of my mother and have her give me such a private demonstration, but by dinner time, I was grateful. I had almost mastered the art of using Tampax by the time I went to bed, but what was more important, I thought maybe, just *maybe*, by starting my periods, I had mastered the art of pleasing my mother.

∅

CHAPTER TWENTY
LADY MARY

The last class of my eighth-grade day was drama with Miss Martin. She was tall like me, only about an inch shorter. She was a slim woman with light brown hair combed in a page boy hairstyle on some days or a small flip-style on others. I loved Miss Martin. She was complimentary of everyone, constantly boosting the moods or eliminating the worries of her students, especially during the long months of winter weather in St. Louis when some years we had uninterrupted weeks of gray days.

Miss Martin was my sun on those gray days. Her voice was musical, like she was saying happy words of dialogue from a comedy rather than teaching, and her laugh was frequent, full, low, and loud. She wore flat shoes instead of high heels like the other female teachers. I wondered if that was because she wasn't married and wanted to be shorter for men she wanted to date or because she needed to move faster than other teachers. A drama teacher was a teacher who had to bob and weave and act out characters all over the classroom.

"Class," she said one dreary Friday afternoon in late February, "this year's eighth-grade play will be *The Admirable Crichton*, a classic English drawing room comedy. Auditions will be after school on

Monday and Tuesday, with callbacks on Wednesday. Rehearsals will start the following Monday, the first of March.

I thought my heart fell out of my chest onto the floor. I wanted so much to be part of the play's production, but how could I attend rehearsals when I had to watch Jimmy and fix dinner every night? It was out of the question.

"Cathy, I want to talk to you after class," Miss Martin said, looking at my long face.

"Yes, mam," I said; we said "mam" in the sixties.

I waited for the other students to leave before walking to her desk. "Cathy, here is a copy of the play. I want you to audition for the female lead of Lady Mary. Study the part over the weekend to be ready for Monday's auditions."

I was stunned. I couldn't speak or thank her; I just took the copy of the play, gathered my books, and went out into the hall. How could I play the lead? I was much too tall for all the boys in the class except Bob Wilkinson, who was exactly my height. Besides, there was no way Mother would permit me to be part of the production.

"I want to do this play, Mother," I pleaded when she got home.

"And how would that be possible?" she asked. "I need you here to take care of Jimmy and start dinner, you know."

"I have taken care of Jimmy after school for two years, Mother. Rick gets to play football and even has a car. I want to do this play!"

"No!" she said.

"Please?" I begged.

"No!" she repeated. I felt my face get hot with anger, but I held back my tears.

"Who do you think you are, God?" I asked. Bam! Mother slapped me hard across the face, the only time she ever did.

"Go to your room, Cathy, and don't come out until you apologize!"

I didn't come out of my room that night to help with dinner or eat it. I cried until I had no more tears. I walked across the hall to the bathroom, washed my face, brushed my teeth, and returned to my room. I was so upset that I couldn't read or call Pam or Mary. All I could do was lie on my bed and stare at the ceiling, quite positive I had the worst life of anyone in the world.

After everyone was settled down for the night, Daddy came into my room. "Tat," he said, "we need to have a grown-up talk, you and I."

"Okay, Daddy, I said, sitting up.

"You are becoming a woman," he began; "you have started your periods, but your mother is approaching the other end of womanhood. She is experiencing the time in a woman's life when she stops having periods, and her body begins to adjust to growing older. Both of you are changing. I want you both to be more understanding of one other and nicer to each other. You two are the only women in this house. Your mother is the only person, Tat, who has been where you are now and where you are heading. Please try to understand that she is working to help our family meet our financial needs while at the same time, she cleans our house, does our laundry, and helps Jimmy every night with his homework. She needs your help; we all do." He kissed my forehead and left the room. We played no games that night. I stayed awake a long time trying to put on my mother's shoes and walk around like Atticus told Scout to do in Boo Radley's shoes.

My rebellion against my mother that day and my father's subsequent counseling over my behavior planted a vital seed that unfortunately didn't grow to full fruition until many years later. Asserting myself over something I badly wanted was my first experience of seeing I was not an appendage of my mother. My father's elaboration over what happened between my mother and me told me that what I did was not wrong and was even normal, but it was how I did it, especially toward the first person on the planet who showed me what love was by giving me life. Still, it was the start of my learning that pain and loss are necessary for becoming a separate self.

The next morning, I went downstairs, where Mother and Daddy were having their Saturday coffee together. My eyes were nearly swollen shut from all my crying; I could barely see to walk into the kitchen.

"Mother," I said, "I want to apologize for using the Lord's name in vain and being so rude to you." It was impossible to have any more tears to cry, but I did cry. "I am so sorry life is so hard for you. I am being selfish. I hope you will forgive me."

"Of course I do, Tat," she said. She got up from the table and walked over to me. She cried too. "And I want you to audition for the play on Monday after school."

"No, Mother," I said.

"No argument," she said. "We will figure out what to do about Jimmy. If you get the part in the play or another part, we will make dinner together when you get home from practice; we will have to eat a bit later than usual, that's all."

I caught a brief glimpse of Daddy behind Mother when he got up to get the coffee pot and refill their cups. I thought I saw tears on his face, but when he started whistling, I figured I must have been wrong.

I got the lead role on Monday, the only one I ever got again. My tall drama teacher knew much more about life than drama. Bob Wilkinson got the male role of Crichton opposite my Lady Mary. The entire experience was fantastic for the Jolly Green Giant, except for the mishap with the tights I was given to wear by one mother helping the costume crew.

It was a dress rehearsal. We had a small, invited audience of Miss Martin's friends, and I wanted to be perfect for her. But in April 1963, *one* size *fits all* pantyhose translated to *no size fit me.* They began creeping down toward my hips by the end of Act One. We didn't take a ten-minute intermission because Miss Martin wanted us to rest that night before opening the next night. We went straight into the second act. I ran behind the stage right curtain leg, hiked up my emerald green velvet gown, and yanked the tights up with all my might to get them closer to my waist. I felt them rip, but I didn't care because my costume covered up whatever tore. There was no taking them off because my size eight and a half feet would not go into my size eight shoes without them.

I stretched out the elastic in the waist by pulling on the tights too hard. My tights began creeping again, only faster, when we were barely into the second act. I counted the times I needed to cross the stage before the final curtain went down, trying not to miss a line. I muffed a few lines with each cross because my tights crept down further, making me panic even more. My steps got shorter and shorter until I made my final cross as England's refined Lady Mary, like a Geisha girl with bound feet. I heard Miss Martin's boisterous laugh ring out above the small applause as soon as the curtain came down. There was no time to make it to my place at the center of the line for bows; I was nailed to the floor. All I could do as the curtain rose for bows was pull up my gown and reveal the twisted tights around my feet. There was a sudden increase in applause from the small audience.

"Well, Carol Burnett," Miss Martin said, "I told you from the start this play was a comedy!"

The actual performances went smoothly. Bob Wilkinson kissed me on the lips behind the curtain as the work lights came up after our last bows of the final performance. My first kiss. But then I had to ruin the memory, thinking Bob might still have been in character and believed he was kissing Lady Mary. Either way, I was thrilled to have accomplished first base! The kiss and wearing tights that Miss Martin bought for me herself should have been enough to paint this moment of my adolescence gold. But it was none of those. It was because my mother came to every single performance and brought every living relative in the St. Louis area with her that made my first theatrical experience golden.

I cleaned my mother's apartment by myself in July 2004 after she died. I wrote and delivered her eulogy at her funeral. Rick and I followed her instructions regarding how she wanted her things distributed among family members and friends. While boxing some of her things one afternoon, I found her brown leather photo album in her hall closet. I sat down to rest for a minute on her pink-flowered sofa and thumbed through her worn, tattered book, her eighty-three years of memories. Two pages under the cover was a yellowed, purple mimeographed theater program from the 1960s. It read: *Hixson Junior High School presents The Admirable Crichton by J.M. Barrie., with Catherine Claire Miller as Lady Mary.*

☙

CHAPTER TWENTY-ONE
POOL DAYS

Early in the summer of 1963, the next best thing that could ever happen, next to going to California with flowers in our hair, happened to Mary, Pam, and me. The Cordeals put a swimming pool in their large backyard. With beach towels, baby oil, and romance novels in hand, the three musketeers were armed and ready the second the workmen dug out that first scoop of rich, black Missouri soil. We watched the workmen's progress every day, counting the minutes until we could be in cool water. It would be much easier to tan by their pool than on the black tar paper on our blazing sunporch at my house.

My mother issued strict orders for the Miller kids when the pool was ready. "Always wait for an invitation from the Cordeals. Do *not* ask them if you can go swimming! Always wait for them to invite you. That is their pool," she said, pointing across our back lawn to it; "that pool is *not* ours! Charlie and Mary Ruth built that pool to control where all their children are during the summer."

Jimmy couldn't wait; our only pool was an old metal cattle tank we filled with water and sat in at night to cool ourselves down before going inside to sleep. Jimmy was the first one in the Cordeals' pool before any Cordeal got near it. Mr. Cordeal found him sitting in only two feet of water, waiting for it to fill. He told Jimmy to come back the next day because it took several days for the pool to be close to full.

Pam, Mary, and I baked daily beside the Cordeal pool every day that first summer. "We are going to be California-tanned babes when school starts," Mary said. The three of us slathered our bodies with baby oil and iodine, something I paid for on my face five times when I got skin cancer in my sixties and melanoma on my back when I was forty-five. My teenage skin could get very dark after the first burn. Pam's skin tanned close to mine, but Mary's skin stayed fair with just a shade of pink. Jimmy's skin got even darker than mine, but Rick's only got beet red depending on how long he stood in the sun waiting for his turn to do cannonballs off the Cordeal's diving board.

My cousin Steve visited us at the end of July before he left for Vietnam in August. Stevie John, as Mother called him, was a diving champion at his high school in Jefferson City and was the most handsome relative on both sides of my family by far. He was my mother's brother, Jack's son. Steve's trim, Johnny Weissmuller's body, and his muscular, tan physique made it impossible to avoid staring at him. He reached Greek god perfection when he got home from the rigors of marine boot camp, and Pam developed a massive crush on him during his visit that summer. Her heart skipped a beat with every jackknife and one-and-a-half twist he did off the diving board. "He is Adonis!" Pam declared the first time she laid eyes on him.

"That's our Stevie John," Mother proudly explained to Pam. Mother was so proud of Steve that she watched him dive into the

Cordeals' pool through the window of our back porch. "I miss my brother," she told me one afternoon while standing there. "We haven't heard from Jack in over ten years. I don't know if he is alive or dead."

Growing up without a father was hard for Steve, but he loved my father, his Uncle Henry. Steve's mother, our Aunt Marylene, loved Mother's brother so much that she married Uncle Jack twice and divorced him twice when his alcoholism grew in severity. Rick, Jimmy, and I did not remember our Uncle Jack, but Aunt Marylene was hands down our favorite aunt, and their children, Sharon and Steve, were our favorite cousins on Mother's side of the family. The rumor was that Uncle Jack was found face down, passed out in the gutter from drinking Mennen Skin Bracer. He was taken to the Missouri State Hospital, where everyone thought he had died.

Once a week, Mr. and Mrs. Cordeal enjoyed their new pool that summer. On their Saturday night date nights, they announced the pool was off-limits to kids. Their message was *No Kids Allowed in the Pool or Pool Area Tonight!* Mr. and Mrs. Cordeal brought drinks and wonderful-smelling foods to the pool and enjoyed themselves until late at night. One night Rick crossed the Cordeals' backyard after midnight when he was sneaking home past his curfew. Mr. Cordeal was naked, jumping on the diving board.

"Hi, Mr. Cordeal!" Rick yelled.

Splash! Was Mr. Cordeal's only response.

Pam, Mary's, and my musketeer's loyalties to one another were tested when one of us had a period. We were not allowed to swim if we were on our periods. On those days, we went shopping to find something extraordinary that our babysitting budgets could afford.

My periods became painful that summer; the pain got worse with each one and gave me paranoia and depression that got so severe that I began to doubt my sanity.

"Do you think I am going crazy?" I asked Pam and Mary.

"No, Cath, you are just fine," they assured me. "You are just fine!"

"Do you think my nose is too big? Mother says I got my big nose from her and that noses keep growing all our lives, same with ears."

"No, Cath," your nose is just fine!" they told me. "Just fine."

Mother called the doctor and told him I was sad too often. He took me off the estrogen/progesterone pill that made me start my periods, but he kept me on my thyroid pills.

"You will have to take these all your life, Cathy," the doctor said. "And you will have to have a blood test yearly to be sure the dosage is correct."

I didn't like the blood tests; they were worse than shots. I was shocked during my first one when I saw the blood tube was a sickening purple and not Valentine red like I thought it would be. After that, I never watched my blood being taken. I did feel better not taking the other pill. I worried a little less about my sanity, my nose, or other parts of my body for a while.

Overall, the summer was free and easy for Pam, Mary, and me. We were too young to have jobs other than babysitting, so we went to the movies and took the bus to the Muny Opera to see every musical that season. We felt high on independence boarding the big green buses that huffed and puffed up and down Lockwood. We waited at the bottom of Woodlawn and rode block after block to Forest Park. We refreshed our tans by the pool before each night at the Muny and preened ourselves for hours to be as beautiful as possible for whatever adventures awaited us. No adventures happened to us, but we were ready for them if they did. We loved every note of every song and sang them on the way home on the bus.

Pam, Mary, and I weren't California surfer girls, and a hot, sticky Missouri summer sure wasn't a breezy California one. Still, the three of us were together in tweener heaven, anyway. We were miserable when we faced the tragedy of breaking our splendid summer pattern and going back to school, Mary to Mary Queen of Peace for eighth grade, and Pam and I separated at Steger and Hixson for ninth grade. Pool days at the Cordeals were summertime when the livin' was easy and at a time in our lives when we could not even comprehend how easy it was.

∅

CHAPTER TWENTY-TWO
THE CURSE OF ROBERT WARNER

Heart throbbing passion for Robert Warner overtook my heart and soul in homeroom on the first day of the ninth grade. Robert went to a private church school for kindergarten through the eighth grade before his parents transferred him to our public school. The first day of the ninth grade and for the following three years, my life, my world, my all-around was Robert Warner. He was gorgeous, all six feet and three inches of him. Robert had pale white skin, auburn hair, glorious green eyes, and a braces-free perfect smile that knocked my nylons off. His legs were so long, sticking out of his red and gray Hixson Spartan basketball uniform, that the other guys' legs looked stumpy.

I was love-bitten the second I saw him, which was the best and worst thing that had happened to a teenage girl in my generation. If the love and attraction were mutual, it was a blessed gift from God, but if it was not reciprocated, or worse, unacknowledged, it was a curse from Satan. "Here you go," Robert said and turned around to pass the stack of health forms handed out by Mrs. Jacobson, our short, plump homeroom teacher with an enormous growth on her chin full of hairs growing out of it. It was impossible to look anywhere else.

"Yeah. Good. Thanks," I warbled to Robert and prayed he didn't notice my hand trembled when I took the forms from him. Robert

Warner wore ironed, blue, buttoned down, oxford cloth shirts like Steve McQueen in *The Thomas Crown Affair.* He wore khaki slacks with perfect creases down the front. The waft of his British Sterling cologne teased me when he turned around. His smiles were perfection and made me dizzy, though they were never directed at me.

I dressed every morning of the ninth grade to please, attract and magnetize Robert Warner. Would Robert Warner like my Villager blouse and pleated skirt? Would Robert Warner like my white tennis shoes? Should I wear nylons or socks? A headband or no headband? My heart ached for Robert Warner, and my passion governed my every thought and action. I always attended one of our junior high basketball games held in our gym after school. I begged Mother to let me stay for them instead of racing home to watch Jimmy.

"Go, Warner, go," the girls in the pep club yelled.

"Go, Robert, go, you stud!" I whispered from my seat on the bleachers.

Robert Warner was instantly part of the "Socies" clique. He sang *The Duke of Earl* with Bill Ryan, a Hixon basketball hero, Bob Wyman, who played all sports, and Skip Weinberger, the star of the football team, but who also played on the basketball team. Skip Weinberger couldn't sing, so Bill, Bob, Robert Warner, and some other guy made up the quartet the girls called the "Big Four." They sang in talent shows, in the halls, and at their exclusive parties. I was told that Robert Warner never went to their make-out parties, and I was glad his church frowned upon them.

Though I never thought I belonged in the popular crowd, in some way, I did because I didn't want to belong to any group; I wanted to belong to them all. I still had my damaged bod and boob to live down and the not-so-jolly childhood nickname that kept me from ever wearing green. I wore baggy sweatshirts or men's shirts whenever I could to hide how Quinton's dodgeball made me feel like a failed female, a distorted girl that I saw in no-funhouse mirrors whenever I caught a glimpse of myself. My warped reflections of myself turned me into Fanny Brice at school. I told jokes, made faces, and tap danced as fast as possible to be "the tall girl with the great personality." The more I made people laugh, the more I helped that reputation. I was acknowledged by the greasers, nerds, drama kids, choir kids, jocks, and socies as "Cathy Miller, who is so nice. She can be a total riot!" they said.

The extent of my social life in the ninth grade consisted of only attending after-school games. I continued to help Mother. I kept track of Jimmy, did laundry, and made dinner. I wanted to be a socie. A girl had to play a big part in school activities like drama, sports, choir, student council, or other clubs. The socie girls had symmetrical budding or bulging breasts that were welcomed with open arms and fingers by all the boys. I fit none of those qualifications.

The ninth grade was my loneliest year at Hixson. Pam called when she had time, but she was busy with her own life. She had a boyfriend and was in lots of activities at Steger. I didn't see Mary often either since we both had a ton of homework all the time. My life amounted to an unmitigated, silent passion for Robert Warner that soared each morning at 7:30 A.M. with the eternal hope that he might say "Hi," to me in the halls and then fell with an unrelenting crash of despair every afternoon at 3:30 p.m. when it didn't happen.

I suffered mercilessly because Robert Warner didn't know I was alive. Every night that freshman year, including weekends, I wrote the day's sad commentary in my diary. At fourteen, going on fifteen,

I didn't know that I was invisible to Robert Warner because I was invisible to myself.

"Did your freshman day of high school treat you any better today, Tat?" Daddy asked me at night.

"Fraid not, Daddy," I answered, night after night.

"Listen here, Tat, when the ninth grade is over and you leave Hixson, tenth grade at Webster Senior High will be much better. There will be the Turkey Day football games, and Pam will be in the same school with you again! Jimmy won't need as much supervision, either. So, honey, this too shall pass; I promise. Now time to go to Chicago, and while you are under those covers, tell yourself that next year will be better!"

"Thank you, Daddy," I said and covered my face, "but I will never leave you and really go to Chicago."

"Don't forget to say your prayers," Daddy said when our game was over. "I may have to stop doing mine on my knees; I fell asleep for three hours on these long ancient legs last night. I almost had to wake Rick up to help me get up! Tat, your old Dad is in his mid-forties; he's getting damn creaky. Night, night, honey."

I began my nightly prayers when I heard shooting and bombs going off on my father's television. *Dear Lord, please bless all my friends and relatives, especially Daddy. And please, please, help Robert Warner discover that you created him for Cathy Miller. Amen.*

✄

PART FOUR

SENIOR HIGH SCHOOL

It is an unforgivable crime for teenagers
not to be able to absolve themselves
for being ridiculous creatures
at the most hazardous time of their lives.

- Pat Conroy

CHAPTER TWENTY-THREE
FIELDCREST DRIVE

My parents put our Woodlawn house up for sale in May 1964. Daddy did not fully bounce back from his heart attack and continued to smoke and drink. "We have to sell our house and move to a house on one floor for your father," Mother told us. We were all sad to leave Woodlawn, but none of us argued. The worst part of moving away from Woodlawn was losing the Cordeals as neighbors. The Cordeals were a family of ten at this time with the additions of Tommy and K.K., and we knew we would miss every one of them.

"I am going to miss your dad," Mary told me. "I will miss his calling across the yards to me every night when I am doing my homework. He has told me 'Goodnight, Abe' since I was little, and I will have more homework than ever in ninth grade. I need your dad to say goodnight and make me laugh, so I don't get too mad at the nuns at school."

The nothing-but-hell ninth grade ended with selling and purchasing a little ranch-style house on Fieldcrest Drive across town. It was only a few blocks from our little yellow house on Grant Road. Mother and Daddy sold the Woodlawn house for nineteen thousand five hundred dollars; they sold it to the parents of a girl in my class whose mother, Mrs. Baylor, was my music teacher at Hixson. One of the earliest changes the Baylors made to our old house was to cut down all the towering oak trees in the front yard. The first time I went back to Woodlawn to visit Mary, I saw the carnage, sat down on the Cordeal's front stone wall, and cried. The absence of our beloved trees felt like murder, and my adolescence needed someone to blame, so I blamed the Baylors for killing my childhood.

Our Woodlawn house was a small old house, and our Fieldcrest house was even smaller but newer. It had a shotgun floor plan. The front door opened into the living room and had a knickknack shelf to the immediate right. It was tricky to open and close the front door gently enough, or it knocked a Miller or Kelly keepsake off the shelf. The coat closet was about three feet across from the front door. The living room had a picture window to the left and a fireplace at the end of the short space. The dining room completed the "L" configuration and had a sliding glass door with a small cement patio outside. The living room and dining room were covered with wall-to-wall muted green carpeting. The move was expensive for my parents, and the money didn't stretch far enough to get more carpeting in the house, except for a remnant used in the thin hallway leading to our three bedrooms and a full bathroom. If the bathroom door was open at the end of the hallway, we could see the bathtub perfectly when we sat on the couch in the living room. "Close the damn bathroom door!" Mother yelled a hundred times daily in her constant struggle to avoid looking straight into the bathroom.

Mother and Daddy's room was even smaller than their room on Woodlawn. The boys had to get rid of their pinball machine and old black and white portable television to fit their beds and dressers into their new room. "Rick will be going to college soon, and Cathy had the smallest room in our old house," Mother said, "so this time, she gets the bigger room." I was ecstatic with joy.

In one of my teen novels, I read about a girl who had a lavender room with snow-white eyelet curtains, a white eyelet bedspread, and deep purple throw pillows. Somehow with no money, Mother made it all happen. My new double bed had no headboard and was pushed against one wall, so I could have room for Mother's old dressing table since there was no room for it in their room. Opposite my bed on the other wall was my dresser. I had two windows that looked out at the baby trees in the neighborhood; no longer could I lie on my bed and watch thunderstorms move through the giant oak trees I loved on Woodlawn. My big blonde desk was sold when we moved, so I did my homework on my bed. My room was to the left of the bathroom if you were facing it, and Mother and Daddy's room was to the right. Rick and Jimmy's room was on the other side of my wall.

The doorway from the dining room led to a smaller kitchen than our old house. Across from the sink, Jimmy's chair was removed from the kitchen table and put in the garage to allow the kitchen table to sit on the wall under the phone. We had to eat in the dining room if more than three people ate together. "Take your books to your rooms!" Mother said daily to keep the dining room table clear. "Damn it, stop putting your things on the dining room table!" I noticed Mother began to curse after we moved to Fieldcrest.

The house had an addition that the previous owner had built. It was on the other side of the kitchen by the stove. It included a small bathroom with a shower stall, sink, and toilet. The short-tiled hall in front of that bathroom led to a large-tiled recreation room with a space heater. We called that room "the back room." Rick and Daddy stapled thick plastic outside the picture window and shrunk it with a hair dryer in the winter to stop the freezing winds from making the room unusable. "Keep the damn door to the back room closed!" Mother ordered in a futile effort to keep our heating bills low. "If you're cold, put on a sweater and more socks!" she yelled if any of us dared to complain.

Though Rick was seldom home during his senior year of high school, we watched Johnny Carson on television in the back room when he was. There was no room for a TV in the living room. Daddy had a small closet in the back room where he housed his extensive 78 record collection. He made a storage cabinet for our LP albums from the old Victrola/television cabinet from Grant Road. He put his hi-fi record player on top of it. Someone gave Mother a small baby grand piano painted white. It never stayed in tune because of the temperature fluctuations in the back room each season. "I want you to take singing lessons, Cathy; you have such a good voice," she said. Mother asked me to sing *Hello Young Lovers* and *Whistle a Happy Tune* from *The King and I*, her favorite musical, for anyone who visited us. I wouldn't say I liked it, but I did as asked. My singing matched the out-of-tune piano, so eventually, she changed her request to a cappella version of *Do-Re-Mi*. Pianos did not like me. Mr. Cordeal strongly suggested I try a different instrument when I took piano lessons from him and practiced on their grand piano in their living room. It was no surprise that when we moved to Fieldcrest, the painted piano in the back room didn't like me either.

Jimmy and I spent part of the summer we moved, helping Mother set up the house because she still needed to work at Doubleday. Daddy looked much older than his forty-six years, and we hoped the single-floor house would help him get healthier. Rick was in independence heaven in his 1957 Ford Fairlane 500 and was ready to roll and rock for his upcoming 1964-65 senior year. Mother raised her hopes that they could stop borrowing money when Daddy returned to work, so Rick could spend some of the money he earned at Boyd's on himself.

That summer, my periods were sporadic and painful. I went for weeks, sometimes months, without one, all the while cramping and feeling I could start bleeding any second. Whenever a period did start, and the Midol pills didn't work, Mother gave me a small shot of whiskey and tied a towel to Daddy's headboard for me to yank on when the cramps peaked. "It is no fun being a woman, that's for damn sure," she told me. "Now, give the whiskey a little time to work, and then get up and get ready for your job."

Mr. Schwartz, one of Daddy's friends, was an accountant who gave Pam and me a job at Commercial Matrix for two summers before we were sixteen. Rick only worked there one summer because he got a lifeguard job at Westborough Country Club, where Daddy "knew a guy." Eight hours a day, Monday through Friday, from June until school started, Pam and I filed pressed paper print mats from Brown Shoes for newspaper advertising. We worked in a cold, dusty basement, filing in rows and small boxes. The best part of our jobs was that my mother's cousin Ruth worked there. Ruthie was more than cool; she was hip. She dressed in tight miniskirts, low-cut animal print blouses, and high heels. Ruthie wore tons of jewelry and lots of makeup and wore her hair in a giant blonde beehive. My family loved her so much that we called her Aunt Ruthie even though she was only a second cousin to Rick, Jimmy, and me.

Ruthie dated a tall, handsome, married man with thick gray hair named Fabian. They went to the Lake of the Ozarks almost every weekend to have wild parties. Talking to Ruthie daily made our jobs tolerable, not to mention informative for Pam and me.

Mr. Schwartz, with his curly blonde hair and mischievous smile, provided bright spots in our humdrum tasks whenever he crossed through the basement. Pam and I thought he could have been a comedian like Carl Reiner or Jackie Gleason. Mr. Schwartz made the long drives to and from work super entertaining. He had a crazy square steering wheel in his car that fit how crazy fun he was. He made faces at Pam and me in the rearview mirror to make us laugh or sang hilarious songs that were borderline naughty to keep Rick in hysterics on the drives to and from work. We didn't make any more money than we did babysitting those two summers, but at least the result was constant and gave us more spending money. My parents couldn't afford to pay us an allowance, so I watched my babysitting and Commercial Matrix money closely during the school year; I had to make it last until the following summer.

Pam, Mary, and I talked on the phone a lot. We were too young to drive, and the Fieldcrest house was too far away to walk to each other's homes. Pam and I made special arrangements with our parents for them to drive us to Cordeal's for swimming or take the three of us to Crestwood Plaza for shopping. Despite the distance between our houses, we kept up our musketeer summer trips to the St. Louis Muny Opera in Forest Park to watch our beloved musicals. We spent hours planning what to wear, plus more hours setting our hair in rollers and polishing our nails and toenails. "You never know just who we might meet tonight!" Pam said.

The two pre-sixteen summers were physically challenging for me. My anxiety, muscular aches, and pains increased as I rode the hormone express. Pam and Mary never lost patience with me, but no matter what they said to help me feel better, the fog in my brain and the pain in my body never went away. I learned it was best not to talk about how I felt. It helped to keep my mind on the upcoming fall, the fact Pam and I were going to be at the same school, and that our years of junior high separation were behind us. We were going to be sophomore Statesmen, part of the graduating Class of '67, and official members of the orange and black nation of Webster Groves High School.

ℒ

CHAPTER TWENTY-FOUR
GO, STATESMEN!

Daddy was excited for one of his children to go to the same high school he did; he could not wait to go to the football and basketball games. The Statesmen played Rick's school, CBC, sometimes too, which made things more exciting for him. The Turkey Day games were on Thanksgiving and were the annual football rivalry of Webster vs. Kirkwood. Daddy went into sports deprivation-depression when the St. Louis Cardinals' seasons ended after spending all summer with the wire from his transistor radio in his ear listening to the Cards. The family always knew where Daddy was in the house because we heard him curse when the Cardinals made errors. "God damn it, guys! What the hell!"

My father loved the radio commentators Harry Carey and Jack Buck, especially when they made sexual innuendos on air. "Look at that couple below us," said one of them. "They must be newlyweds because he is hugging her on the strikes, and she is kissing him on the balls!" Daddy's contagious laughter told us the Cardinals were at least doing okay.

On the first day that the Statesmen Athletic Schedule was available, Daddy and I went to the high school office to get one he could take home. "Look, Tat; the Statesmen will play CBC in basketball this year! Rick goes to CBC, but you and I must root for our alma mater, so go Statesmen!"

Pam and I spent the week before school discussing how we wanted to look on the first day of school. "You've got to look great when you see Robert Warner for the first time," she said. Oh God, Robert Warner, my heart pounded at the mere mention of his name. There was no chance of my forgetting him over the summer. All I did was dream about him since the last minute of Hixson's last day of school.

Our first day at "Webby G," as we called it, held many changes. The freshmen from the three junior high schools, Plymouth, Steger, and Hixon, were all poured into the senior high school to form our sophomore class. I was not prepared for so much change. A small fraction of the kids from Bristol and Hixson were African American, but the percentage of Black students increased dramatically at the high school. The only Black people I knew personally were Lucille, our cleaning lady, and Zoupy and Priscilla, two girls in my cabin at YMCA summer camp during grade school. At first, the change made me slightly fearful if I was alone in a hall with Black male students, but I got over that fear fast when the star basketball and football player, Clarence Thornhill, came by my locker and told me funny jokes. He was one of the nicest upperclassmen I knew and always gave me a friendly smile wherever I saw him at school. Clarence was much more of a gentleman than most of the Caucasian junior high boys I knew at Hixson. Soon, some of his male and female friends were my friends too.

The principal at Webster High was Howard A. Latta. He was the principal of WGHS for over twenty years. Mr. Latta's speech to the incoming class of sophomores was the same each year from 1955 forward. *Students, every class is unique. Every class makes a distinct contribution to the life, leadership, and history of a school. For each member of your class, may your years invested here be an introduction and a challenge to greater opportunities and a rewarding life.* Mr. Latta was a forward-thinking principal who believed in interracial groups and that all classes and activities were to be open to all students. Midwestern America struggled to include African American students in all upper-level honors classes and extracurricular clubs in the mid-sixties. Still, Mr. Latta saw that equality on every level was our policy at Webster High. The national civil rights campaign was gaining momentum, and Mr. Latta wanted our school to lead the way. Mother and I listened to KMOX radio programs in the car whenever she drove me to school. "Thank God," she said when the news was good about the progress of the civil rights movement. "It's about time!"

On the first day of my sophomore year, I was also unprepared for the cornucopia of handsome junior and senior *men* of any color. They were absolute dreamboats clad in yellow and blue, buttoned-down collared shirts and khaki pants, just like Robert Warner's clothes at Hixson. I thought I had died and gone to heaven when I walked down the hall with many boys taller than me. Our sophomore class alone had more than six hundred students, so the number of tall guys total at Webster High was unimaginable for me.

My biggest surprise was when I found out that I wasn't the tallest girl in school. There were, just in my class, Terry Shaw and Peggy Southworth, who stood almost as tall as me, and Leslie Cummings and Mary Todd Lincoln, who were taller. Terry was my hero when she was voted on to the cheerleading squad among all the tiny socie girls. I vowed to try out myself the following year. After all, Pam and I had dressed as cheerleaders in the sixth grade; the last Halloween, we wore costumes and went trick or treating. Our trick was to do a cheer. I thought maybe it was my destiny to be a cheerleader. Our trick was to do a cheer at each house. *V I C T O R Y is our Webster battle cry! Go, Team!* Very few people let Pam and I into their living rooms to perform; they preferred we stayed in the front yards or on their porches, away from lamps or precious heirlooms. I only hoped I was destined to be a cheerleader in high school, but Terry *was* a cheerleader for actual junior varsity and then varsity! On the first day of my sophomore year, I told Mother, "I am going to try out for my junior year for cheerleading!"

"No, Cathy, you will not," she said. "No daughter of mine is going to bend over in public every weekend." So that was that.

Just the size of the buildings at the high school was intimidating on my first day. Two entrances faced Selma Avenue, the senior entrance and the junior entrance. "Hey, newbie," some junior girl yelled at me on my way into school. "Sophomores, go in the side doors!" The halls were so long that the rows of lockers seemed to go on forever. My class members were easy to spot on the first day because we could not even find our lockers. Most of us spent much of the day looking down at our schedules and trying to look cool by writing our locker combinations on the palms of our hands; we didn't want to look like nerds by glancing at the paper each time. It was mind-boggling trying to find our classrooms. I didn't see Pam once that day, but I did see Robert Warner.

"If you see him, Cath, go for it," Pam advised me the night before. I vowed I would do as she instructed. I rehearsed what Pam and I planned for me to say. It was supposed to be a new day, school, and life for Cathy Miller! The new confident Cathy was determined to speak to him, but I was shaking like Don Knotts as I stood behind him at his locker.

"Hi, Robert," I said when he turned and saw me.

"Hi Cathy," he said.

Dear God in heaven, he said my name! Nobody pronounced my name better, not Cary Grant saying "Cathy" to Doris Day in *That Touch of Mink*, not Gregory Peck saying "Cathy" to Sophia Loren in *Arabesque*. When Robert Warner's smiling lips uttered, "Cathy, it was spoken nectar from the most virile of mythological gods and made my first-day new school panties wet. I almost walked away, but then I heard Pam's voice in my brain, "Don't you wimp out, Cath!" So, I sucked in my breath and went for it.

"Do you have a girlfriend, Robert?"

"Yeah," he said, "she doesn't go here, though; she goes to my church. We've been boyfriend and girlfriend since eighth grade."

Whaaaaat? I thought, but before I threw up, I managed to form a few intelligible words.

"Oh, that's nice. Bye, have a good next class," I said and then ran to the nearest girls' restroom.

"How did it go?" Pam asked me over the phone after school.

"God is a traitor," I answered.

I carried a blazing, burning torch for Robert Warner for six years. Even after I found out he had a girlfriend, the flames of passion in my heart for Robert Warner remained in full blaze. It was a fact; life and I were both ugly.

At our fiftieth high school reunion in 2017, Robert Warner was there. He had not been at our tenth, twenty-fifth, or any other reunion, but he was there that night, sixty-eight years old with thinning hair. "Cath," Pam said in a whisper that sent us straight back to our high school days. "Robert Warner is *here!*"

Pam grabbed my hands and fixed her still beautiful brown eyes on mine. I held my breath and turned to look at Robert Warner. I did not feel an inkling of desire to speak to him; the flames burned out years before. Robert Warner didn't even create a spark. Instead of talking to him, I walked back to my handsome, six-foot, six-inch tall, slim husband, looking drop-dead gorgeous in his black leather sports coat, waiting patiently for me beside our table places.

"Are you having fun?" my husband asked with his blue eyes twinkling.

"Only when you came into my life," I told him. Truer words I had never spoken.

ℒ

CHAPTER TWENTY-FIVE
REALITY MORE THAN BITES

The sophomores were asked to attend an assembly one Friday after school to see a film that sent me into a severe hypersensitive shock and affected me physically for two days. Our history teachers met us at the auditorium doors, took our parental permission slips, and paraded us to our seats to watch actual news footage of World War II.

"What you are going to see in this film is true," said Mr. Rodenbaugh. "It happened during World War II in Europe twenty years ago. Students, following the film, you may go home for the weekend, and we advise you to talk to your parents about what you will see here today. This presentation will be disturbing, frightening, and graphic. If you need to leave the auditorium during the film, your counselors will be outside in the lobby, but we need you to remain quiet and pay attention.

"Twenty years ago" was ancient history for a fifteen-year-old. We baby boomers were a protected generation by parents who needed to put the horrors of war behind them and give us a happier life than they had. Though my father shared much of his time in WWII with us, I knew few specifics and nothing at all about what I was about to see.

No sound was made in the auditorium when the lights went down; there was none of the usual clownings around by boys, chatter between girls, the scraping and shifting of feet or books dropped on the floor for attention. The black-and-white news footage of the concentration camps was so nauseating that I looked down at my lap for much of the film. The images of teeth with gold fillings in huge piles, the lampshades made from human skin, the medical experiments performed on people with no anesthetics, the boxcars tightly loaded with crying adults, small children, and babies like cattle or sheep. What I saw on the screen in front of me were not pictures or film; I felt inside the footage and part of what I was watching. The stripped bodies of the living lying on rough, splintery wooden slats of bunk beds, the gas chambers spewing ashes from burned flesh into the air like snow, the mass shootings, and graves full of hundreds of bodies were people, not strangers to me; I felt I knew them. I did know them! Suddenly I saw the black tattooed numbers on their arms; I saw Mr. and Mrs. Otterman standing over the burning trash can; I felt the heat of their fire. Mr. and Mrs. Otterman were on the screen, and what I was watching really happened. I was going to be sick. I wanted to flee the auditorium, but I was in the middle of the long row of seats and had to trample over everyone else to leave. I had to sit there while everything got more extensive and horrid than my psyche could absorb or comprehend. All I did to avoid the pain was put my hands over my ears, stare at my lap and go to the secret place inside myself that denies reality. But I felt it all continue, scene after scene, horror after horror, for another half an hour.

The twenty years before that day in the auditorium was a finger snap of time for the adults in the room. Still, it was the second worst *now* I had ever experienced, almost as soul-shattering as when Daddy confided in me that our family might be better off if he died.

There is no designated time in life we are magically considered "old enough" to process all realities. People mature and actualize at different rates and sensitivity levels, and that afternoon, my HPS became overloaded. I wanted to cry out, "Stop!"

People can see, hear, and experience things before they are intellectually sound and emotionally stable enough to handle what I was watching that day. I didn't learn until I was over forty that intrusion and constriction are invisible and can produce unconscious behaviors that can happen at any age. I realized I was moaning when the auditorium lights came up. I did my best not to look at anyone when I got to the aisle and walked out of the auditorium. I tried not to think about the film or cry as I walked home. I wasn't successful. I went straight to my room and was glad nobody else was in the house. I didn't want to talk to my parents; I didn't want to speak at all. My emotional dam broke, and I went into uncontrollable sobs that made it hard for me to breathe.

I heard Mother come in the kitchen door from the garage. I was borderline panicky when I ran to meet her in the dining room. One picture after another was flashing in my mind; I couldn't stop seeing the horror. "This movie we saw today after school," I said and choked on my words, "none of that happened, did it?" I demanded. "Mother, tell me what we saw today in that film never happened, that human beings never did those horrible things to other human beings?"

"I'm so sorry, honey," she said, "but yes, it did happen." She saw the trauma on my face and sat me down at the table. She sat across from me and tried to explain the holocaust. "Man's inhumanity to man is evil and terrifying, but knowing about it is important, so good people never let such things ever happen again."

"Why would they show us this at school? I don't want to know about such awful things," I said, still hoping for a negation of the film.

"It is history, Tat; as human beings, we are supposed to learn from history, so we don't repeat it."

"Why did you sign that permission slip and make me see that movie, Mother?" My body was aching all over.

"Knowledge can cause a loss of innocence, and that does hurt sometimes, but what doesn't kill us, Tat, makes us stronger." She had said that phrase a thousand times to us, but I had never heard it before that moment. "Cathy, you now know one of life's ugliest truths, and you didn't die. See? You are still here; you need to be strong enough to face life, real life."

I went back to my room. I did not come out for dinner. I couldn't eat. I sat on my bed and waited for my father to come home; he had to have a better answer for what was happening to me than Mother did.

"I want to show you something, Tat," Daddy said when he entered my room. I followed him to the back room, where he opened the cedar box we used as a window seat. Inside were newspapers, the Globe-Democrat and Post-Dispatch, with the bleak and bolded word **WAR!** on their front pages. Beneath the headlines were the words, *The United States goes to war in Europe*!

"What you saw at school today is why I joined the army and went to France and Africa for four years. America wanted to stop the Nazis from doing the atrocities you saw at school today. Those heinous acts were part of their efforts to take over the world. The United States went to stop them, and we did stop them, too." I stared at the newspapers as my father took a bright red folded flag from the cedar box. He unfurled it, and my stomach turned over. "I got this flag in France when our U.S. troops defeated the Nazis there. It is the enemy's flag. Maybe I shouldn't have taken it, but we fought for the right to take it down once and for all. I believed I had the right to keep it, not as a souvenir, but as a reminder of what all the allies who died in the war accomplished."

The black swastika in the black and white film I saw earlier that day frightened me enough, but the terrorizing symbol on blood-red cloth in front of me was so hideous, so repulsive, I got nauseated, ran to the bathroom, and vomited. I sat on the floor until I thought I could wash my face, brush my teeth, and return to my room.

"This was the most awful day of my life," I said when Daddy came in after me. He put his arms around me and held me close.

"I know it was, Tat. The truth can hurt, but accepting the truth can also set us free from fear and become stronger so we can face reality with more courage."

It was the same thing Mother said, but I did not want to face reality; I wasn't built for it. There was something wrong inside of me that always made me weak. It was why I was panicky and petrified so much of the time. I wanted, needed, to stay forever in the safety of my father's presence, and I prayed he had enough courage for both of us.

I had no appetite and had diarrhea the whole weekend. I didn't talk on the phone to my friends. I tried to do my homework but couldn't concentrate; I kept seeing Jewish people and all the atrocities done to them. I stayed in my room on Saturday, afraid of the realism outside my door. On Sunday, Daddy came in to talk to me again. "Tat, you need to be brave," he said. "You must come out of your room and be with the rest of the family. Tomorrow, you need to go to school like the rest of your classmates, and when you are all together, you will find out why all of you love America more than ever."

The Pied Piper worked his magic again. I came out of my room to be with my family and went to school. I trusted what my father told me, and he was right.

The spring of my sophomore year was, in a way, about flowers but also about much more than that. One of the most joyous events for a sophomore girl was when she turned sixteen at Webster High School; she received a corsage from her parents from Wichman's Florist. The corsages were beautiful roses surrounded with colorful ribbons and sugar cubes. The parents had their corsages delivered to their daughters during homeroom on the mornings of their birthdays. All day long, the birthday girl got whistles and winks from all the upper-class boys, hugs from all her girlfriends, and Happy Sweet Sixteen Birthday wishes from all her teachers. It was a rite of passage and a jubilant tradition. Pam's birthday was April sixth, so she had her special day a few weeks before mine. Her corsage was pink and white and lovely beyond words. I prepared myself the day before my birthday on the twenty-ninth not to receive a corsage; they were expensive, and I was sure my parents didn't have money for such extravagance. I knew I would walk around school on my birthday without one.

On the twenty-eighth, Mother picked me up after school. Jimmy was already in the front seat, so I climbed into the back seat of Mother's little white Comet car behind him. "Mother," I said when I noticed we turned the wrong way to go home, "are we going to the grocery store?"

"No," she answered in a flat tone. "We must go to Wichman's to pick up your damn sweet sixteen corsage!" I was shocked by the venom in her statement, and her poison struck deep in my heart. I resisted the urge to cry. I looked out my side window to cover how hurt I was by her cruel words. I didn't speak again.

"What's the matter, Claire?" Jimmy said while he stared back at me while Mother was inside Wichman's shop. "It's almost your birthday; you will get to drive!"

Mother got back in the car, reached over the car seat, and tossed the corsage box toward me. I had no voice to say thank you when it bounced on the seat and no courage to tell her I didn't want it. The tension grew between my mother and me, and it kept all three of us silent for the rest of the drive home. I looked down at the corsage sitting on the seat. I stared at the beautiful, fragile yellow roses through the plastic top of the box. I wanted to love them but instead felt shamed by them.

My corsage was not delivered to my homeroom. I pinned it to my blouse myself in the car on the way to school. My sweet sixteen was not sweet at all, but at least Daddy drove me to school that day instead of Mother.

"Have a wonderful day today, birthday girl," Daddy said in front of the school. "I asked Wichman's to ensure your corsage was made from yellow roses. I wanted you to have your favorite color to wear all day!"

My father's happy words on my birthday did not erase my mother's bitter ones, but I appreciated that he tried to rescue me again. "Thank you, Daddy," I said as I got out of the car; "thank you for putting the sweet back into my sixteen."

Todd Prybil, one of the sophomore boys, started calling me shortly after my tarnished birthday. I was dumbfounded. Stanley, my old friend from junior high, told me, "Todd Prybil likes you, Livingston; he told me at lunch today." I didn't believe her at first. I liked Todd more than most of the guys in our class, except for the never-gonna-happen Robert Warner. I thought about how Todd and I talked at school in the halls from time to time, but did Sue mean, *like*, like? Todd was good-looking with bright eyes and a brain to match. He had light brown hair, a perfect complexion, Crest-white teeth, and was almost my height. We talked about intelligent things together. Summer was around the corner, so we didn't talk about high school; we talked about our families, what made us laugh and how we would meet at the Webster pool on opening day.

"I love talking to you," Todd said one night. My heart skipped a beat. Throughout May, we walked together in the halls and sat together in assemblies. One Friday night, he kissed me at a party at Sue's house while we were double clutch dancing to *The Twelfth of Never*. My seventh-grade pact with Pam was sealed. At last, I had a boyfriend, even if he arrived four years late. Todd and I were considered on the fringe of the socies by the end of May. I was friends with Sue Lance and her boyfriend, Bobby Gill. They were part of the socies, as was Pam dating Bill Garland. Pam and Mary were thrilled for me. I was thrilled for myself, too; I could not remember when I was so happy.

The boys all went on a camping trip in mid-June. Todd was supposed to call me on Sunday after they got home. Sunday night, I waited and waited. There was no call from Todd. For once, I wasn't worried about myself or leaping to self-deprecating conclusions. Todd was far too sweet and genuine not to call. He would never forget to call me. I couldn't sleep; my intuition kept kicking in, making me fearful. Something was wrong. Sue called me just before midnight. She was crying.

"Cath," she said, not calling me Livingston like she always did, "Todd died today. Bobby told me the guys were playing around, and Quinton jumped out of a tree to scare Todd. It scared him so bad that he had a heart attack and died. Oh, Cath, this is so sad."

I have no memory of hanging up the phone if Sue told me anything more, if Daddy came to my room to see who called so late, or if I said my prayers. There was only Sue's voice, "Todd died today."

On Monday, we were told that Todd had an undiagnosed hole in his heart, a defect that was there when he was born. It was not Quinton's fault; the heart attack was going to happen at some point; it was just that it happened that night. All of Todd's family, relatives, our friends, and their parents went to the funeral home two days later. Daddy drove me to the funeral home for the wake, and we stopped to get a long-stemmed red rose at Wichman's. "Do you want me to go in with you, Tat?" he asked as he pulled up to the curb.

"No, I'm all right," I told him. Todd was the first dead person I saw, but I wasn't frightened to see his body. I felt brave and safe, like God was walking beside me as I went inside the funeral home. I signed the guest book and walked up to the casket. Todd looked pale but peaceful, sleeping on soft peach-colored satin. "I was just tired, Cathy, so tired," I heard him say above me. He was still Todd, handsome in his blue dress suit, his face so kind, his hands resting on his chest. I put the rose next to him, leaned over him, and whispered, "Thank you, Todd, for how happy you made me just by knowing you. I am going to miss you; we all are."

Later, I discovered that other friends waited for their turns to give me time to say goodbye. It was Sue who touched my shoulder and turned me around. I walked over to Todd's parents and tried not to cry. I shook their hands, walked outside, and sat beside Sue on the concrete wall at the bottom of the stairs.

"We never said it, but I loved Todd," I told her; "I hope he knew it, for real."

"I know you did, Livingston, and I know he knew it, for real," she said.

Daddy drove up to take me home. Sue and I hugged each other, and as I got in the car, I wondered if we would ever dance in her recreation room again

✍

CHAPTER TWENTY-SIX
THE DRIVING TEST

Most sophomores at Webster High took Driver's Education. The athletic coaches taught Drivers Ed. We sat in small demonstration cars with steering wheels, gear shifts, brake pedals, gas pedals, rearview mirrors, and side mirrors. Pam called me after our first day during the spring semester of 1965. "I got Coach Jones for my teacher, Cath! He is such a hunk!" she said.

"I got Coach Moss, of course," I told her. Coach Moss was as old as my father. His daughter, Candy, was in our class.

"Well, that's okay, Cath," Pam said. "Coach Moss is a legend; he's been the head coach in the Athletic Department since 1940, and he does have charisma, Cath."

"Yeah, right," I said. "You got 1965 Coach Hunk, and I got 1940 Coach Charisma."

I was alone with Coach Moss in the school car on my assigned driving day toward the end of the semester. Undoubtedly, I benefited from his patience and wisdom from all his years of teaching kids how to drive. We drove down Lockwood Avenue from one end to the other. "Your parallel parking is excellent, Cathy," he told me, but when we drove down Swon to go back to school, Coach Moss told me to make a right and turn onto Blackmer Drive. "It is a dead-end street, so drive to the end, Cathy, and practice turning around." There were flashing yellow *Men are Working* signs around an open utility hole at the end of the dead-end street. Two workmen in hardhats were standing beside the utility hole with equipment all around them.

"Cathy, we need to turn around now!" Coach Moss instructed. "Go into the driveway on the right, then back out and turn around."

"Okay, Coach," I said. I did exactly as he told me, but when I backed up, I knocked one of the *Men are Working* signs down the utility hole. The workmen got angry, not to mention the one who popped out of the hole, shaking his fist. All three men shouted and cursed, and the two men on the street started walking toward the car.

"Floor it, Cathy; let's get out of here!" Coach Moss told me, "Floor it!"

From that moment on, Coach Moss was way cooler to me than Pam's Coach Jones. I couldn't wait to get home that day and call Pam and Mary to tell them of my adventure in the car with Coach Charisma. It is a scientific fact that tenth-grade girls laugh harder and longer than any other homo sapiens on the planet, especially when girls are on their phones.

I passed my written test on the first of June with flying colors. I had my temporary license to drive with an adult in the car. Mother did not let me drive her Comet because she said I hit every pothole in Webster, and Daddy said, "You are not ready to drive one of the company cars yet, Tat."

"She's not driving my car!" Rick said. "No way!" But when school ended, I struggled to get over Todd's death, so Mother,

Daddy, and Rick continued to help me practice my driving. I missed everything about Todd, and though I made many new friends when we were considered a couple, once school was out, everyone but Pam and Mary scattered to vacation plans. In the ten days following his funeral, my grieving reached its worst.

"Cathy, it is time to put all your energy into practicing for your driver's test," Mother said. "You may as well use the Comet; it will be the car you use the most, anyway." Mother still refused to do the teaching, so it fell to Daddy. It was humorous when he tried to fold his six feet, seven inches into the little Comet. There was one time, though, I drove with Rick. When we returned from his tutelage, I overheard him talking to Daddy in the kitchen.

"God, Dad," Rick said, "Cathy's rollercoaster driving makes me sick to my stomach, and she acts like she's gonna cry when I try to help her."

"I know, Nick," Daddy said, "Cathy has no sense of driving rhythm. What is getting to you is her accelerate, brake, accelerate, brake, approach to driving; it's like riding waves on the high seas. We only have three more days before her driving test. I won't ask you to help her again."

"Okay, but if she doesn't pass, you must drive with her till she does; I can't take it."

We had Bob and Liz over for barbecued ribs on the Fourth of July. Bob was Daddy's nephew. He and his wife, Liz, lived on Crossbrook Circle, down and around the corner from our house. Mother loved Liz. She looked like Elizabeth Taylor with her tiny waist and raven black hair. Her eyes were huge, brown, not lavender, but her breasts were as big as Liz Taylor's. Bob's wife, Liz, was a nurse and a hard worker. "She is one smart cookie," Mother said, "except for her taste in men. If Bob didn't have Liz for a wife, he would end up in the gutter!"

Bob believed he had the best and most infectious personality in the world. He called my mother "Tiger or Tige" and grabbed her and crushed her to him while he said it. Bob's nightly visits on Fieldcrest replaced Harold Milton's weeknight visits on Woodlawn. It was like Mother could not avoid visitors during her busiest time of the day. Bob came over for a cocktail or three, right on time, like Mr. Milton, when he came over for one cocktail five times a week without fail. Everyone in our family knew Mother was not a physical person and that every time Bob hugged and squeezed her, we saw her go wild with silent anger. I always thought Bob knew he made Mother angry but couldn't resist doing it.

Mother's only defense was her words. Every night she spoke to Bob through gritted teeth. "Robert, this is my busiest time of night after I have been working at Doubleday all day. I am trying to make dinner, help Jimmy with his homework, do laundry, and a thousand other things!"

"Well then, Tiger, you just go ahead," he answered. "I'll just sit with Uncle Henry and have cocktails."

Mother never got the message to Bob that he outstayed his welcome; he just came right back the next night and the next.

Pam, Mary, and I loved Bob and Liz. We liked to go over to their house whenever we got the chance. Bob played records and danced with us in their recreation room, always with a drink in his hand. He never offered us any alcohol or did anything offensive; he just danced with all of us and made us laugh. We loved having a house to go to that didn't belong to the three of us. Bob and Liz's house became our teenage haven that summer.

The night of our Fourth of July barbecue was the day before my driving test. Liz brought a salad and her German mother's famous cheesecake, my mother's favorite dessert. Mother made au gratin potatoes, fresh green beans, and rolls. The smell of the sizzling pork ribs on the grill combined with my nervous anxiety over my driving test and resulted in my eating too many of them.

That night when I went to bed, I believed I had a heart attack. I was positive about it. No position was comfortable; my chest felt like it was on fire. Daddy had so many heart attacks that I thought I must have inherited his bad heart or had a hole in mine like Todd's. *Dear Lord,* I prayed, *please don't take me to heaven before I can even drive!*

"What's the matter, Tat," Daddy said when he sat down on my bed to kiss me goodnight. "Can't sleep? Too nervous before your driving test, I bet."

"Daddy," I said, "I am sick, horribly sick. I need to go to the hospital. I had a heart attack, and I am scared, really scared."

"You did not have a heart attack, Cathy," he said. "I have had more than one; I know the symptoms." His face looked so loving, and his voice sounded so sincere that I wanted to believe him. He got up and went round the corner to the bathroom. But when I closed my eyes, I felt the flames in my chest surge higher. "Chew these up," Daddy said, handing me two Tums when he returned. "You are having heartburn from too many pork ribs. Wait a few minutes, and it will subside, I promise. Now, get some sleep so you will be sharp! Tomorrow you must drive better than James Clark, Jr.!" Tomorrow night, I will be kissing our family's newest driver goodnight!"

"Who is James Clark, Jr., Daddy?" I asked while I was waiting for the fire to go out.

"He's the guy who won the Indianapolis 500 on Memorial Day, that's who! Night honey."

I heard uproarious laughter from both my parents coming from their bedroom after Daddy left my room. I knew he told Mother I thought I was dying and that they found it funny. But I didn't care if I was being laughed at; I was so happy not to die and that I would be alive to take my driver's test. *Thank you, God,*" I prayed; *thank you, dear Lord, for Tums.*

I passed the driving test, not with one hundred percent, but I passed. It helped that I impressed the man who gave me the test that I knew who James Clark, Jr. was.

The rest of the summer, every chance we got, either Pam drove her mother's car or I drove Mother's Comet, but we always went by and picked up Mary. We went to each other's houses or *Steak 'n Shake ("Steak")*, the teenage hangout on Manchester Road. I ran every errand my parents needed. Pam and I never complained once if we had to drive our little brothers anywhere. The three musketeers drove and drove with our car radios blaring and sang every song at the top of our teenage lungs. We were *Feelin' Groovy* and having a hot down summer in Webster. There was no need to drink or smoke; we were high on our new independence. Being sixteen grew sweeter by the minute.

♌

CHAPTER TWENTY-SEVEN

"SIXTEEN IN WEBSTER GROVES"

We heard rumors over the summer, but we didn't believe them. On the first day of our junior year, the Class of '67 got a surprise. The Columbia Broadcasting System, CBS, was going to do a documentary on what it was like to be a sixteen-year-old in Webster Groves, Missouri. The program focused on the baby boomer juniors, all six hundred and eighty-eight of us.

Minnie Belle Phillips and Patricia Voss detailed *Sixteen in Webster Groves* in their book *100 Selma . . . 100 years.* Their book covered how the CBS television crew took twenty-two hours of footage during their twelve weeks in Webster. The producers, cameramen, and crews were given a hearty welcome with enthusiasm and hospitality offered in every home. The program cost was one hundred and thirty thousand dollars, but the money they spent meant nothing compared to our community's anger when the program aired on February 8, 1966. Dr. Arthur Barron, sociologist, and producer of the program, led everyone in town to believe his findings, based on a questionnaire, interviews, and observations, that were supposed to show average teenagers in a typical midwestern middle-class suburb. His study included academic pressure, cheating, dating, social life, parental control, racial relations, and future goals.

The February 8 show was postponed because a news special on the Vietnam War preempted it. We had to wait until the program aired on Friday, February 25, to see what they had done to us. Everyone all over town sat in disbelief and silence in front of their television sets during the nationally televised hour. Charles Kuralt was the narrator. He depicted the Class of 1967 as sheltered, materialistic, parent-driven teenagers who only wanted a "good job, money, and success." The community went into outrage; letters flowed into CBS, the Post-Dispatch, and Globe Democrat newspapers. Parents and students were furious at their depiction of us as mere labels: socies, normies, weirdos, intellectuals, or fringe, and their report that the socies ruled our school.

CBS presented a follow-up airing on April 8 called *An Evening with St. James and the MacGreevys*. It didn't help calm the fuming frustrations; few people even remember that program; they only remember *Sixteen in Webster Groves* with none of its emphasis on our junior class doing community service, families sponsoring travel exchange programs, the inclusion of African American students in upper-level courses and all extracurricular clubs, our Christmas Vespers services, the quality of our teachers and their student-centered teaching methods, or our large number of national merit scholars. CBS ignored our long list of positive accomplishments in every way they could do it.

Clarissa Start explained it well in her book *Webster Groves*. She said that CBS looked for a Black student who would say she felt discrimination and that it took CBS almost twelve weeks to find one Black student who would say what they wanted to say. "Ya wanna be on network television, doncha?" the interviewer asked. The aired documentary showed how CBS used our high school choir singing *This is My Country* in the background for their contrived criticism of us. The CBS director of the program told us repeatedly in numerous situations, "Let's go through it one more time, only sadder this time like you're gonna cry. Come on try again."

One of my English teachers found the show an excellent way to teach our class about slant, bias, and quoting out of context. "Class, we can talk about slant in selection and bias in quoting out of context, but as your teacher, I could never find a way to get the idea across to you better than the way *Sixteen in Webster Groves* did it."

Webster High School was rated "superior" in American High Schools for academics. According to the National Research Council of the National Academy of Sciences, it ranked second in the state for the most graduates earning doctoral degrees. Our school was deemed "a school of the future" with quality teaching, a research-based curriculum, technology, and student-centered instruction. But there was none of that in *Sixteen in Webster Groves*.

The limelight CBS gave that ten percent of our junior class only heightened ill feelings the other ninety percent may or may not have had about them. The months of filming made many of us feel left out; we didn't know why CBS was focusing almost exclusively on the socies. We didn't know about their biased agenda; we felt ignored and unworthy of interviews. It was not until the program aired in the spring that those of us in the ninety percent were glad to be left out of it.

The citizens of Webster Groves never lost confidence or pride in our town, but I lost my naïve trust in television news. The winds of disgust over the injustice done to us by CBS blew over, but as a junior in high school, I discovered my parents were right; either we learn from history, or we are doomed to repeat it. Fifty-six years later, that little wind still blows.

∅

CHAPTER TWENTY-EIGHT
SPACE PANTIES

Pam and Bill were socies at Steger and remained in that group when they arrived at Webster High. I was invited to a few of the socie parties at the beginning of our junior year, but I didn't last without Todd. One truth about being a socie was that a girl needed a boyfriend to feel included.

Madison Bruker took pity on my sad wallflower self at one socie party and asked me to dance a slow dance. I was excited to get off that wall and into his strong football player arms. Madison was a big guy in every way. He held my body close to his, so close, it was impossible not to notice that he liked me or, at the very least, was attracted to me. It was a first for me to become aware of that compliment. But Madison and I were not destined to be a couple. He most likely felt the shock that went through my good Catholic girl body during that dance, so a few weeks later, he fell for Becka, a short, blonde, pretty girl who lived in my subdivision. Disappointed, I chalked it up to one of life's unexplainable mysteries; why do so many big, tall guys like short, petite girls? Once Madison found Becka, they dated the rest of our junior and senior years, probably to infinity and beyond.

As a big fat zero in the boyfriend department, I drifted away from the socies and returned to the fringes and my former identity of "Cathy Miller is a riot" so I could be somewhat comfortable in every group. There was a song called *Cathy's Clown*, but in my case, I *was* the clown. I made people laugh and deflected my poor self-esteem to deal with my loneliness. I determined it was time for the Jolly Green Giant to find girlfriends with whom she had more in common. I needed friends to hang out with at school and on school activity weekends. Pam, Mary, and I remained close friends; the Woodlawn musketeers still talked on the phone, celebrated our birthdays, and exchanged Christmas presents, but it wasn't easy to be together since Mary was in a Catholic high school and Pam and I were in a public one.

Eleanor Hughes and I were in grade school together at Bristol. The kids called her Baby Hughie because she was fat then. Her nickname, like mine, haunted her in junior high too. Eleanor and I didn't become friends until our junior year in high school. Our sensitive natures and bullied self-images leeched on to each other's life forces to sap enough strength to get through the collective years of our "no boyfriends" hell of high school. The *Echo*, our Webster High School Yearbooks from 1964 through 1967, document on slick, grainy, black, and white pages that "Baby Hughie" grew from a fat, freckled, Irish girl into a true Celtic beauty. Eleanor's hair was so shiny black that it looked indigo blue in the sunlight. Her pale skin was smooth with beguiling, freckled flawlessness that lacked any sign of adolescent pimpled graffiti. Her emerald green eyes and long, black, mascara-free eyelashes were showstoppers, especially when combined with her dazzling, flirtatious smile. In high school,

Eleanor was irresistible to college men and boys from other high schools whose minds and memories never knew her nickname. Rick and his friends noticed Eleanor's change from seventh-grade larvae into a high school butterfly the first time she came to our house after school. Rick and Eleanor had one date together before one of his friends moved in on his territory and started dating her.

The Jolly Green Giant got thinner in high school, but she still had ample hips and kept her uneven breasts hidden for most of the climb up the teenage ladder. I would have faded away entirely in the back row of our sophomore class photograph in the *Echo* if I hadn't worn a headband, used London white lipstick, white nail polish, and thick black English Mod eyeliner. Thanks to my friendship with Eleanor during my junior year, I abandoned my mod look and returned to my Aqua Net flip, light brown Maybelline mascara, and Love U Babe pink lipstick.

I had three to four hours of homework every night at Webster High, and the only club I belonged to was the pep club. Eleanor joined the drama club and was busy acting in plays, but we had fun together at her house when she didn't have rehearsals. Sometimes our other girlfriends, Becky and Barb, joined us. Eleanor lived only a few blocks from school. She had one younger sister, and her mother was divorced, so her house was girl heaven after school, and before we went home to hit the books.

The summer after my junior year, I was tired of never having enough spending money to keep up with my friends. I needed a higher-paying job than Commercial Matrix or babysitting; one dollar an hour wasn't cutting it, so I went to work at Burger Chef for $1.25 an hour. I was happy to have more money and no longer felt guilty about needing money. Daddy never knew about the heartbreak corsage incident with my mother in the car; that day dealt me the most emotional pain I had ever experienced up to that time. I felt horrible over what I financially cost the family during that time; I vowed never to take a dime from my mother again. I kept that vow. After I was hired at Burger Chef, I refused to take money from Daddy when he tried to slip it to me. Money was a dirty word in our house.

Burger Chef was a better job, mainly because I worked with Barb. We had fun at work when we shared shifts. We had shared interests too. We both learned to sew in Home Economics in the eighth grade. I made almost all my clothes out of necessity because of my height, and I made some for my mother out of the hope that she would be proud of me. Barb was almost as tall as I was and needed to sew many of her outfits. We bought patterns and materials together, which made sewing more fun and creative. I went camping with Barb's family and loved her parents and her younger sister, Mev. My family didn't have the money to take vacations or have a family interest like camping. Barb's mother made me laugh every time Barb wanted to do something her mother didn't like. "Barbara Jean's not going!" she said. "Listen here, girls, that's a big fat NOPE for Barbara Jean!" I loved spending time at Barb's house.

My first purchase with my own money from Burger Chef arrived through the mail. I ordered from the back of a Photoplay magazine. This purchase happened when getting a crushed manila envelope from Beverly Hills, California, was an outta sight cheap thrill for a Missouri girl. It was an act of liberation from the torture of the teenage captivity I felt from being governed by a heavy-hearted Catholic mother.

"It is my money!" I told Mother whenever I bought something. "I earned it myself!" I was proud of my job six blocks from our house, where Highway 66 joined Grant Road. I worked at the counter and cleaned the fryers at Burger Chef. Mondays, Wednesdays, and Fridays after school and all day on Saturdays, my crinkled paper hat and stained apron were not just parts of my uniform; they were my orange and white badges of courage.

The package arrived after three weeks of agonized waiting and checking the mail daily. I usually walked home from school since I didn't have a car. On a Thursday afternoon, just when I was about to give up hope, I spotted the envelope sticking out of our mailbox a half block away. There it was! I raced up our short, steep driveway, ran across the walk, and jumped on our little square concrete front porch slab. I yanked the envelope out of the mailbox, placed it on top of my blue cloth ring binder, and opened the front door. Mother was at Doubleday; Jimmy was at Hixson playing seventh-grade baseball; Rick was at community college looking for girls in tight sweater sets to impress; and Daddy was at Keehn's Chevrolet leasing cars. I dumped my stack of homework on my bed and sat down to enjoy my quiet excitement.

I studied the pink and white labels. *To: Cathy Miller, Fieldcrest Drive, Webster Groves, Missouri, 63119. From: Lucy's, The Lingerie Experts, Box 1457, Beverly Hills, California, 92126.* I carefully tore open the envelope and saved the label. I tacked it to my bulletin board beside the black-and-white photo strip of Eleanor, Barb, and I crammed in a booth making funny faces. I pulled out the clear cellophane bag and heard a faint drumroll in my brain. Ta-da! It was my *Days of the Week* panties!

My months of coveting the panties I saw on other girls in gym class were over. I had my own, and Saturday and Sunday! Each panty representing the seven days of the week was rolled tight, nestled against each other, and proudly displayed its special day. Of course, the other girls' sizes were petite twos and fours, and mine were big-ass size sevens, but that didn't matter, not that day; I was making feminine progress. *God*, I prayed, *please let them fit!* I took them out of the bag, shook their folds, and spread them across my white eyelet bedspread. Sunday was Dolphin Blue, Monday was Lovely Lilac, Tuesday was Salmon Pink, Wednesday was Sunshine Yellow, Thursday was Lemon-lime Green, Friday was Perfect Purple, and Saturday was Candy Apple Red. Each day was emblazoned in fiery stitching encircled by embroidered flowers in darker complementary colors on the side of the left leg hole. They were beyond beautiful, and they were nylon! All I could think of was that I could finally throw my white cotton Lollipops in the Goodwill bag at last.

My spirits soared until they nosedived and crashed. How was I going to defend my purchase to my mother? Mother and all the nuns in her past placed total faith in the modesty of cotton Lollipops. I was determined to plead my case like Perry Mason. Poor Mother, I thought; she still parted her shiny blonde hair in the middle and curled it with bobby pins. I thought it was my sole responsibility to get her movin' and groovin' into the sixties, where maybe she could leave her old ice queen self behind, but the task was hard to do since we seldom talked. But heck, if I won this argument, I vowed to buy a pair of black patent leather high heels at Baker's shoes with my next two paychecks so Robert Warner could look up my dress and find out what day of the week it was! Of course, the heels couldn't be too high, maybe only an inch and a half; I would be six foot, one and a half inches tall even at that, and I could not be as tall as Robert Warner in case things changed with his church girlfriend.

There was a crack of optimism in the next sunrise. It was Perfect Purple Friday. The new confident Cathy said "Hi," to every boy she passed in the halls she knew. Some spoke, and some didn't, but it didn't tarnish my sunshine that day.

"Cathy, there is an envelope on the secretary addressed to you," Mother said when I got home from school. I picked up the envelope, took it to my room, and threw it on the bed. I closed my door, kicked off my flats, and changed into my Burger Chef uniform; all the while, I stared at the envelope. I sat down and carefully looked at it. No return address, but the postage meter mark said Webster Groves, Missouri. It was mailed from somewhere in Webster Groves. I opened the envelope and looked at the unsigned card: *This coupon entitles you to a free pair of Space Panties! Happy summer to a girl whose ass is out-of-this-world!*

I was breathless, not with insult, but with excitement that someone liked my fat bottom. "Who would send me such a thing?" I asked Barb on the phone. I thought she might have an idea because she and her boyfriend, Patrick, had been dating since the ninth grade and were more advanced about rounding some of the bases than I was.

"I don't know, Cath," she said, "but far out, baby! Way to go!" I was delighted at Barb's reaction until I heard Mother's voice.

"It is time to go to work, Cathy," she said on the other side of my closed door.

"Be right there," I said. I tucked the card under my stack of Days of the Week panties in my drawer. Mother and I rode the six blocks to Burger Chef in usual silence. "Daddy will pick you up at ten, Cathy. Don't eat too many French fries or drink too many milkshakes," she said before she drove away.

"Fine," I muttered under my breath while I watched her drive away, but not even her criticism of my weight took away my newfound confidence from the mysterious coupon I got in the mail. I swung my *out-of-this-world-ass* from side to side, crossed the parking, and whistled my way inside to work.

∅

CHAPTER TWENTY-NINE
THE COLLEGE "MAN"

I saw little of Rick the summer after my junior year in high school; he whirl-winded through the house on his way to work or somewhere else that was important to a junior college freshman on summer break. Rick and the other members of his 1965 high school graduating class across America had to stay on top of their grades in college or answer draft calls. The conflict escalated in Vietnam that summer, and our cousin Steve was already an active-duty marine there.

Jimmy finished the eighth- grade at Hixson and spent most of his summer days with his old pals from Woodlawn, Mike Cordeal and Tony Whiphold. He was old enough to take care of himself until Mother came home from work, so I got to spend more time with girlfriends when I wasn't mopping the floors or cleaning the hamburger grill at Burger Chef.

Daddy was working as the leasing manager at Keehn's Auto up on Highway 66, but he was unhappy there. He looked tired every night when he came home. One night in early June, I met Mr. Keehn's son, Paul, at *Steak 'n Shake*. He was a tall Paul, a preppy guy with wavy brown hair, big brown eyes, and eyelashes that went halfway down his cheeks when he blinked. We chatted out our car windows over attached trays laden with milkshakes, burgers, and fries.

Steak 'n Shake didn't just lure teenagers with high-caloric food; it was also our place to rule the earth; it was a high-drama teenage environment. Our radios blared, boyfriends and girlfriends fought or laughed, car motors roared, and tires squealed. The air seduced us with a mixture of smells: hamburgers sizzling hot from the grill and perfumes, colognes and hair sprays freshly applied. We called the parking lot "the meat market," and it beckoned to those who were single and looking for dates.

Life at *Steak 'n Shake* held the fascination of a highly charged, sensual teen soap opera when the kids got out of their cars, leaned against them, and flirted their brains out with each other. Life got even more interesting when a guy got out of his car and got into a girl's car. Everyone watched everyone and every vehicle at *Steak 'n Shake*. A girl never went to *Steak 'n Shake* by herself unless the girl was a "slut." Good girls went there with a crowd or at least one girlfriend; it was a risky reputation business to be seen at the meat market alone. Whatever happened at *Steak* lit up the teen phone lines across our St. Louis suburb each night, and whatever name was gossiped about was then talked about all over school the next day.

The night I met Paul Keehn was my most exciting night at *Steak* to date. He got out of his car and came over to my side window of Barb's car. "Hey, want to get out of our cars and talk?" he said. I was nervous as hell, but I got out of her car and leaned against the trunk next to Paul. "Thank God for a little privacy," he said. "I'm Paul Keehn, by the way." I was already flattered just to be talking to a college guy and far too naïve to notice what a smooth operator he was in the girl pickup department.

"What's your name?" he asked.

"Cathy Miller," I told him. "Yeah, this is more private out here." Oh Lord, the sound of my voice sounded ludicrous and undoubtedly inexperienced.

Barb was all ears and poked her head out of her window while Paul and I talked. Close girlfriends told each other *everything,* but Barb couldn't wait until I got back in the car. She was champing at the bit to tell Eleanor and Becky about Paul and didn't want to miss a word of our conversation.

"My father works for your dad; he's the leasing manager at Keehn's," I said.

"Yeah, I know your dad; I work there part-time. Mr. Miller makes everybody laugh at work with his crazy jokes."

"I bet," I said and then giggled way too much. "Are any of them clean jokes?"

"Well, not always," Paul said and laughed. He was too handsome to describe when he laughed. "So, Cathy Miller, you wanna go out sometime?"

"Are you sure?" I asked.

"Of course, I'm sure," he said with hunkier laughter. "How about next Friday? We could go to a movie at the Crestwood Theater or something."

"Sounds great," I croaked. How could my throat be so dry? I just drank a Cherry Coke.

"So, can I have your number, Cathy Miller?"

"Um, yeah," I said. Barb thrust a paper out her window with my number already on it. I was mortified.

"Woodland 1-7806," Paul said, "that right?" Paul laughed again, took the paper from Barb, and then stood closer to me. His English Leather cologne made me perspire even more than the intense midwestern humidity.

"Yep, that's it," I said.

"I gotta go," he said and opened the front passenger door to let me back into Barb's car. "Got a night class on Tuesdays and Thursdays. I gotta make up for something I failed last year in high school. I must pass it before I can enroll in college. I'll call ya, Cathy Miller, later in the week," he said, then closed my door and smacked the top of Barb's mother's car.

"Sounds fine," I said out the window. Sounds fine? What teenage girl says sounds fine? "I mean, that would be outta sight." He smiled at my correction, but I thought it was the most stupid thing I had said all night. I told Barb, "Outta sight! What am I anyway, a rock star?"

I turned and looked at Barb's ecstatic face; the second Paul drove off. "Outta sight," I said and pretended to gag myself. "I am such a dumb butt! Do you believe I said that, Barb? Oh lord, not too geeky!"

Barb and I did not stop swooning over Paul all the way home. We sat outside my house for an hour and went over every detail of my lucky night.

I ran inside; I could not wait to tell Daddy about Paul Keehn. "Great, Tat," he said, "you look really happy!" From where I was on cloud nine, I didn't notice how forced his enthusiasm was.

"He's a total babe, Daddy," I said, "a total babe!"

Paul called me as promised. We decided he would pick me up at 7:00 p.m. on Friday night. "We can go to the 8:00 p.m. show of *How to Steal a Million* and then to Luigi's for a pizza after? How does that sound?"

"Perfect," I said and gave him my address. I figured the fewer words from me, the better.

"Great, see you on Friday! Tell your dad I said hello; Mr. Miller's been cranky toward me at work the last few days," Paul said and hung up.

Daddy, cranky? That didn't sound like my father. "Daddy," I yelled from my bedroom, "it is really going to happen! I have an actual date with Paul Keehn, a college man!" There was no answer. I just figured he didn't hear me.

That Friday night, Barb took my shift at Burger Chef. I started dressing at 4:00 p.m. after I talked to her about what to wear, what Paul and I should talk about, what to do if he tried to kiss me, and other vital matters. For three hours, I worked at looking natural while ignoring Jimmy's constant knocks on the bathroom door."

"I need to get into the bathroom, Claire!" he hollered.

"Use the other one!" I hollered back. I knew he didn't need to get into the bathroom; he was being a brat, like when he flipped off the light switch for my ceiling light when I was covered with books on my bed doing homework. "Mother, make Jimmy stop bothering me," I yelled. "I need every second to bathe, shave my legs, shampoo my hair, roll it up in curlers, dry it, polish my toenails and fingernails if I am going to be ready when Paul comes!"

"Cathy, the more you shave your legs, the more you will have to shave your legs. Don't do it so often," Mother said from the other side of the bathroom door. I found out later in life that she was right again.

Daddy was sitting on the couch reading the paper when I emerged from my room at 6:45 p.m. "Wow, honey, you look so pretty." For once, I thought I did too. My hair turned out well, my legs were smooth and tan enough to wear sandals, and I wore my favorite yellow sun dress with spaghetti straps. "I want to sit here until Paul arrives," Daddy said; "a good father meets his daughter's dates."

"You better take a sweater; the air conditioner makes it cold when you are in the movie theater," Mother said on her way to the kitchen carrying a basket of dirty clothes to wash in the basement.

"I have my white one," I told her; "it's with my purse on the chair." I sat in the armchair across from Daddy to look out the window and see Paul's car drive up and park. I was more excited than nervous.

"Tat, look at this," he said, handing me the paper. "Today is 6/6/66!" That enumeration won't happen again until it is 7/7/77."

"Mmm, hmm," I said, staring out the window, not interested in numerations. It was almost 7:00 p.m.

"Then it will be 8/8/88, then 9/9/99," Daddy continued.

"Wow, Daddy, amazing," I said. The clock on the mantle clanged seven times. No sign of Paul's car. Daddy was on to the sports section.

"Cards blew it again," he said. I got up and started pacing when the clock clanged once at 7:30 p.m. "Mother, has anyone called?" I yelled to her.

"No, Tat, you are sitting right there; you would have heard it if the phone rang," she answered.

The clock on the mantle clanged eight times. The movie was supposed to start at 8:00 p.m. My hands were shaking. I felt like crying but was afraid it would ruin my mascara; I bit my tongue to cause enough pain to stay composed. Daddy, still on the couch, was reading the editorials. I had no more excuses for Paul. My lips started quivering as I tried to hold back my humiliation. At 8:30 p.m., there was no call, no car, and no Paul. It was apparent I was stood up by the college man. My ill-disguised humiliation became devastation.

"Well, looks like I've been stood up," I said quietly and walked down the hall to my room before Daddy could say anything. I didn't cry. I closed my door, sat on my bed, and leaned against my pillows where I could see myself in the mirror. "You are such a joke," I said aloud to my reflection and continued to ridicule myself with self-loathing. Any semblance of self-worth I had was left in the living room.

Daddy knocked on my door. "Can I come in, Tat?"

"No, Daddy," I need to be by myself." I was miserable and too embarrassed to be with my father. I didn't want any part of the male of the species, not even him.

"Tat," Daddy said, "Paul Keehn is a bum. He was a bum in high school, and he's a bum now. I watched him for two years at work. Please trust me on this. He's a loser, a spoiled brat user, and not good enough for you, not even close."

"Go away, Daddy, please," I begged. He stood outside my door a few minutes before he left and walked back down the hall.

I wanted him to leave me alone, yet I was lonely without him. Jokes about myself turned into insults, and I became much more my enemy. Night fears began. I frightened myself to numbness, complete immobility, where I didn't dare to blink. I asked God to help me work harder to hide my emotions from everyone, especially my family; they had enough problems.

✒

CHAPTER THIRTY
KENTUCKY FRIED DATE

Three days after Paul stood me up, Tim Burns, one of Rick's best friends, called me and asked me to go out with him the following Friday. "Uh, Cathy," he said, "would you go to a movie with me on Friday?" It sounded strange for Tim to call me Cathy. He always called me Cath for at least ten years. "I thought we could go to Flaming Pit for some surf and turf action before we go to the movies." Tim never once showed any interest in dating me. I was Rick's kid sister, period. Flaming Pit was way too expensive, and the mention of lobster and steak made his invitation even more suspicious. Furthermore, Tim didn't have the money to take me to the Flaming Pit Restaurant; he worked at Kentucky Fried Chicken. Tim needed his Kentucky Fried Chicken paychecks as much as I needed mine from Burger Chef.

Daddy set up the date to make me feel better. He was the benefactor for this "date," an expense I knew our family couldn't afford. Mother and Daddy never even went out themselves. I also knew Daddy would be disappointed if his brilliant plan didn't raise my spirits, so I agreed to go out with Tim and put on a big happy act when I got home.

I thought my father gave away all his secret tactics and antics to me when I was ten years old and "won" a cake in a cakewalk at the Girl Scout Bazaar. I was thrilled when Mr. Lawrence called my number; I had never won *anything*! Daddy's mistake was not being more discreet when he paid off Mr. Lawrence while I chose my cake. Mr. Lawrence's belly laughs at the joke Daddy told him made everyone turn around. My whole lucky win was a sham and anything but secretive.

My date with Tim was exhausting for both of us. We never had a moment of awkwardness in all the years we knew each other, but that night, neither of us could think of a word to say. Tim's blonde hair was still wet when he arrived to pick me up after a quick shower that followed his shift at Kentucky Fried Chicken. The collar of his shirt was soaked, and there were water spots on his tie. Tim's conversation with Daddy in the kitchen before we left could have been a comedy sketch on *Rowan & Martin's Laugh-In.*

"Good evening, Mr. Miller," Tim said.

"Good evening, Tim," Daddy answered. Tim was over at our house four nights a week. He was Rick's best friend. Their formality on this night was geepy, a cross between geeky and creepy.

"Well, I guess we better be going, Cathy," Tim said and then opened our front door to let me go out first. Dinner was ordered, served, and eaten in almost complete silence, except for both of us clearing our throats, often at the same time. We couldn't wait for the previews to start when we sat at the movies. I smelled Kentucky Fried chicken emanating from his pores, and he probably smelled Burger Chef emanating from mine. His bath in Brut cologne and my half bottle of Wind Song perfume didn't cover how we reeked from our fast-food places of employment. The mixture of our food and cologne scents was so pungent that it drew a comment from an older couple sitting behind us.

"We should have eaten before the movie," the woman said. "Now we will ruin our dinner after eating this tub of popcorn!"

"Nonsense," the male voice replied, "We won't overeat. Besides, I have a craving for fried chicken."

After the movie, Tim took me straight home. He pulled up in front of our house, and in a simultaneous moment of magic, the living room light in the house went off at the same time the porch light went on. "Tim," I said, "you do not need to walk me to the door."

"Oh yes, I do, Cathy," he said and got out of the car. He came around to my side and opened my door. I was glad it was dark in the street so that we couldn't see the awkwardness in each other's eyes.

The most excruciating moment of the night happened under our porch light. I could not stand to see Tim in misery any longer. "Look, Tim, mission accomplished, okay?" I said, opening the front door.

"What do you mean, Cathy? I had a perfect time."

"You are such a liar, Tim, but I love you, and I love Daddy for trying. Thank you. I do mean that."

"Thanks, Cath," he said with total relief. "You are my favorite sister Rick has," he said, patting my arm. We both laughed for the first time that night; dear God, I thought, was a kiss required in his paid contract with Daddy?

"Lucky for you, Tim, I am Rick's only sister!" The second I closed the door, he was off in a shot to his car.

I turned off the porch light as Tim's taillights disappeared around the corner. I walked down the hall to my room. "Did you have a nice time on your date, Tat?" Daddy asked like a bad actor as I passed his door.

"Oh man, did we ever!" I said equally as horrible an actress. "Only Daddy, see Tim and I decided we have more fun together being friends instead of boyfriend and girlfriend."

"Well, you gotta kiss a lot of frogs to find that prince, honey. Night, night," Daddy said and went back to the bombing of London. There was no bedtime visit from my father that night. The acting was hard work, and I was glad I didn't have to think of ways to turn the embarrassing date with Tim into a fabulous and fun evening.

I never found out for sure if my father threatened Paul Keehn to "never darken my daughter's doorway for a date" or if it was how long I moped around wearing my hurt feelings on my sleeve that made my father "find" the money somewhere for my flameless Flaming Pit date. Maybe Paul really was a "bum," but either way, I came to believe that as years accumulated, neither Paul Keehn nor any other man could ever love me as much as my father did.

☒

CHAPTER THIRTY-ONE

FIRST CLASS OR COACH?

Once my dating was a reality for my father, our conversations before I went to sleep changed. Rick told me the sexual advice he got from Daddy was, "Nick, you've got to be very careful about pregnancy, and never, under any circumstances, start a girl down that path if she has not already traveled there." My father and Rick talked about many things, like when Rick and his friends went downtown St. Louis to the World Theater to see a burlesque show that was advertised nightly in the newspapers. They saw *Evelyn West and Her Fifty-thousand-dollar Treasure Chest.* It said in the advertisement that her breasts were insured for that amount by Lloyd's of London. I was jealous of Rick's freedoms, but I knew I would also be jealous of Evelyn West if I went to see her breasts. Her breasts were sure to make me feel worse about mine. Rick got to go to Sunset Teen Nights and watch Ike and Tina Turner do the "dirty dog" dance. I was forbidden to go.

Daddy never said the word "sex" to me. He said, "Tat, if you are ever tempted to have intercourse with a boy, look around at your surroundings first. If what you see isn't first class, like the bridal suite at the Ritz, don't do it. My daughter only flies first class and *never* coach, so if everything isn't top-drawer, Tat, don't make the trip. No daughter of mine needs to ever settle for the backseat of a car or end up in one of those fleabag motels on Route 66."

My father's tactic with me was clever on three counts. First, he used "intercourse" instead of "sex." The word "intercourse" was not romantic at all; it sounded scientific, and I was terrible at science. The second was about those awful bungalow places we drove by on our way to the Route 66 Drive-in movie. My girlfriends and I believed those places could give people social diseases if they slept in filthy beds, much less had intercourse on one of them. The third and most important thing was that Daddy called me Tat and said, "my daughter;" I loved being my father's daughter more than anything in the world; I would have died rather than do anything to disappoint him.

Looking back at my junior year, all my "dates" were innocent friends, except for the date I almost had in June with Paul Keehn, which might have had the potential for my father's concern. So, Daddy had no real reason to have the "sex talk" with me. I went to the Fortnightly dances at Miss Condit's studio during the school year with Rick Watkins. Rick and his twin brother Bruce were born two days after I was at St. Mary's Hospital. The three of us knew each other from birth. A date with them was the same as going out with Rick or Jimmy. I was fixed up with a former Webster High graduate who was a freshman in engineering at Rolla. The most exciting things that happened that night were that Charlie took me to his home and showed me his Lionel train collection, and then later when the braces on my lower teeth locked with his retainer on his upper teeth when he tried to kiss me goodnight. We were both too embarrassed for him to complete the move by the time we finally got unhooked from one another. Suffice it to say; it was a great relief to get my lower braces off that spring.

I had a date that started the fun with one of the Canda twins on the Admiral riverboat in May until I walked by someone putting mustard on his hotdog from an almost empty but huge pump bottle. The guy turned the nozzle and slammed the pump down as hard as he could, and I got splattered from neck to waist in his line of fire. The rest of that night, I felt ridiculous and reeked to high heaven of mustard. That year, my other "dates" were with boys and girls who were friends. We went out in groups everywhere: the St. Louis Zoo and art museum, even to the top of the arch on the day it opened to the public in 1965. I wore my candy-striped shorts and looked down at a very unsexy vein popping out of my thigh when I felt the arch sway back and forth. The next day in the paper, it said they would close the arch for a few months due to "technical problems." I never went back to the top of the arch again, but I did have that vein removed.

Sex between human bodies was not real, still just romantic imaginings for Pam, Mary, and I. until August arrived that summer. One night, we went to Schneithorst's Restaurant off Lindbergh Boulevard and drove into their drive-up area. It was a daring night because we were out of Webster Groves and almost halfway to Lambert Airport. I was driving Mother's Comet and was too scared to drive on busy Lindbergh Blvd., so we took the back roads through Ladue. Pam, Mary, and I talked to four older boys in a car next to us when we parked, but we found them immature and not worth breaking our parents' rule to stay in Webster, so we decided to go back home right after drinking our milkshakes.

It was dark when we got back on the back roads. Mary and Pam noticed we were followed. The headlights from the car behind us got closer and closer. The three of us got scared. "We shouldn't have done this," Mary said. I sped up and tried to lose them.

"You are going too fast, Cath," Pam warned, "if we get in an accident, our parents will know we left Webster." I slowed down, and their car revved up and passed us. "It's those dumb guys who were . . .," Pam said, but before she got out all her words, we saw two naked male butts framed in their back window glorified by the high beams of the Comet's headlights. Two bare male butts, complete with the backs of hairy balls swinging away. We were horrified. How the glass in all four of Mother's car windows didn't break from the three of us screaming was a miracle.

"I think I am going to throw up," Mary said. "Turn off your brights, Cath!"

"I am so grossed out I can't believe it," I said.

"Girls, I think we just got mooned big time; I'm never going to stop gagging!" Pam said.

"I've never seen my father or brothers naked before!" Mary said.

"Me neither," Pam said, not my dad or Tommy ever!" Pam referred to her parents as Mom and Dad, but sometimes, Mary called her parents Mary Ruth and Charlie. I always loved it when Mary did that; it never failed to make me laugh. I tried to do it for my parents, but I could not form the words Hank and Mary, so they were always Mother and Daddy.

"I've seen my brothers' penises and balls before," Mary proclaimed, "but Mike's, John's, and Tommy's were not hairy!"

"What about your dad's?" Pam asked.

"Are you kidding? There are eight kids in my family, and to this day, none of us know how Mary Ruth and Charlie found the time or place to conceive any of us!"

The din of our Catholic girls' shock and awe chatter stayed full force all the way home. "What a way to start the last month of our summer!" Pam said as she got out of the car at her house. "I am still totally grossed out!"

"I am probably going to be blind the rest of my life after tonight," Mary said at her house. "I don't think I have opened my eyes since it happened."

Daddy sat on my bed later that night and asked, "You three musketeers have fun cruisin' around tonight?"

"Not exactly, Daddy," I said, pulling my pillow over my face to block out the night's anatomical memory, still too vivid in my brain. There was no way I could tell my father what we saw without his seeing the dwindling of innocence drain from my face. We played our Chicago game, which helped me hang on to little girl me a while longer. I had a serious talk with God after Daddy went to his room. *Lord, please tell me Paul Newman and Steve McQueen have nothing like what we saw tonight on their bodies.* I was awake for a long time waiting for an answer but got zilch. It took until morning to understand that no answer was His answer. I didn't like that a bit.

Some girls were not as innocent as the three musketeers; some girls didn't believe they would go to hell if they were not virgins when they got married, but the three of us thought it, and I, for one, was not sure I wasn't headed for hell just from seeing butts and balls.

I did a horrible thing a week later. "Never, ever, chose a boy over a girlfriend," Mother told me, but I did that awful thing, and it could have ruined my friendship with Pam were it not for her goodness to forgive me.

The Saturday night following our "b and b night," Pam and I mustered our courage and returned to Schneithorst. We had to go without Mary because it was Mr. and Mrs. Cordeal's date night, so they were barricaded in their bedroom, and Mary had to fend off the younger kids from disturbing them. I pulled Mother's Comet into a vacant parking spot next to two guys in a green sedan. The guys rolled their windows down before I even turned off the motor. "Hey girls," said the super handsome guy sitting on the car's passenger side. He had light brown hair and a Kirk Douglas cleft on his chin.

I rolled down my window and said, "Hey," back.

"I'm Rex," said the passenger, "and this is Jay," he said and pointed to the driver, who had coal black hair and a friendly smile.

"I'm Cathy, and this is Pam," I said louder than my heartbeat and gestured to Pam beside me. These guys were older, college guys, for sure. They were gentlemen, unlike the idiot moon guys we saw with Mary earlier that summer. The four of us talked for quite a while through our open windows. They bought burgers and Cokes for themselves and asked if they could buy us something. Pam and I looked at each other in utter disbelief; boys our age were too cheap for such generosity. "Let's just order two cherry Cokes," I whispered to Pam.

"Two cherry Cokes would be great," Pam told the attendant, "Thanks a lot, guys," she said to Rex and Jay.

Both guys were going to be juniors in college that fall; Rex was going to the Utah State University in Logan, Utah, and Jay was going to Missouri University in Columbia. They had been friends since they went to high school together in nearby Baldwin, Missouri.

"Can I come over and talk to you, Cathy?" Jay asked.

I looked at Pam, and she nodded. "Sure," I said.

"Hey Pam," Rex said, "why don't you come to our car and talk to me?" Pam looked at me, and I nodded; we decided these guys were safe enough for us to do it. Pam and Jay got out of their cars and passed each other. Jay was tall, but not as tall as Rex. I noticed that when Rex got out of their vehicle and opened the door for Pam.

Jay and I talked about college life and where I wanted to go after graduation. I told him I might go to Central Missouri State College in Warrensburg. "That's not too far from Mizzou," he said. At first, I thought Rex was far more handsome than Jay; after all, his name was Rex Steele, a name good enough to be a movie star's name. Jay's last name was Gunther, hardly a movie star's name. It was almost impossible to believe Rex's name and his good looks were real. But the longer Jay and I talked, his sweet manner convinced me he was a doll too. Jay said he hoped he wouldn't have to go into the service after he graduated, but if he did, since he was in ROTC, he would go to officers' school.

It felt like we talked for five minutes, so I was stunned when I looked at Jay's watch and saw it was 11:30 p.m. Our curfew was 11:00 p.m. "Pam, we gotta go," I called out my window to her. "Look at the time!"

"Yikes, okay," she said and got out of their car.

Before Jay got out of my car, he leaned over and kissed me. It was a lovely kiss, long enough for me to notice the warmth of his soft mouth. It was my first sensual kiss, the kind that stirs a girl so much inside that it sealed the deal on my developing crush.

"This was fun, Cathy," he said. "You are a real sweet girl. I hope I see you again."

I started Mother's Comet as soon as Pam got back in the car. What was more important than getting home was that I couldn't wait to tell Pam that Jay kissed me.

"Hey girls," Jay said, still outside their car. "Want to go to the Cardinals' game at Busch Stadium next weekend?" I looked at Pam, and she looked at me.

"Let's do it, Cath," Pam said. I nodded. It was decided; that we were going against parental rules.

Trying to maintain our façade of being experienced and cool, we gave the guys our phone numbers and took off for home, squawking like magpies the whole way. We agreed that both guys were winners, and we could not believe our luck in meeting them. We also decided that our parents would disapprove of our dating college juniors since we had just turned seventeen in April. "Okay, Cath, what will we do about this little problem?" Pam asked. Not missing a beat, we decided that if the guys did call, we would tell them to meet us at Schneithorst; we would park our car and go with them to the game from there.

"What do we tell our parents?" I asked. Pam's mom and dad, nor my mother and father, had ever called Barb's parents before, so we believed our story was airtight. We decided we would tell them we were going to an all-girls party at Barb's house and needed a midnight curfew.

I called Barb; it was an automatic, "Hell yes!" She agreed to cover for us, but then she called later and said her parents sprung a camping trip on her.

"Crap!" I said to Pam on the phone. We decided to hit up Jenny; she was the wildest of all our friends; Jenny loved to be in cahoots about anything and always agreed to everything.

The guys called, and our plan went off without a hitch. It was fun to double date with one of my two best friends. Pam, Rex, Jay, and I had a great time at the ballgame and riding in Jay's car, going to and from Busch Stadium. Jay had to drive because they said Rex's classic MG was too small for four people. The night baseball game in St. Louis was beautiful, even with the heat and humidity. Whether the Cardinals won or lost that night was immaterial, I was too busy talking to Jay and hoping I was interesting enough that he might kiss me again.

Back at Schneithorst, the guys walked us to our car. I didn't see if Pam got a goodnight kiss from Rex, but I got another exciting one from Jay and a hug. "Bye Cathy, so glad you went to the game with me," he said. I was cooked, utterly crazy about him.

Five days later, Pam and her parents left town and went on their yearly summer vacation for two weeks. Jay and I talked on the phone those five nights, but after Pam left, Jay suddenly stopped calling, and Rex started.

"Jay is returning to his old girlfriend," Rex told me. My heart sank. Rex called me for the next three nights. At first, we talked about Jay, but then the subjects changed.

"We shouldn't be talking so much, Rex," I told him, "Not with Pam gone." There were no cell phones then, no way to reach Pam, but even if there were, I couldn't resist Rex's persistent phone calls. No boy ever pursued me as he did, and there was no aphrodisiac like it.

"Come on, Cathy, Pam won't mind if we date. I will explain everything when she gets back. Jay is sorry about returning to his girlfriend at Mizzou, and he told me to tell you. Pam is out of town for almost the rest of the summer. There is no reason why we can't have fun with what's left of it!"

I saw Rex every night for the rest of the two weeks Pam was gone. Each night I fell more infatuated with Rex than the night before. My affection for Jay dwindled, and my selfish rationalization of deserved happiness kicked in and replaced it. It didn't even matter when Rick and Jimmy made fun of his name. "It is a fake name, Claire," Jimmy said.

"Rex Steele? It sounds like Rip Torn," Rick teased.

"Wasn't he the one Pam liked?" Mother asked one afternoon. I acted like I didn't hear her. It didn't matter what anyone said, none of them. My hormones surged like the motor of his red MG convertible every time he roared up our steep drive to pick me up for our dates. His kisses made Jay's kisses feel like grade school pecks. He was at least two inches taller than I was, and for the first time in my life, I felt petite and feminine in a male's arms other than my father's.

Rex and I took drives, went to the movies, played tennis, went bowling, and played miniature golf. I never felt I was pretty before I dated Rex, but with Rex, I felt like Lesley Ann Warren in Rodgers and Hammerstein's *Cinderella*. I was so wild about him; I even hoped he would touch my good breast, I yearned for him to do it, but he was too much of a gentleman to try.

"It is so cool to go out with you, Cathy. I am crazy about you and proud that you are a good girl and a groovy girl," he said. But I didn't want to be a good girl with Rex, not even a little. Good wasn't at all what I was thinking or feeling.

Daddy must have noticed how lost I was over Rex. Before Rex left for college, Daddy told me he didn't want me to see him anymore. I was furious. "I am just looking out for you, Tat," he said. "Rex is too old for you. Older boys want to do things you are not ready to do yet.

"Not Rex, Daddy," I pleaded, "He is a total gentleman."

"Next summer after you graduate will be a better time," Daddy said. "If Rex likes you enough, he will wait to date you until after you graduate high school." After that talk with Daddy, Mother started on the subject, and then all three of us had a huge fight.

"I only have one date left with him before he returns to college," I told them, "And I'm going to keep it!"

I never disobeyed my parents before the night of the ball game, so I decided that if I had already done that, I might as well keep the date. Rex and I promised each other we would write every night the first semester, and he would see me at Christmas. My knees got so weak I could barely stand inside the hall by our front door after he kissed me goodnight and goodbye. I figured it was all part of the same sin.

"This one has to last, Cathy," he said. "Please make this kiss last."

I wept when I heard his car drive away. After closing the front door, I turned around, and Mother, not Daddy, was sitting on the couch waiting for me. I was miserable that I disobeyed my mother and father, but I was more heartbroken over already missing Rex.

"Pam comes home tomorrow from vacation," she said. "What do you plan to tell her?"

"The truth, Mother. I need to tell her the truth."

"She is going to be very hurt, you know, Cathy. I hope Mr. Steele was worth hurting your best friend," she said and then got up and went to bed without looking at me.

There was no visit from Daddy that night. I tossed, turned, and tried to rationalize some more. Pam had a million boyfriends since the sixth grade, and my only boyfriend died; plus, I got stood up, and Pam never got stood up. My selfish logic was that I deserved happiness and had waited too long. I told myself that Pam would have her pick of a million guys our senior year.

The next night, I didn't wait for Pam to call me. I called her. My guilty conscience devoured me. I couldn't take another breath until I told Pam the truth. "Hi Cath," she said. "Have you been dating Jay while I was gone? I can't wait for Rex to call me . . . .."

"Pam, I said, interrupting her, "Jay went back to his girlfriend at Mizzou, and Rex started calling me."

"About me?" she asked.

"No. He wanted to date me," I said.

"And did you date him?"

"Yes, I'm sorry, Pam, but we fell for each other. The tears formed in my eyes; I knew I hurt her and felt the worst kind of guilty. We couldn't help it."

"I never thought you could do something like that to me, Cath. Never in a million years," she said and hung up.

The next morning, I called Pam, and we talked for a long time about boys and our friendship. She was light years ahead of me in maturity, and even though I knew she was still very hurt and felt terrible about hurting her, Rex's magnetic pull was too much for me when he called at 1:00 p.m. that afternoon. "It's okay, Cath; I want you to go out with him. We won't let a guy ruin our friendship."

"We aren't leaving for Utah until tomorrow! I get to see you one more time!" He picked me up in front of Bob and Liz's house around the corner from my house. We went to Shakey's for pizza, and then to his house to listen to records and talk. We sat on his couch and just held each other song after song. We kissed repeatedly and wanted to do more than kiss, but Rex got up and changed the record each time we felt that wave of desire overcome us. Later, we pulled up in front of Bob and Liz's house, and Rex kissed me again, a kiss that I knew had to last until he got home at Christmas. I watched and waved until his MG disappeared around their corner, down Fieldcrest, and onto Grant Road. I walked home and tried to memorize every moment of our time together.

The next night, I went to the Ozark and saw the film, *A Patch of Blue* with Pam. I watched the blind white girl fall in love with Sidney Poitier and loved that his race did not matter to her. She could see what others refused to see. Just like Rex and me, I thought. I know what Mother and Daddy do not. Pam and I talked about the movie for a long time on the phone. We were mesmerized by the complicated love we saw in the movie. "I wish love were simple," I told her.

"It should be, Cath," she said.

I knew she was still disappointed in me, but I also knew that Pam, above all others, was, and would always be, my favorite person to watch movies with and to try and understand life. I didn't know I would still feel that way fifty years later.

I discovered that summer, I had the selfish capacity to hurt a best friend and that I needed more of a conscience to learn selfishness and that being the queen of denial was sneaky and dangerous not just to myself but to others. I discovered it but didn't learn it. Looking back, my lack of self-control with Rex was foreshadowing, a warning of what was to come in my thirties. God protected me from making a mistake with Rex when I was seventeen, but it was a mistake I repeated and cost my future children's lives.

On August 31 that summer, the entry in my diary was: *Thank you, God, for Pam and her ability to forgive me for what I cannot forgive in myself. This summer was the best and worst of my life. I learned how wonderful and terrible it is to be a woman. The good was that I found out that a boy could find me physically attractive and how wonderful it feels to be physically attracted to that boy. The bad was that I also learned that those good feelings can be so strong that they can make me selfish enough to hurt one of my best friends. Most of all, thank God for giving Rex self-control this summer. You both saved me from traveling coach and wrecking my chances for traveling first class.*

CHAPTER THIRTY-TWO

OUR TIMES, THEY WERE A-CHANGIN'

Children in the sixties did not live at home with their parents after high school; we left our wombs for jobs, college, or the military. My last year of high school had much in common with my first year of life. I found my hands, feet, and voice as a baby. I learned to hold my bottle and spoon and how to eat by myself. I laughed and cried and identified those who loved me. I learned to reach, grab, and hold on to things. I stood unassisted, and then I learned to let go and walk.

In my senior year, I had to learn how to sleep. I was restless at night, awake more than ever. My subconscious did not shut down; it kept me awake, trying to visualize my future. Where will I be next year? What will my room look like? What will my bed feel like? And what about the next year and all the following years? Night after night, I tried to answer those questions, while daily I worked to assure Mother that she raised me right and affirm with Daddy that he prepared me well for the real world. I grabbed whatever I could to stand by myself, walk at graduation, and find the courage to walk away from my home in the spring.

The year started with a lot of letter writing. I wrote to Rex at Utah State, Rick at Southeast Missouri State in Cape Girardeau when he transferred from Meramec, my Aunt Marylene in Jefferson City, Aunt EB in New York, and my cousin Steve in Vietnam. I told Rex how much I missed him; I asked Rick about how to survive in college with no money; I made plans with Aunt Marylene to drive to Warrensburg and see Central Missouri State College; I asked EB if she was happy in New York; and, I kept Steve up to date with our family's news. The school year was busy, and my friendships with Mary, Pam, Eleanor, Becky, Jenny, and Barb, kept my social life alive. I auditioned and made it into "A Choir" and got to do all the choir events. Senior English and my teacher, Mrs. Bernard, became the highlights of my classes. I was active in Pep Club, joined French Club, and still worked at Burger Chef. My senior year busy-ness and waiting for Rex to come home for Christmas kept my fears of my future at bay in the daylight.

Eleanor and I took the train and visited Aunt Marylene in Jefferson City one weekend in September. We solidified our plans to visit Central Missouri State College at the end of October to be sure we wanted to go there. Eleanor and I wrote to five colleges and were invited to tour all of them, but we both needed to go to in-state colleges because of our families' financial situations. Neither of us could afford any schools out of state and, indeed, no private colleges. I applied for a National Defense Act Loan at all five in-state colleges and was accepted. Eleanor's family had enough money to pay for all her in-state college expenses.

In the first part of October, against orders from our parents, Jenny, Becky, and I drove to Southeast Missouri State on a

Saturday. Jenny wanted to visit her current boyfriend, who was a freshman there. We got up at 5:00 A.M. and took off before our parents knew anything about our journey. None of us, even as seniors, were allowed to drive downtown St. Louis, much less out of the city, but sneaking out of Webster at sunrise gave the trip more allure.

Jenny planned to spend the day with her boyfriend, so when we arrived on campus around 9:00 A.M., Rick gave Becky and me a tour. He took off for whatever he planned in the afternoon, so Becky and I found things to do. We played touch football with some guys in the park. Becky was a short, cute-as-all-get-out-blonde from Tennessee. Her accent always gained attention. Becky's fabulous southern expressions made everyone laugh. "Cath, see that poor guy over there? Dang, he's homely. I bet he must sneak up on a water fountain to get a drink!" There was never a problem filling time with Becky.

Daytime depression set in when there was no letter from Rex in our mailbox. I wrote him every night as promised, but fewer and fewer letters came to me from him. I sorted our Fieldcrest mail every afternoon, and my emotions went beyond disappointment when there was no letter from him. My anxiety shot through the roof, and my imagination went rampant. I didn't talk to Mother for fear of hearing, "I told you so." I didn't talk to Daddy because I disobeyed him and saw Rex that last time, and I couldn't talk to Pam; I refused to hurt her again by mentioning his name. I poured my heart out in my letters to Aunt Marylene; I needed affectionate guidance. At home, I just stuffed my fears and emotions inside and acted on the outside like I was okay.

The day before Thanksgiving and the Turkey Day game, I finally got a letter from Rex after waiting to hear from him for weeks. It was a "Dear Jane" letter, we called it. He explained in female psyche-shattering detail that he'd met a girl at college. *She looks just like Cher, her figure, her hair, everything! I'm glad you and I had fun together this summer, but I am with her now. Cathy, have fun your senior year! Love ya, Rex.*

Everything inside me went dark! All my old brain tapes of worthlessness started playing in my brain again. *I'm too tall; I'm too fat; I'm too ugly. Welcome back, Jolly Green Giant!* I played Simon and Garfunkel's *I am a Rock* a million times a day on the hi-fi in the back room, but I wasn't a rock, and I wasn't an island. This rock felt pain, and this island cried a lot, and I did a ton of both alone in my room. Convinced again that I was nothing, I dwelled on how I deserved to be a zero since I was not strong, desirable, or even kind since I hurt Pam. I was convinced I was not my parents' good girl or even a nice girl.

I didn't understand that I was raised by a generation of women who believed they were nothing without men and that my mother was not a card-carrying member of that club. Her daily insistence on my becoming an independent woman translated at my fragile age of sixteen as a cold and unloving opinion of me. What I couldn't know was the future, that Rex would stand on our porch again one day in his Air Force officer's uniform and that he would ring our doorbell and Daddy would answer the door.

"Hello, Mr. Miller. Do you remember me? I dated Cathy the summer before her senior year in high school. Is she home?"

"Of course, I remember you, Rex. I'm so sorry, Cathy doesn't live here anymore. She got married two weeks ago." Rex had become everything Daddy wanted for me, a strong man, a patriot, and a gentleman. All I could think of when Daddy told me this story was that Rex's Cher must have broken his heart as he broke mine. If I had known my future, I would have written a letter of comfort to myself.

I went to the annual Turkey Day game with Barb on Thanksgiving, and Webster lost to Kirkwood. It was the only Turkey Day game we lost during our three years at Webster High, but it fits perfectly into the unhappiness of my senior year's first semester.

The sad beat went on, of course. Besides losing Rex to a Cher lookalike, Rick enlisted in the Naval Reserves, and I thought our family could lose him to Vietnam. He told me he had too much fun at both colleges and that his grades had to be higher to stay out of the draft. "If I have to go into the military, I want to choose the branch myself," he said. Rick continued to work at Boyd's until he left for boot camp. He was sent to the Great Lakes in the freezing January of 1967, and my imaginings of Rick dying in Vietnam increased my night terrors.

The 6:00 p.m. national news on television covered the conflict nobody called a war in more vivid detail than any war before. The broadcasts were all about the enemy and the deaths of American boys. This visual coverage shocked American households. No combat scenes from any war or military action had ever been seen on live television, only newsreels at movie theaters. Death came right into our homes and sat down with us at dinner. I felt as divided about the war inside me as the country was outside. I watched CBS,

ABC, or NBC with Mother and Daddy. The news brought back all the fear and trauma I experienced when I saw the holocaust film my sophomore year, the newspaper headlines lying on our dining room table about the Cuban missiles pointed at the U.S., and when we hid under our desks at Bristol for protection from Communist nuclear bombs. The nightly Vietnam news was worse than all because it was about my age group, my peers, my cousin, and my brother. I watched injured American boys cry for their mothers, and my heart broke over and over from worry and fear.

My father believed in answering our country's call to defend the world from evil, but he often sounded as confused as I was about it. He yelled at the television, "If the damn government is only going to give our boys pea shooters to fight this damn thing, then get them the hell out of it!" My father's Greatest Generation's patriotism and pride in what America and the allies did during World War II was understandable. Still, the times were a-changin,' and both his generation and mine felt it. The boys shown on TV fighting and suffering were their children, the kids of those who survived WWII. Mother sat silent when the news was on, but it wasn't because she didn't have an opinion; instead, Mother lived her life with her finger in the hole of a virtual dam of anger. She was my role model for doing that.

Rick felt the country had changed when he came home from boot camp, but he had also changed as well. It was more than how he looked with his pink-shaved head that felt like peach fuzz. He was older and trimmer, and there was no remaining Ricky Miller baby fat. He looked like a man, no longer a nineteen-year-old college party guy. During the time between boot camp and leaving for active duty, Rick was given a store to manage in Clayton. He dated Joanna Lombardo, a beautiful girl with creamy mocha-colored skin, coal-black hair, and a voluptuous European figure. Joanna Lombardo's father was a big shot in the produce industry in St. Louis and one hundred percent Italian. He did not like my Irish-looking brother dating his daughter, though Joanna's mother, a blonde woman of German descent, loved my pale, freckled brother and his strawberry-blonde hair.

One night Rick came home and looked a little shaken up; his face flushed and serious, not his usual happy and clear. "I cannot see Joanna anymore," he said. "Some of Mr. Lombardo's associates met me at my car after I walked Joanna to her door tonight. They convinced me, waving their fists and more, that Mr. Lombardo would allow a mick like me to date his daughter under any terms."

The changin' kept coming my senior year. Two weeks after the brutal demise of my relationship with Rex, I got a hold of myself and changed my life by finding a new job. I stopped working at Burger Chef and took a job at Crestwood Plaza in J.C. Penney's Drapery Department. I worked the evening shifts and had to wait for Mother to come home from Doubleday to use her car for my job. I was home from 3:45 to 5:30 by myself. Daddy, Mother, and Rick were still at work, and Jimmy was out with his friends from school or Woodlawn. The phone often rang between 4:00 p.m. and 5:00 p.m., with strange, scary callers on the other end of the line. Home by myself, and the calls were upsetting. "Is your deadbeat father there?" one voice said. Another said, "If that bastard doesn't pay right away, tell your mother a moving van will be there Friday to pick up all your furniture." Each call was more shocking and threatening than the last. "Are you the asshole loser's only daughter?" Are you home alone?" I was going to go to Rick, but he was seldom home, and I didn't think he knew anything about the calls. I didn't go to Daddy, I was too afraid he would have another heart attack, so I went to Mother.

"What is going on with these phone calls?" I asked her. "I am scared to death! Are you answering them too?" Her face instantly went from ash gray to bright crimson as her mama bear let out its roar and rage.

"Your father owes these people money, Cathy! Listen to me; I promise I will see that they stop calling. Do not think about them for one more minute, do you hear me?"

"Yes, mam," I said. I never learned what she did, but after our conversation, the calls stopped.

Money continued to be a dirty word in our house. The only time Mother talked about money was to complain about our lack of it or blame Daddy for not earning it. Daddy only said, "someday, this family will have money again." His words only reminded me of the night he told me that we would get insurance money if he died. My father always hoped to replace the wealth his family lost, and his failure to do so, especially to please my mother, put great stress on him. I absorbed every ounce or vibration of it during my senior year. No wonder my father was in and out of the hospital with nose bleeds or because his heart kept collapsing. Not only had Daddy's ship not come in, but he missed the boat so often that his life was endangered, and I began to be afraid for him all the time, scared the mafia would come after him for not paying loans or gambling debts. I thought we all needed to move where nobody knew or could find us.

Mother and Daddy discussed moving to Granite City, Illinois, the previous summer. "Your father has been offered a job," Mother said. I did not want to leave my friends and move away my senior year, but the calls I answered made me wish Daddy had taken that job if that job existed. A few days after the last call, our house settled down a bit. "Mother, things are better now," I said to her. "What did you do to make them stop?"

"I took care of it, Cathy; that is all you need to know. Just concentrate on the rest of your high school senior year and prepare for college."

It was nice not to always smell like Ode to Grease from Burger Chef and wear real clothes to work instead of a food-stained orange and white outfit with a paper hat. The job was boring as hell, but it paid a bit more, and I got to shop at stores close to it on my shift breaks. Seventeen Magazine sponsored fashion shows at Crestwood Plaza from time to time, so because I was a tall teen in their employ, J. C. Penney's asked me to model their clothing when their store was featured. I was excited until I did the first fashion show. Talk about boring; modeling was the worst, all that standing around, plus I was self-conscious about my hips and uneven breasts and was not remotely in the 34-22-34 category of the other girls. I felt like a circus freak on display.

On Saturdays, I worked eight-hour shifts, 12:00 p.m. to 8:00 p.m., or if I had to close, 2:00 p.m. to 10:00 p.m. Two weeks before Christmas, I was working the earlier Saturday shift. I took my break at 5:00 p.m. and thought I would run across the hall from J.C. Penney's to Lerners Clothing store, where I never found a single thing that fit me but passed the time there regardless. Two uniformed Army guys from Ft. Leonard Wood stopped me and asked for directions to Stix Baer & Fuller before I got inside the store. Mother's voice rang in my ears, "You are such a sucker for a uniform, Cathy; I bet you would date a garbage collector if he wore a clean uniform."

These two Army guys were polite and cute, so I blocked Mother's words from my mind and stopped walking. "Well, you have to go all the way to the opposite end of the plaza from Penney's," I said. "It is faster if you cut through Sears." I smiled, turned, and walked into Lerners.

"Hey, wait," the shorter one said behind me, "I'm John, and this is my buddy, Richard McIntyre; he wants to ask you another question."

"Sure, what's your question, Richard?" I said, looking up. Yes *up*! Richard stood somewhere around six feet, four inches tall. His short military-cut hair was a little redder than Rick's, and he had a few small scars from teenage acne that dotted his fair complexion. I liked his shy "aw shucks" manner and his pinkish face, even if it wasn't as handsome as his shorter, darker-complected, confident friend's face. There was something about the sincere look in Richard's blue-gray eyes that worked for me.

"I have two questions," Richard said. "First, can you tell me your name? Second, if I wait around the plaza until you get off work, could I buy you a coke or coffee at the food court?"

"Well, I have three more hours before I get off work," I said. "Don't you guys have a curfew or something?"

"It's okay," Richard said, encouraged. That will give me time to drop John off at his folks' house in Ladue and come back. Both our families live in the St. Louis suburbs, and we are on a weekend pass. We don't have to go back to base until midnight tomorrow night".

I was flattered. Wow. He was willing to wait three hours for a coke with me, while Rex didn't wait a single day for me when he got back to college. I thought about it. I'd be safe in the food court. I wouldn't let him walk me to Mother's car. I would only tell him my first name. I was in military training, too, because after Rick returned from boot camp, he kept warning me about military guys. "You gotta listen to your gut alarm, Claire," he said and repeated, "military guys are *not* high school boys!" I looked at Richard and waited. Nope. No alarm went off about Private Richard McIntyre. Besides, he looked kind and hopeful standing there.

"Sure, okay, Richard, sounds nice. My name is Cathy. I will meet you back here at 9:00 p.m." I was glad I wasn't closing that night.

Richard and I began dating as soon as we had that Coke date in the food court. My father liked Richard; he was as old as Rex, but Daddy admired Richard for serving his country right out of high school. He talked to Richard often about the military and WWII whenever Richard was at our house. They joked and laughed together. While dating him, I learned much about Richard and more about myself.

I had a hard time getting used to Richard's relatively poor grammar. He ended words with prepositions like, "Cathy, where are you at?" or "Hey John, what you got that for?" I never heard the word "ain't" used in everyday conversations, only in books or movies about uneducated people. But I loved Richard's parents when he took me home to meet them. They were such lovely people and did everything possible to make me feel at home, but their grammar was worse than Richard's, and it was apparent that good housekeeping was not a priority. TV dinner trays were everywhere, and the living room smelled like burned grease and cigarettes. The furniture looked as if they used it instead of napkins. I was never in a living room or home quite like it. Even Mrs. Lester's house across the tracks in Webster was not like this one.

Gertrude Lester worked in the shoe department at Lambert's. Mother and I were in her home once when we returned some shoes to her that didn't fit Rick. Her son, Barney, was considered a hood at Webster High. Most of the hoods at school were poor and lived on "the other side of the tracks," as everyone called that part of town. We were poor enough to live there, too, but my parents worked hard to disguise that.

After Richard took me home, I thought about how much I liked Richard and his family and wrote in my diary that *I am a snob.* I hated my reaction to Richard and his family's grammar and home conditions. I didn't like knowing this about myself and prayed about it: *Lord, I vow to overcome my critical attitude and to work extra hard to show that I like Richard and his family; they are all honest and good people.*

The fact that snobbery was wrong but can be cured was not the only thing I learned about Cathy Miller while dating Richard McIntyre. I knew that no matter how hard I tried, I couldn't put romantic love in my heart for him if it wasn't there. His kisses did nothing to me like Rex's, even when I closed my eyes. It wasn't only because he smelled like cigarettes; my parents and Rick smelled that way too, but kissing a smoker was a turnoff for me. On each date, it grew more difficult to kiss Richard because I knew I was doing it to make him feel good about himself and not because I was attracted to him.

One cold night before Valentine's Day, when Richard was over, we had a fire in the fireplace. Jimmy was in the dining room doing something at the dining room table. Mother was reading, and Daddy was watching television in their bedroom. Rick was out as usual. Richard and I went to the back room to watch tv. It was so cold that we didn't sit on the couch in front of the picture window with the plastic on it; we sat in the two small armchairs on opposite sides of the space heater.

"Cathy, Daddy wants you to go see him in their bedroom," Jimmy said when he burst unannounced into the back room. I got up, and Jimmy sat in my chair opposite Richard and started talking to him the minute I left the room. Jimmy was always up to something. One of his favorite things to do was to call any date I had by a different name than the right one, prompting my date to interrogate me after we left.

"Bye, Bobby," Jimmy said once when I went out with a boy named Charlie.

"Who is Bobby?" Charlie asked suspiciously, so I had to defend myself.

"There is no Bobby," I said. That's just Jimmy being a younger brother."

My parents' bedroom door was open when I got there after Daddy's summons. Daddy was standing in the hall. "What is it, Daddy?" I asked.

"Jimmy says you and Richard are rolling around on the floor in front of the fireplace in the living room. Is that true?"

"It is absolutely not true!" I said. "Richard and I are in the back room in the chairs beside the heater, watching television!" I stopped a second and looked into my father's eyes. "But what is true, Daddy is that I am much more like you in the romance department than Mother."

"Well, Tat," my father responded, "If that's true, I think it is time for Richard to leave; besides, it's getting late!

The next day was Valentine's Day, and I knew I was in trouble. Richard took me to Cheshire Inn for an expensive dinner. He reached across the table and gave me a small royal blue velvet box with a tiny red taffeta bow. "No, Richard," I said, "this dinner must have cost a fortune."

"Please, Cathy, take it and open it." His eyes shone with excitement; I could not disappoint him and refuse his gift. Inside the box on a thin gold chain was a tiny gold pendant with a sliver of green jade in the middle of it. It was lovely and precious to him. No boy had ever given me a gift before. I knew the pendant and the dinner cost Richard hard-earned military wages, and that brought tears to my eyes. "It is beautiful, Richard," I said, "thank you."

"What are those tears for?" he said. "I wanted to get this for you, Cathy; I want you to know I am serious about you."

Oh no, I thought. I knew how painful it was to care more for someone than they cared for me. Never from the depths of my low self-esteem did I ever contemplate that I might find myself in the position. I didn't have the courage to speak that truth to Richard and hurt him the way Rex hurt me. At that moment, with Richard's Valentine's gift in front of me on the table, I understood how much more painful it was to hurt someone than to hurt myself. I didn't tell Richard my truth that night; I was a coward. He was too proud and excited about the perfect Valentine's Day he had planned for us. I had no guts, no bravery, and I had no idea that it would only get harder to tell Richard the truth.

I wrote in my diary about it but seeing the words on paper only made me feel worse. I needed to talk to someone, and Daddy was always there.

"Don't put this off any longer, Tat," Daddy said. "It will only be more painful for Richard. He's a soldier; he will be strong and honorable about it."

"What will I say, Daddy? Is there anything that won't hurt his feelings?"

"No, Tat," there isn't. Pain is a part of life; it is one of the most critical ways we know we are alive. This isn't supposed to be easy. Just tell Richard what is really in your heart, whether he feels the same way or not, even if you wish things were different."

That Friday, when Richard came to pick me up for our date, I asked him if we could sit in his car awhile before we left. "Richard," I said, I don't want to mislead you." I saw in his face that he knew exactly what was coming, that he had been down this road before, like me. "I am not going to tell you I want to be friends; I want to tell you I am already your friend, and I am proud to be your friend. You are one of the best guys, no best men I have ever met in my life, and if I could pick a man I want to be in love with, it would be you." I couldn't stop my tears. "But life doesn't work that way, does it?"

"No, it doesn't," he said quietly.

"Richard, I want you to take back this beautiful necklace and save it for a girl who deserves it. It is not a friendship necklace. It is a love necklace, and there is a girl who will love wearing it because she loves you." I put the velvet box on his dashboard and started to get out of the car.

"Hold on there, Cathy," he said. "I am, no want, to walk you to your door."

I was still determining how I would hold it together until we got to the porch. My knees felt weak, but it would have only made everything worse if I had grabbed his arm.

"May I kiss you goodbye?" he asked on the porch.

"Yes, of course, Richard," I said. Cigarettes or not, I would not be cruel and deny him the only thing he asked of me that night. He put his arms around my waist, and I put my arms around his neck, the way we kissed each time during our brief relationship, but that kiss was one of the sweetest, most meaningful kisses I ever received, not just up until that night, but ever.

Two weeks later, a small package arrived addressed to me in the mail. It was the small royal blue velvet box with the tiny red taffeta bow and a folded piece of paper.

Cathy,

I wanted my favorite friend to have this. I got my orders and am leaving for Vietnam. When you wear it, pray for me. I hope you will.

- Richard

Daddy was right. Richard was a soldier; he was honorable, and I felt fortunate to know him.

ॐ

CHAPTER THIRTY-THREE

WHY THEY CALL
IT COMMENCEMENT

Time picked up speed during my last semester of high school. After Christmas, we lost another class member. Ray was a fantastic athlete, student, and friend. He and his girlfriend, Candy, were loved by everyone, no matter what group they were in at school. Ray was interviewed for athletic scholarships from all over the United States; we all knew Candy would go to school wherever Ray went to college; their love was true love to all of us.

St. Louis and its surrounding suburbs were hit with a big snowstorm. Winter snowstorms in Webster meant sledding, skating parties, and another party afterward. I was six feet two inches tall in ice skates, so I opted for snow boots and sledding parties. We had favorite places to sled in Webster; some paths were on steep, bumpy hills and the boys loved those spots the best. Ray and Candy took a sled down one of the most prominent hills in Webster. Ray laid down on the sled first, and then Candy laid on top of him for the "danger ride" on the steepest hill. They hit a big bump on the way down, but both seemed fine when they got to the bottom and for the rest of the sledding that afternoon.

Ray collapsed from a heart attack during the afterparty that night. His heart was severely bruised from hitting that bump. Nobody, not even Ray himself, knew how gravely he was injured that afternoon. The entire school took the news hard, especially the members of our class. We felt horrible for Candy and both families. It was difficult for us to absorb the loss of another friend so young after losing Todd when we were sophomores. Ray's funeral and the war news brought us more confusion and sadness.

The curriculum in our senior classes second semester at Webster High got more complicated. All the teachers piled on the work to be positive that they covered every inch of what was required for students to graduate. I was tired of high school and more fearful of the future. Jenny asked me to explore Washington University with her. She also had a boyfriend going there, and since my father did two years at "Wash Out U," as he called it, I agreed to go out of curiosity. Jenny, with her Doris Day good looks and personality, persuaded me to go on a blind date with a friend of her boyfriend.

Washington University got the nickname Wash Out U, not only because it was a tough school academically but because it was also a party school. Their parties were wild keggers. The taste of beer gagged me as soon as I smelled it. I didn't drink at all until I was twenty-four years old. Nobody in high school, or college for that matter, could afford mixed drinks or wine, just beer, horrible, cheap, warm disgusting beer.

My date was a sophomore guy named Bud Weissberg from the Sammi fraternity. Jenny and I went to their fraternity house on a late Saturday afternoon. As soon as she introduced me to Bud, she disappeared to find her boyfriend somewhere else and left Bud and me alone in the study. The room was beautiful; it was apparent the fraternity had lots of money. The wood paneling was dark walnut, the mahogany chairs were covered in deep burgundy brocade, and the forest green carpeting was thick enough to wrap the sides of my shoes when I walked on it. The bookcases were packed floor to ceiling with classics, all with titles in shiny gold lettering.

I skimmed through a few titles and took a book off the shelf when Bud came up behind me, reached over my shoulder, and took it out of my hands. He placed it back on the shelf and said, "Come sit on the sofa with me, Cathy. Let's talk awhile and get to know each other before I show you around the campus." I followed him to a lush gold velvet sofa and sat down. He sat beside me, and at first, we just talked. It was "no biggie," as we used to say. Bud had black hair and was my height, but he was a stocky guy, a wrestler who weighed at least forty pounds more than my one hundred and fifty-five. Bud's face and arms were hairy; he was one of those guys who probably had to shave three times by noon and probably started shaving when he was ten.

Bud suddenly stopped talking and tried to kiss me. It was way too fast a move for me, even if I had wanted a kiss from him, which I did not. I pushed him back and scooted to the arm of the sofa. He took hold of my legs and slid me down, so my head was flat on the cushion. Before I knew it, he was on top of me and tried to force my legs apart. I panicked. My mind raced to think of something I could say to stop him from going further. Then, like magic, a genius lie that would fix everything came to mind, at least, I hoped so.

"No, Bud, stop it. I'm on my period!" I exclaimed.

"That's okay," he said, "that never bothers me," he whispered.

"Oh, my God!" I screamed in his ear. I was grossed out and shocked that I thought I would throw up all over him and the gold velvet sofa. I slapped his face with all my might. He jerked away in total surprise. It was the moment I needed to jump off the couch, grab my purse and run out of the room. I ran up and down the halls trying to hear or find Jenny or anyone. I heard, imagined, and feared Bud was right behind me and started opening doors to rooms but found nobody in any of them. I turned a corner, ran down another hallway, and opened another door. A guy was cooking on a hot plate in a kitchenette.

"Are you okay?" he said. "Are you looking for someone? The kegger isn't until a little later."

"No," I said and tried not to sound breathless. "I'm here with a girlfriend, but I'm not feeling well; I just need a phone to call for a ride home."

"There's a phone," he said, pointing to one on the wall.

"Thank you." I dialed home and thanked God that Daddy answered. "Hi, Daddy, I'm with Jenny at Washington U. and need a ride home," I said with a shaking voice I couldn't control. "I don't feel well, but I don't want to ruin Jenny's date with her boyfriend."

"Okay, honey, I will be right there. Where are you?"

"I'm at the Sammi House."

"I know where it is. Go out the front door and meet me across the street. I will come in and find you if you are not there."

Oh no, I thought, I have got to be out there; I didn't want my father to come inside. I walked to the front door, and Bud was waiting for me there.

"I've been looking for you everywhere," he said. "Don't go; the party hasn't started yet."

"I called my dad," I said. "He went to Washington U. He was a Sigma Chi. He's coming to pick me up out front. He said he would come in and find me if I was not there. My father is six foot seven." Bud Weissberg didn't say another word. He just opened the door and held it open for me.

It was dark already, and I had to wait forty-five minutes for my father to drive from Webster to Washington University. I was still shaking when I climbed into the front seat with Daddy. I was ready for the boom to drop and Daddy's hard questions to begin after we turned around and headed for home.

"Hi Tat," he said finally, "I don't know what happened while you were at the Sammi house, but you did exactly right. I'm proud of you." Relief and tears. On the way home, he told me about Jenny's Dad, Russ, an entertainer in St. Louis, and how they knew each other when they grew up. He asked me about school and my girlfriends and told me about the movie he wanted to watch when we got home. "I don't think we need to tell your mother anything about this evening, do you?"

"Thank you, Daddy," I whispered. "Can I come and watch the movie with you in your room?"

"Of course, Tat, he said. It was almost nine. "Why don't you get ready for bed, honey? I will fill you in if you miss anything important."

Once in my pajamas, I grabbed my comb, curler caddy, and Grandma Miller's silver hand mirror and went to my parents' furniture-crowded bedroom. I couldn't get ready fast enough; I just wanted to sit beside my father, feel his warmth and smell his

Daddy smell. I slid down at the foot of his bed on the floor beside his long legs that protruded from his recliner and almost touched the television set. I leaned against his bed, balanced my hand mirror on my knees, and started to roll up my hair.

"I don't know how you sleep on those brush rollers and big orange juice cans, Tat," he said. "Why do you want straight hair? I like your wavy hair just the way it is."

Odd for a teenage girl, though not for me, when I climbed into bed after the movie, I thought about the word *safety*, the tier above physiological needs on Maslow's climb up to self-actualization displayed in his *Hierarchy of Human Need* pyramid. I learned about the pyramid in science but never understood it until Mrs. Bernard discussed it in senior English when we discussed Shakespeare's *Hamlet* in class. We talked about Hamlet's father and Hamlet's confusion over what was happening in his maturation world. I grabbed my diary and wrote,

I don't care if Daddy isn't good with money, exaggerates, and even lies sometimes because safety, in my world, equals Daddy.

The night at the Sammi House was my last escapade with Jenny. I didn't blame her for what happened; I wasn't mad at her; she didn't know what kind of guy Bud was, but the fury of events in our second semester caused changes that made some of our oldest relationships drift apart, especially those relationships between the naïve like me and those not so naïve.

Eleanor and I visited Karen, one of my neighbors, at Missouri University one weekend. Karen was a year older than we were and invited us to see Mizzou. The Friday night we arrived, Karen had blind dates lined up for us. After Bud, I was leery, but we were all going to be together, so I agreed. Eleanor's date, Bob, was about her height; he was a friendly guy dressed in a yellow V-neck sweater, corduroy slacks, and loafers; he was very preppy. I was sitting down when my date walked into the room and was introduced to me. I was taller than Robbie, and I was sitting down!

Robbie was also preppy in his olive-green vest, herringbone slacks, and loafers. He was not only a short young guy but would also become a short older guy. He was small-boned, almost fragile. My height didn't faze him. I dreaded standing up. I was afraid he would bolt for the door the second I stood. He sat beside me, and we all chatted for a long while in the greeting room of Karen's dorm. When we stood up to leave for the movies, Robbie didn't bolt for the door; he just looked up at me and said, "Cathy, I was so glad Karen invited me on this blind date, and now that I've met you, I am even more glad."

The six of us went to see *A Man and A Woman* at the Art Theater in Columbia. I had heard the theme song countless times on the radio and loved it. The movie was better than the song. We went to a local steak house for dinner afterward and couldn't stop discussing the film. It was exciting to talk about art, acting, movies vs. live theater, favorite books, and not about the next football or basketball game or what might be Kasey Kason's top twenty hit songs the following week. Robbie was intelligent and fascinating to talk to; the evening was successful. The next day Robbie and Bob gave us a tour around the campus and pointed out buildings where they had classes. We went to the student union to have Cokes and then spent the rest of the day discussing the differences between high school and college. Bob was taken with Eleanor and wanted to see her again; that became obvious when the guys walked us back to the dorm. Eleanor thanked him for the great weekend and explained that she was getting serious about her boyfriend at home but would let him know if things changed between them. Robbie and I were friends from the start; we exchanged addresses and wrote to each other for almost a year. My friendship with short Robbie and his colossal brain showed me the benefits of having platonic friendships with members of the opposite sex. Years later, I learned that Robbie became a successful neurosurgeon. He was, indeed, a gentleman and a scholar.

As much as I wanted to go to Washington University or Missouri University, there was no way my family could afford those schools. I didn't think I was smart enough. The competition for scholarships in 1967 was stiff among students with 4.0 averages. There were so many baby boomers. The possibilities for those scholarships were beyond my grasp, though I graduated in the upper third of my class. My only hope for college was to garner forms of financial aid that required paybacks with interest.

My mother's powerful pointer finger shook an inch from my nose throughout high school and at least a thousand times during my senior year. Bitter over many of her life choices, she said, "By hook or crook, you are going to college, Cathy. You will have something to fall back on when life gets hard. Somehow, some way, we will find the money!" I was going to a state college with a National Defense Act Loan and needed to work many hours while I was going to school. The writing was on the wall.

After Eleanor and I visited Central Missouri State College with Aunt Marylene, we decided to go there. The weekend of our visit,

I met one of my cousin Sharon's friends, Scotty. Sharon was Aunt Marylene's daughter; Scotty had been Sharon's friend for years. Both Sharon and Scotty became English teachers. Sharon went to teach English in Texas after graduation from college, and Scotty took an English position at CMSC. The weekend we were there, Scotty helped me secure two jobs for the fall, one in the dorm kitchen and one as a student assistant in the English Department. Eleanor was set financially and would not need to work.

Eleanor and I defied all advice and decided to be roommates. Everyone from counselors to family friends told us, "Don't room in college with a high school friend; your friendship won't last!" We found their assumptions absurd, filled out the dormitory paperwork to be roomies, and started planning day and night. We decorated and redecorated our room by passing notes during French class while Mrs. Bolay shook pencils out of her white bun in an animated effort to help us speak the language. Eleanor and I went through reams of paper writing notes that we passed to each other in the hall between choir and English, notes filled with ideas for color combinations and fabric suggestions for our bedspreads. Hours after school were spent at each other's houses speculating about our new suitemates, the dorm mother, or the resident assistant. We tied up our home telephone lines, discussing our college wardrobes and praying we could turn small budgets into a line of clothing we could mix and match in endless combinations. We couldn't share clothing; I was much taller than Eleanor.

April brought Pam's and my eighteenth birthdays. Mr. and Mrs. Shontz, Pam's brother Tommy, Mary, and I celebrated Pam's on April 6 with dinner, cake, and gifts at the Shontz's. The three musketeers never broke our tradition of celebrating birthdays together. We repeated the celebration at my house for my birthday on April 29. Rick, Jimmy, Bob, Liz, Mother, Daddy, Pam, Mary, and I gathered around our dining room table. Mother and Daddy gave me a jade ring and a watch. I could not believe my eyes. These adult gifts were precious to me in an instant. I had never received anything expensive from my family before that birthday. I was taken aback. I refused to let my mind entertain the thought of whether Daddy "got a deal" from some crooked jeweler; I didn't want to know; I just wanted to treasure the jewelry and my family for giving them to me.

May was Senior everything: Senior Prom, Senior Class parties, Senior Class Day, Baccalaureate, Graduation, and All-Night Graduate Party. The Senior Prom was called *Moonlight and Cherry Blossoms*. Each senior received a formal engraved invitation with an enchanting Asian scene on the cover, complete with a river, a bridge, a cherry blossom branch, and the moon. Eleanor invited her boyfriend, Henry; Barb and Patrick were dates, and Craig Uthoff asked Pam to go with him because her relationship with Bill was over. I was, as usual, very single, so I asked Bill Daniels, a junior in the choir, to go with me. Bill said, "I'd love to go with you, Cathy." I went to Stix Baer & Fuller and bought a long white brocade dress after school, then to Bakers Shoes and bought a pair of one-inch white cloth "heels" and a clutch purse. Since I saved money with my discount at Stix buying my dress, I asked the saleswoman at Bakers to have my shoes dyed turquoise.

Pam, Barb, and I went to Joe Weiman's Salon in Stix Baer & Fuller on prom day and had our hair styled. I darkened my long, dishwater blonde hair with a bottle of Raven Black Roux temporary hair coloring the night before. Most of the color stayed in after my Joe Weiman appointment, but my hair hadn't exactly achieved my goal of Raven Black. I wanted my hair color and style to look like Elizabeth Taylor's hair in the film, *The VIPs*. I brought the stylist a picture of Liz Taylor from Photoplay magazine, and silk turquoise flowers to wind through my braided hair instead of white flowers like Liz wore in her photo. My earrings were exciting, very Mod, white ivory-looking balls on the end of long chains.

The prom was formal attire, so most girls wore floor-length gowns, and the boys wore tuxes if they could afford them or dark suits. Pam's mother made her dress from white pique. I was so proud that from my wages at work, I was going to wear a dress I didn't make myself. Barb's dress was brocade, a soft pink shade she had made with her mother's expert help.

Pam, Eleanor, and Barb went to prom in separate cars with their dates. Bill and I went with other seniors from the choir in three vehicles. We arrived at the courtyard at school to find the courtyard had disappeared. The junior class magically turned it into an elegant Japanese Garden. Bill gave me a beautiful white orchid corsage with turquoise ribbons, and I gave him a white rose boutonniere trimmed in turquoise to wear on his white tux. Some of my classmates were practically unrecognizable. They looked so stunning. I might have been unrecognizable, but at six feet one inch tall in turquoise shoes, an all-white floor-length formal, and black hair piled on my head, it was not hard to figure out it was me. That night in the moonlight amid the cherry blossoms, the Class of '67 were no longer boys and girls who had known each other since grade school; we were senior men and women.

It was darker than usual around 8:00 p.m. on the night we all waited twelve years to experience. Still, other than that, prom began as picture perfect, a fairytale with characters heralding from Royal kingdoms across our grand land called Webster Groves. We were happy, the faculty was delighted, and the junior class was ecstatic over their success. Then, unexpectedly, the weather turned everything into a dripping nightmare. All our brand-new gowns with corsages, expensive hairstyles, dyed shoes, and purses were hit with a torrential downpour of rain. Senior men and women ran in all directions from the rain, and the juniors ran into the shower to try and save some of their decorations. Only about half of the Royal kingdom made it to shelter while others didn't, including the six-foot, one-inch girl in the white brocade dress who lost one of her turquoise-dyed, not-so-high, high heels. I found my shoe in the crowd, grabbed it, yanked up my brocade skirt, and did an awkward fifty-yard dash to the girls' bathroom. I was afraid to look in the mirror once I got inside. My friend, Julie, from choir, came running in right behind me. "Oh my God, Cathy, look at us!" she said.

I'm afraid to look!" I said. We held hands and turned to look in the mirror together. My face, neck, shoulders, and white brocade bodice were streaked with running rivers of Raven Black colored water; I was a drowned mess. Julie's ironed hair looked like a Toni Home Permanent gone wrong; her corsage and clutch purse were missing. We stood looking at each other in the mirror, still holding hands, and burst out laughing.

"Hey, Cath, let's find the other choir kids and see who wants to go home. We can all change and go to Luigi's for dinner."

"Deal," I said. A few of our entourage were waiting for us outside the bathroom, some dry, some not. We bounced the plan off them and received immediate approval. The guys threw us the car keys and went to get everyone else. There was no chance in hell that Julie and I would cross through the gym among all those who survived the storm and were dancing; we just looked at each other and ran right back out in the rain. Barb and Pat, Pam and Craig stayed and danced the night away.

All the prom kids with romantic dates went to dinner before 8:00 p.m. When we got to Luigi's at 10:00 p.m., there were only a few tables with people, so our choir gang had our choice of where to sit. We feasted upon Italian dinners with all the fixings. The wait crew enjoyed our tale of wet woe so much that they treated us to frozen spumoni desserts.

Luigi's let us use a banquet room after dinner to hold our own prom until 1:00 A.M. One of our choir guys went home and got his record player and a stack of records. We danced to the Temptations, the Four Tops, the Supremes, Little Richard, and many more. We sang and laughed and hugged one another until the employees told us it was time to go home. We wanted to thank them, so we helped them clean up the banquet room and any other tasks they gave us to do before closing for the night. I got home at 2:30 A.M., and even Daddy was asleep.

I wrote in my Graduation Memories book before I turned off my light: *Ever since seventh grade, I dreamed about how romantic Senior Prom would be, how I would be dancing every slow dance in the arms of my high school boyfriend, who could not take his eyes off my beauty. Tonight was the best prom ever! It is the first night I remember that I am happy not to have a boyfriend. During all my boy-crazy years, I never imagined how grateful I could be tonight to spend my evening of Moonlight and Cherry Blossoms in an Italian restaurant dancing to Motown with my friends.*

But prom night wasn't the best, not by a long shot. I confirmed later that on May 13, 1967, I saw my reflection in a high school restroom mirror and had my first healthy laugh at myself. But it was only a glimpse of a woman-to-be, a woman I did not become for over twenty-five years in the future. Poor self-esteem continued to hover over me like the dark clouds on prom night. It would take more than a high school diploma to teach me how to love myself; it would take a Magna cum Laude diploma from the School of Hard Knocks.

It rained again on June eighth, graduation day, but it cleared off by the time *Pomp and Circumstance* boomed over the P.A. system on the football field. Excitement and fears about our futures rose with the temperature during rehearsal until we walked at 6:00 p.m. I could not determine whether our red faces were from anticipation or the ninety-five degrees and eighty-five percent humidity. The girls reported to our senior class sponsor, Mrs. Bernard, in the girls' gym before the ceremony, and the boys reported to Coach Jones in the main gym.

Mother and Mary Cordeal sat in the front row. Jimmy was with Daddy standing on the track under the home team goalpost. Rick was absent because he had to work. Five hundred and ninety-seven seniors received a diploma. The P.A. system played *Pomp and Circumstance* so many times that it became slapstick by the time we all took our seats. The choir members sat in the front rows, and the entire class filed by us. There was a moment I realized how few people I took the trouble to know. Pam reached out and squeezed my hand when she went by me. Eleanor was a soprano and sat in a different row from Barb and me because we were second sopranos.

Dr. Spivey gave the invocation after *The Star-Spangled Banner,* and the audience stood as the Webster Groves High School Acapella Choir filed onto the risers on stage to sing the selections chosen. Miss Replogle chose *A Mighty Fortress is Our God,* and the senior choir members chose the *Hallelujah Chorus* from the *Messiah.* It was moving for the audience and for us to sing with our beloved and legendary Miss Rep one last time. She was so proud. Earlier in the year, our choir sang both selections at Kiel Auditorium with the St. Louis Philharmonic Orchestra, a thrilling first for Miss Replogle and her Webster Groves High School choir.

Susan Maxey and Doug Wheeler were our commencement speakers. They left us with this at the end of their speeches.

"God said, "Your task is to build a better world!

'How?' came the response of the people. 'The world is such a vast place. It is so complicated now, and I am so small . . . there is nothing I can do!'

But God, in all His wisdom, said, "Just build a better you!"

The concert band played *America, the Beautiful,* Principal Latta and Superintendent Brown presented us with diplomas, and Dr. Spivey said the benediction. The Class of 1967 moved our tassels and threw our caps high in the air with no hope of finding our own again. Our eighteen-year-old minds believed throwing our mortarboards in the air meant, "We are outta here!" We had yet to comprehend that this age-old tradition symbolized the many directions our lives were about to take.

Daddy and Jimmy at the top of the hill whistled and clapped during the recessional. "Smile, Tat," Daddy ordered and snapped my picture when I passed him. "Hip, hip, hooray for my sister and Pam!" Jimmy added and kept on whistling and clapping.

Mother and Mary were waiting for me in the girls' gym when I returned my robe to Mrs. Bernard. "Have you finished your grading yet, Mrs. Bernard?" I asked her.

"Not yet, Cathy; final grades for the semester will be posted on Monday," she said. I was anxious to know my grade from her; I wanted an A from Mrs. Bernard; I worked so hard to get one. I was praying for it. "All we had to turn in so far were the names of those graduating."

"Bye, Mrs. Bernard; I loved your class and having you as my teacher. You were my all-time favorite!" I hoped I didn't sound overly butt-kissy because I meant those words with all my heart.

"Don't forget what I wrote in your yearbook, Cathy!" she whispered when she hugged me.

Eleanor stopped Mother, Mary, and me on our way to the car. We had been fighting all week but made up on the phone the night before. "Cat, we are going to be great roommates!" she said. Eleanor always called me Cat. I never liked it, but I never said so.

"We can't miss!" I told her.

Later, Pam invited Mary and me over to her house for a champagne toast with her parents before Pam and I went to the All-Night Senior Party. I wrote in my *Graduation Memories* book: *The Shontz family gave me a lovely onyx necklace and card, and the Cordeals gave Pam and me both monogrammed handkerchiefs and gift certificates.* I didn't write down what I gave Pam, but I hope I gave her something half as lovely as the two musketeers gave me.

Bruce Watkins, one of the twins born across the hall from me, was madly in love with Mary. We were good friends, and he was my date for the party since it was only for senior class members. The theme was *Music,* and the gym was decorated like a Gay Nineties city. Bruce and I danced until our feet ached to *Bob Kuban and the In Men* that the PTA hired to play for us. Between dances, Bruce talked about nothing but Mary and his plans to be her boyfriend during her senior year because he planned to stay in town. He spoke of Mary when we all went swimming at the Webster pool after the band finished playing, too. All night I promised I would do an excellent job of cheerleading for him whenever I talked to Mary. I wondered my last night at Webster High how many times I played matchmaker for classmates during my three years there while I walked the halls without a match of my own.

Breakfast was served to the seniors at 7:00 A.M. in the gym for our last event together. No matter how hard we hugged each other or how often we promised to write from college, sadness was attached to each hug and promise.

Mother was making French toast for Jimmy when I got home. "Did you have a good time?" she asked.

"I did," I said, "I did; everything was super fun, but it was also strangely sad."

"That's why they call it commencement," Mother said. "Sadness is part of it because you are leaving your old way of life and starting a new one. Hey, guess what Mrs. Bernard whispered to me during graduation? Tell Cathy she got her A in English!'"

"Really?" I said in disbelief. "Oh, my goodness!" I ran to my room to find my yearbook. I turned to the faculty section and read Mrs. Bernard's message beneath her picture. She wrote in her familiar shaky handwriting:

Cathy dear,

You were an excellent student. I loved having you in my class for this last year before I retired. Now, you go be a teacher! You were born to do it! `

Fondly, Jane Bernard.

𝔂

CHAPTER THIRTY-FOUR
THE SUMMER OF LOVE

June 1967 expelled thousands of baby boomers into the world from America's urban and rural birth canals. It was known as the *Summer of Love*. But only some of my generation went their ways of *California Dreamin'*. Just a few kids I knew went hitchin' and groovin' to San Francisco wearing flowers in their hair, wanting to make love, not war. The rest of us spent those three months in the establishment earning money for college, joining the military, or working to help at home. Fresh out of our nests, the baby bird boomers divided ourselves into two sides: them and us.

Mary, Pam, and I still had our pool days that summer, but fewer than in previous summers. I continued to work at Stix Baer & Fuller and was given full-time hours. I was grateful for the extra work to save money for college. Our musketeer time together was precious, with fall looming and Pam going to Southwest Missouri State College in Springfield; Mary to be a senior at St. Joseph's Academy at home in Webster, and my leaving for CMSC in Warrensburg. Fall meant separation, a permanent one, we feared.

The music the three of us listened to changed that summer as the antiwar movement increased. I always listened to the radio – in the car, at home on my transistor, or lying on my beach towel by the pool with Pam and Mary. We always shared a love for music; Broadway musicals and our funny little shows brought us close together. Mary's father was a musician, so her home was filled with the finest piano and organ music. Mr. Cordeal even wrote a Requiem Mass for John Fitzgerald Kennedy after the president was killed. It was played at Mary Queen of Peace and other churches in St. Louis. Pam's father had a fantastic record collection of seventy-eights, forty-fives, and LPs. We spent hours listening to music at her house. One night when we heard Connie Francis, I sat on Mr. Shontz's seventy-eight record of *Harbor Lights* and broke it.

"My big bottom strikes again!" I said in total embarrassment. After that, Mr. Shontz teased me about sitting on *Harbor Lights* whenever I was at their house.

"Cathy's here," he said, "put the records away!" He meant to be playful; he didn't know I didn't hear it that way.

At my house, my father played Big Band music; the works of Tommy Dorsey, Count Basie, Glenn Miller, Pete Fountain, and Louie Armstrong were just a few of his favorites. Our hi-fi was rarely silent. The voices of Ella Fitzgerald, Nat King Cole, Frank Sinatra, the Ink Spots, Lena Horne, Doris Day, and other vocalists kept me in my constant state of romanticism. Once I saw my mother and father dance in the backroom, and for a fleeting moment, I saw why they fell in love.

Rick played his favorite albums of Bobby Darin and Elvis. I listened to love songs from Frankie Valli and the Four Seasons, Andy Williams, Johnny Mathis, and Dionne Warwick when I got my chance at the turntable. I sang along with every song. My family went insane with my continuous singing. I had the song, *Alfie*, stuck in my head during the summer of love and sang it nonstop until Jimmy banged on the bathroom door one night and yelled, "Please, Claire, *please,* knock it off with *Alfie!* We can't stand it anymore!"

It was a rare Saturday afternoon when Pam, Mary, and I were not working and tanned by the Cordeal's pool. Frankie Valli's *Can't Take My Eyes Off of You* came on the radio while Pam and Mary were in the water, and I was on my beach towel. I fell in love with the song; it was the first time I heard it. I tried to find it again on other stations after they came back to their towels but had no luck. It came back on the radio when I drove home from Mary's house. I got goosebumps that hot summer day when the song hit its crescendo of saxophones, and Frankie Valli's voice came over the top of them. In the driveway, I didn't turn the motor off in Mother's car until the last note faded. *I love you, baby, and if it's quite all right, I need you, baby, to warm the lonely night.*

The following Monday evening, after I got off work at five o'clock, I drove out of the Crestwood parking lot and pulled onto Highway 66. I went straight to Korvettes to buy a forty-five copy of my new favorite song.

"There are none out front here, but just a second, and I will check in the back," said the dark blonde curly-headed sales associate.

"Thank you, Joe," I said, reading his name tag; "I just love that song."

"It's really popular," he said. Joe had clear blue eyes, was slim to almost skinny, and stood about two inches shorter than me. He was no Rex and not close to the tall, athletic guys I was usually attracted to, but he had the college preppy look that always got to me. Truth be known, it was the sincerity of his natural smile that set off my hormonal fireworks.

"Oh wow, I hope there's one in the back!" I said and crossed my fingers when he went around the corner. Yes, cute, that's the right word. He's cute; I thought while he was gone.

"You're in luck; there were three of them back there!" he said when he returned. I gave him the money for the record, and he rang up the sale on the register. I must have been grinning as he slid the record into a bag and handed it to me. "I don't think I've ever made a customer so happy," he said, laughing.

"Thank you, Joe," I said and changed my grin to a smile before leaving.

"What's your name?" he asked.

"Cathy Miller," I answered. "What's your last name?'

"Eckert, nice to meet you." We both shook hands, but it felt sappy, so we didn't. "So, Cathy Miller, would you like to go out sometime?"

I didn't hesitate. "You bet," I said and gave him my phone number.

The second I got home, I put my new treasure on my bedroom portable turntable. I sat on my bed and played the record over and over. Each time Mr. Valli and his saxophone hit that crescendo, I swooned. The phone rang at about 10:30 p.m.

"Who in the hell is calling us this late?" Daddy said from his recliner.

"I've got it, Daddy!" I said.

"Hi, is this Cathy?" the voice said. "This is Joe Eckert. Want to catch a movie tomorrow?"

We talked for almost an hour about the things guys and girls usually share on their first phone call. Joe was a year older and would be a sophomore at Mizzou in the fall. He wanted to be an electrical engineer like his father. I told him my goal was to major in business at CMSC and be an artistic director for a theater. We decided a specific time for our date the next night as we ended the call, and I returned to my room. I played the record again and wondered if Joe, like the song, was too good to be true.

The Eckert's house was in the group of expensive homes behind the stonewall that enclosed the land across from the Bird Park, once owned by my Blackmer relatives before the depression. Joe and his family moved to Webster from Michigan. Joe was the oldest child, followed by his brother, James, and his sister, Joanie. I was comfortable around all the members of his family except his father. He differed significantly from my father and any of my friends' fathers; he was cold and disapproving toward everyone, whether family members or not. Joe and I spent little time in his home, and I was glad for it.

Most evenings the rest of June and all of July, Joe and I spent together, if we weren't working, either at my house or out with friends. We laughed a lot and had fun wherever we were, but mainly we confided worries about our fathers, our families, and our futures. We didn't realize we were two sexually charged kids craving romantic love to escape uncomfortable realities. Daddy's recurring heart problems and money worries dominated me, and the fears of disappointing his father and draft possibilities haunted Joe. We were in love with love. Neither of us had anyone close to a steady in high school, and we were hungry to make up for what we thought we missed or lost.

Mary and Bruce Watkins began dating, and Pam was busy getting ready for college and spending time visiting her grandparents in Illinois. Time with Mary and Pam grew less and less as the summer progressed. The summer of love moved toward fall until it stopped when Daddy had a stroke the first week of August.

I was in the living room waiting for Joe when it happened. He would pick me up and go to his house for dinner. Jimmy was sitting at the dining room table waiting for us to drop him off at Tony's on Woodlawn on our way, and Rick was at work in Clayton. Daddy was standing at the front door looking out for Joe's car, but when he closed it and walked to the couch, I noticed one side of his mouth was drooping. He tried to say Joe was pulling into the driveway, but I couldn't understand him. I knew something terrible was happening and walked over to see what was wrong. Jimmy saw Daddy, too, and yelled for Mother in the kitchen.

"Something is wrong with Daddy," Jimmy told her. "He's talking out of just one side of his mouth!" Mother came rushing into the room and looked at my father.

"Hank," she said, "Sit down. Are you feeling all right?" He sat down and tried to say he was fine, but he had no control of his mouth. She wiped the drool from his chin and said, "I'm calling Dr. Jones!"

I sat down beside Daddy on the couch and held his shaking hand. Jimmy went to the door and let Joe inside. Joe knew something was very wrong with my father and sat on the other side of him. Jimmy paced between Mother on the phone and the three of us on the couch. After Mother hung up the phone, she returned to the living room. "Cathy, you and Joe go to the Eckert's for dinner and drop Jimmy at Tony's. Everything is going to be fine. Go, have a good time."

I tried to eat but couldn't eat anything. I felt terrible because Mrs. Eckert went to so much trouble, but I could not concentrate at Joe's house. I told Joe's mother about my worries over my father, and she completely understood. I helped her with the dishes, and she chatted with me to help me feel better while we did them. There were no cell phones to keep in touch with Mother about what was happening; we only had house phones. Joe and I sat with his family in their TV room for a while before I asked him to take me home. I thanked Mrs. Eckert and said goodnight to everyone. Mr. Eckert made a point of telling Joe not to be late for his curfew.

There was nobody there when we arrived. Mother called just as we sat down to wait for news. "Cathy, Daddy is fine, but Dr. Jones wants him to spend tonight in the hospital. I will be home after he is settled in his room. Rick is still at work, and Jimmy is at Tony's. I will pick Jimmy up on my way home."

This time Daddy was only in the hospital for two days. Mother brought him home, helped him to his room to rest, and then met me in the kitchen. She told me Dr. Jones wanted him to stay home for a few months until he was better. "He will not be able to work, so that he will be on disability again." I studied my mother's face carefully; she looked so thin, her hair lacked her pin curls, and she was not wearing her red lipstick. She avoided my eyes while she talked; I believed nothing she told me.

"Mother," I said, "I am not going to college. I am staying home to help, and since Daddy won't be working, we will need my paycheck from Stix. Rick's paycheck will not be enough."

"Absolutely not!" she said, and this time she looked directly into my eyes and shook her pointer finger at me. "Cathy, you are going to college. We will receive money from the government until your father is better; it will all be okay. Do not argue with me; I have enough on my plate!" I turned and went to my room and tried to make her harsh words not feel like a slap of rejection, but I was hurt not to be needed by my mother. Her cold tone only pushed me closer to Joe for warmth and affection.

Daddy went back to wearing his robe and slippers full-time. His speech was normal again; his color returned somewhat, and his sense of humor was never gone, but the thought of leaving my father, especially at that time, created a constant ache in my heart. Mother made me sad, too. She didn't laugh much anymore, and to add to her weariness, Bob still came over for drinks almost every evening to "cheer up Daddy." Mother was exhausted all the time.

Our family custom in August was to celebrate Jimmy's birthday. It was the only time of the year that we went out for dinner and a movie as a family. We never had the money to do it for anyone else. "It's the kid's birthday!" Daddy announced each year. "Time to celebrate!" We went to fancy restaurants like Yugari's or the dining room at the Coronado Hotel for Jimmy's birthdays. We followed dinner with movies like *The Guns of Navarone, The Longest Day; It's a Mad, Mad World*, etc. But there was no restaurant and no movie in August that summer. All of us felt the heaviness of the atmosphere. Our nights of celebration for Jimmy's birthday always served as touchstones for our family. We never had enough money for much, so our dinner and movie nights were our mini vacations before school year chaos began each fall.

The sudden turn in my father's health and the continuous tension from Joe's father about Joe's education cemented Joe and me to one another. Joe's father was a wealthy, formidable German patriarch who was not crazy about his son getting serious over me. I was sure Mr. Eckert hated me; he couldn't hide his disdain and the thought I would drag Joe down until he flunked out of Mizzou. Joe had come perilously close to failing his freshman year.

The first time I was at the Eckert house, I sensed how much pressure Joe was under about school. I felt sorry for him the way his father treated him. Joe's mother, Janie, was always cheerful and welcoming. It was obvious where Joe inherited his personality and kind disposition. His younger brother and sister were both fun to be around and made me feel welcome. Nothing the rest of the family did could compensate for Mr. Eckert's angry cloud that hovered over their house when I was there.

On each date we had, Joe and I became more intimate, but we were raised to be "good kids," which in the sixties meant staying virgins. Our restrained summer was out of sync with the summer of free love. I had to remain a virgin until I got married; I did not want to go to hell or disappoint my father, and I was terrified to bring any form of shame or any more problems to my mother. I didn't realize I was not physically attracted to Joe like Rex. I loved Joe because I needed to love Joe. I wanted to deserve to wear the white dress and have the fairy tale of my father beside me when I walked down the aisle toward my husband. Daddy was my first true love, and the romantic dream of his giving me away was all I had ever wanted since the first Chicago game we played. I would not tarnish my father's suit of armor or the marital experience

Daddy wanted for me in any way, especially after he became so sick.

Joe honored my wishes. He told me his father would disown him if he ever made a girl pregnant before he graduated and had his degree in electrical engineering. It was a full year later before Pope Paul VI stunned the world in July 1968 and reaffirmed the church's ban on modern contraceptives in the Humanae Vitae. The church still had not approved birth control other than the rhythm method. Pregnancy was a constant possibility. Joe and I settled for French kissing and fondling one another until our car windows steamed over, and we forced ourselves to stop.

Joe left to return to school and gave me his Mizzou lavalier on a silver chain on our last date during our version of the summer of love. He told me how serious he was about us. A lavalier in 1967 meant we were engaged to be engaged. I never took it off my neck after he put it on me, not even in the shower. Columbia was about three hours from Warrensburg, but since neither of us had a car, it may have been across the world. The months until we could be home together for Thanksgiving felt lifetimes away. I played *Can't Take My Eyes Off of You* thousands of times during my remaining days at home after Joe left. If I couldn't have Joe, Frankie Valli had to do.

♌

CHAPTER THIRTY-FIVE
CHICAGO

I didn't want to leave my lavender bedroom and its fluffy, white, frosting-like eyelet curtains and go to college after Daddy's stroke, but Mother gave me no choice. I sat on my bed, held one of my royal purple throw pillows to my chest, and waited for Eleanor's mother to pick me up for Warrensburg.

The night before, I sat on the floor next to Daddy's recliner and watched *The Secret Life of Walter Mitty* with him on my last night at home. I envied Walter Mitty's ability to escape reality and live romantic adventures as a brain surgeon, a secret agent, or a World War I Flying Ace. I read *The Secret Life of Walter Mitty* in sophomore English. It soothed my fears to watch the movie with Daddy and laugh at Walter; I needed to be near my father. I leaned my head on his knee and marveled at how Danny Kaye brought Thurber's words from a printed page to a living, breathing presence on the screen. My nervous heartbeats about leaving the next day went *ta-pocketa, ta-pocketa,* just like Thurber's short story and the sound effects in the movie that emphasized Walter Mitty's challenges.

My father was too tired to come to my room after the movie, so I kissed him goodnight and hugged him in his recliner before I went to bed. That night, when I finally fell asleep, I dreamed Walter

Mitty saved me from leaving my father. I had a lot in common with Walter Mitty. He was frightened of life and crazy, too, just like I thought I was. Walter Mitty may well have been the reason I made it to Central Missouri State College.

I believed God sent Walter to me in my dreams because He wanted me to take Walter to college for as long as I needed him. God knew I would be lonely without my hero at home in his recliner and that I needed another hero to take his place as a confidante, therapist, cheerleader, and protector. I didn't know how to be without the man who saved me for eighteen years from the terminal tender feelings and anxieties that spun me into sensitivity overloads.

The following morning, I wasn't sure if I was certifiably insane or just in the process of going there as I sat on my bed clutching my pillow and waited for Eleanor and her mother to arrive.

"Walter, I'm scared," I whispered.

"Of what?" said, my imaginary hero.

"Of everything. Rick going to war. Daddy is sick. Not being with my family or Joe."

"Tell you what," Walter said, "we'll make an adventure out of it. Believe you are going to an enchanted land called Academia, where there is a kingdom full of happy, funny friends."

"Okay, Walter," I whispered; "if you help me, I will do it."

"Cathy! It is eight A.M.," Mother called from the living room. "Eleanor's mother will be here any minute! Are you ready?"

"Yes, I mean, no; I don't know. I guess I'm as ready as I'll ever be," I finally said. I left my lavender security behind and walked down the hall to the living room.

"Cathy, stop being so dramatic," Mother said when I arrived. "This is a wonderful opportunity. You're just too sensitive for your own good. You've seen too many movies and read too many romance novels. It is time to go learn something useful and have some fun doing it."

"Fine, I will," I said, but I wanted to scream. *Have I ever done anything the way you wanted me to do it?*

"Be sure to stop at the student loan office when you settle in your room and ask for the National Defense Act Loan representative. He will give you your work-study job assignments when you sign your final papers. Now, smile. You and Eleanor will love college." With that, Mother handed me my round blue suitcase and went to the window to watch for Eleanor's mother.

"Are you ready, Tat?" Daddy said from his chair at the dining room table. He looked forcibly animated in his gold, terrycloth robe with ragged white binding. A huge safety pin closed the collar at his neck; it seemed the only thing holding him together.

"I have to keep my neck safe and warm," he said and patted the pin. "Here, honey, I have your train letter for you."

Since my first trip to Illinois to visit Lori, I never left home for more than two nights that my father didn't write me "a train letter." It didn't matter whether I went to summer camp, visited Aunt Marylene in Jefferson City, or when Aunt EB paid for me to visit her in New York for the World's Fair in the summer of 1964. No matter how, when, or where I traveled, my father wrote me a letter to read while I was gone. "What a world you will see in your lifetime, Tat!" he always said.

"Thank you, Daddy, I said and tucked his letter inside my purse. "I could never leave without one of your train letters." Rick and Jimmy hugged me goodbye earlier that morning, but I missed them not being there when I heard Eleanor's mother honk her horn.

"There they are," Mother said.

"Time for you to have a Walter Mitty adventure," Daddy said when he stood up.

I was determined not to cry; it would be selfish, so I just reached up and hugged my father. "I'm going to miss you so much, Daddy. Please get well soon and write to me often." I felt I was hugging an imposter from the smell of the medicinal ointment Dr. Jones prescribed for the surfaces of Daddy's dry, cracked skin on his hands, legs, and ankles, the direct results of the poor circulation that came with Edema.

The pungent odor won the struggle and overtook the smell of my real father, clean from his shower and smelling of soap, shampoo, and aftershave lotion. I hugged him as hard as possible and whispered in his ear, "I love you. I will be home for the Turkey Day game. Don't watch too many movies without me, Daddy, especially Danny Kaye movies."

"I love you, Tat," he whispered back.

Mother and I carried my shiny new, black patent leather footlocker down to Mrs. Hughes' dark blue sedan. Eleanor was in the front seat with her green eyes bright with excitement.

Mother and I took two more trips to the house to get everything. Eleanor slid next to her mother in the front seat to make room for me as my mother slammed the trunk closed. The back seat was packed to the roof with Eleanor's things and some in the trunk.

"Bye, Mother," I said, knowing I was going to miss her but had no idea why. Maybe it was my fault that I was intimidated by her. Perhaps it came from my efforts to please her and never feeling I succeeded. I knew my mother loved me; I didn't believe she liked me. "I love you, Tat," she said, giving me one of her brief hugs. "Here is five dollars, Daddy, and I will mail you five dollars weekly. I wish we could send more, and maybe we can when he goes back to work." Mother squeezed my shoulders and opened the car door. Daddy was standing in the front doorway waving, and I took a forever photo of him in my memory.

I closed the car door and pressed the palm of my hand to the glass of my window.

"That's it, Ellen," Mother said to Mrs. Hughes; "thank you for driving the girls. Be careful, and have a safe trip. Bye, Eleanor, you girls have a good first semester, and Cathy, call me tonight when you settle in at the dorm."

I pantomimed *I will* and clutched my purse with Daddy's plane letter inside. I watched my mother wave until we turned right onto Grant Road, drove up and down the hills to Big Bend Road, made a left, and drove to Highway 40 toward Warrensburg and adulthood.

"Here we go, Walter," I whispered.

We drove four hours plus a lifetime to the enchanted land of Academia near Kansas City. We stopped for nineteen-cent McDonald's hamburgers in Columbia to break up the drive and calm our butterflies. I thought about Joe somewhere in town, maybe blocks away, and I wanted to jump out of the car. Back on the road, I reached for my neck and patted Joe's lavalier necklace as we passed each of the exits that read *Missouri University.*

Two hours later, we missed the exit off highway thirteen for the main campus entrance in Warrensburg. Mrs. Hughes passed it by mistake. We drove into town just as farmers were unloading their trucks filled with large, squirming, smelly hogs to herd them onto a waiting train. Mrs. Hughes turned off her motor and said, "Roll up the windows, girls! This won't be a pleasant wait." All three of us pinched our noses as hard as we could stand. My city girl worries turned into shock at the rural sights in front of the car. The squealing hogs caused near panic inside me. I wanted to read Daddy's train letter to calm myself, but Walter told me, "Wait, you'll need it much more later."

"Look, there's a movie theater!" I warbled, still clenching my nose. It looked ancient, but it had a marquee.

"Thank God!" Eleanor said. "We never saw this part of town when we came to look at the campus with your aunt, Cat!" The theater was a sign from God. His personal message was that there was a tiny bit of civilization in Warrensburg and that I might survive my freshman year after all. "I bet it's the only movie theater in this one-horse town," Eleanor said.

Once the train started moving, and Mrs. Hughes started the car, I closed my eyes, afraid to see anything else, afraid my fragile heart couldn't take any more worry that day. I didn't open them until Eleanor said, "We're here!"

Only a week past Labor Day, it was too early for the leaves on the campus trees to change. The September sun was beating down and lighting up the alternate patterns of crunched summer-bleached grass and bright golf-course-green patches where sprinklers reached and rescued. We drove through fraternity row, and Eleanor immediately surveyed the testosterone terrain.

"Look at him!" Eleanor said, "that guy looks like an advertisement for Brooks Brothers." He did, too, with his bleached blonde attempt at California surfer hair and his pink knit shirt, madras shorts, and brown sandals. "He looks like one of the Beach Boys! Yum!" Eleanor drooled.

"Hey, taken woman!" I said. "Don't forget about Henry. You can look, but you can't touch, Miss-almost-engaged."

"Honk, Mom!" Eleanor ordered, "let's see if he looks up."

"Behave, Eleanor," her mother said.

The parking lot of Nattinger/Bradshaw Hall for freshmen was full of families unloading their precious cargo, kids from all around the state, the new bottom-tier men and women of the collegiate pecking order. There were no microwaves in 1967 or computers or any other technology to unload, not because they were forbidden but because they didn't exist.

There was a television and a phone at the end of each hall. Eleanor and I carried the heaviest objects to room 116 in Nattinger: our footlockers, record albums, portable stereos, and popcorn poppers. Everything else was transported with relative ease in suitcases and open cardboard boxes. CMSC had large dorm rooms with a bathroom between every two rooms. We had superior accommodations and actual suites compared to other Webster High grads who went to Mizzou, SMS, or other state universities and schools. Our room was huge compared to their tiny rooms, with one big bathroom per floor, which they all had to share.

Eleanor hugged her mother goodbye, and I thanked Mrs. Hughes in the parking lot after everything was unloaded; then, we two freshies went inside and watched through our wall of windows over our side-by-side desks while she drove out of the parking lot.

There were no co-ed dorms when I went to college; the boys were in Bradshaw Hall, adjacent to Nattinger. A shared lounge area hooked the two buildings together. Freshmen were not allowed to have cars, so the expansive, vacant, blacktop parking lot resembled an airstrip at Lambert Airport. Eleanor took the closet and the bed closest to the window, so I sat down on the bed by the painted olive-green cement block wall. We had a large brown wooden nightstand with two drawers between our twin beds and two full-size dressers on the opposite wall. Our room differed from those we saw at other colleges, with bunk beds and no dressers.

"Hey Eleanor, I've got to call home really quick," I said. "I'll be right back." I used the call to procrastinate; I was unprepared to accept my immediate fate by unpacking. I ran to the hall phone and waited in line to make a collect call to my parents. The sound of my mother's voice was an automatic trigger for homesickness. I imagined Daddy lying down and Mother in the basement doing laundry before she helped Jimmy with his ninth-grade homework while she cooked dinner.

"Hi Tat, how is everything?"

"Just great, Mother," I lied. "How is Daddy?"

"He's tired today," she said, "but he's fine."

"The financial aid office was closed today, Mother, but I will go first thing tomorrow after freshmen convocation."

"That's good, honey. This is a long-distance call, so we must keep it short; time is money. Bye-bye. We will talk next Sunday again. Good luck this week," she said and hung up before I could say or feel anything more.

Eleanor and I finished unpacking and decorating our room just before midnight. We heard our suitemates, Patti and Betsy, snoring through their bathroom door. Eleanor and I christened my popcorn popper and saved hers for canned soups on Sunday nights when there was only a noon meal for students. We sat on our new celery green bedspreads in our new, still-creased pajamas and surveyed the color scheme we designed for our room. Powder pink accessories on Eleanor's side and soft yellow on my side. We took the sales stickers off the bottoms of our new pink and yellow mugs, clinked them together, and toasted our first night as roommates.

"To Ellie and Cat," Eleanor said, using the nicknames she made up for us, names no one else was allowed to use and names I never did.

"To us," I said, "and our future adventures in this new land called Academia!"

I took my turn in the bathroom while Eleanor wrote Henry a letter. "Do you think he gets letters in boot camp?" she asked.

"Rick did when he was there," I gargled through Listerine. "They must get letters; they just aren't allowed to write back yet," I said, clicking my upper retainer into place.

"I'm exhausted," Eleanor said as she licked the stamp, kissed the envelope's seal, and wrote S.W.A.K. (sealed with a kiss) on it. "Are you going to write Joe tonight?"

"I already did while you were down the hall with Patti and Betsy," I said.

"How do you end your letters to Joe, Cat?" Eleanor asked.

"More than yesterday and less than tomorrow," I said and immediately regretted it.

"That's great," she said, "I'll use that tomorrow night in my next letter to Henry."

"Eleanor, I'll set the alarm so we don't miss breakfast. I'll turn out my reading light in a minute," I said, but Eleanor's breathing was already in slow rhythm; it was safe to pull Daddy's letter from under my pillow. I didn't want Eleanor to feel bad since she didn't have a father.

I held my father's letter for a long time and stared at the envelope. The tears I held back all day started to flow just looking at his words: *A train letter for Tat.* Daddy's warm personality showed in his printing; it was precise, neat, and happy. I nestled back into my new foam rubber pillow and traced his words with my fingers.

Dear Tatter,

I know you are scared but don't be. Remember when you were a little girl and would have a bad dream? I'd go into your room and sit on your bed, and you would pull the covers over your face. "Where is my Tatter?" I asked. "Where is she? Has anybody seen Cathy? I hope she hasn't gone to Chicago. I would be so sad and lonely if she went to Chicago." Then I would lie down and pretend to put my weight all on you, and you would giggle and yank the covers down from your face and hug me.

Honey, there's nothing to be afraid of in Warrensburg or college or your future, but if things get scary, pull those covers over your face and go to Chicago. Just pretend I'm there to bring you back. I'm so proud of you, Tat. I'll write again soon.

Love, Daddy

I placed the letter back in its envelope and put it under my pillow. I turned off my light and pulled the covers over my face. "Walter," I whispered, "are you still there?"

"I'm here," he whispered back.

"Do you have a crystal ball, Walter?" I asked him.

"No, I'm sorry, I don't."

"Then, will you play Daddy's game with me?"

"Yes," he said. "Are you going to go to Chicago?"

"I am," I whispered.

The next morning Walter was gone, and I was on my own.

∅

ACKNOWLEDGMENTS

Thank you to the college and university professors who encouraged me to write, especially Professor Hinton, Advanced Composition instructor at KU in 1980; *Writing in Place* instructor at Yavapai College in 1991, whose name sadly escapes me; and special thanks to Yavapai College creative writing instructor, fiction, and nonfiction author, Laraine Herring.

Loving thanks to Dr. Melinda Martin for handing me a copy of *The Atonement Child* by Francine Rivers on my first visit to her as a patient thirty years ago and who remains my Woman's Health doctor today.

Sincere appreciation to the Professional Writers of Prescott and the Hassayampa Writers Club for awarding me first and second places for nonfiction writing in their 2008, 2009, and 2010 contests.

Heartfelt recognition goes to Senior Pastor Michael Cannon at Mt. Zion Tabernacle, Prescott, Arizona, for his inspirational sermon that started this memoir.

God bless my tactful readers of early drafts; those I consider saints: Frank Hahn, my incredible, loving, and supportive husband; Molly, my loyal four-legged writing companion; Chadwick Fritz, my son-in-law who never stopped asking, "Are you still writing your memoir?" Martha Steeves, my dear friend; the fabulous two musketeers, Mary Cordeal and Pam Shontz; my brothers, Rick and

Jimmy Miller, and their brave wives, Michele and Ann; and my loving niece, Jennifer Miller Guthrie, for all her prayers.

Grateful acknowledgment to my friend and writer Ed Gates for his advice about publishing the first book and to my hero son and business agent, Dan Renfro, whose expertise in guiding me through this *entire* process was irreplaceable.

Affection and gratitude go to my poetic, encouraging daughter, Mary Renfro, my little miss spider, for her lifetime of love and loyalty.

Thank you to my stepdaughter, Kristi Fritz; my stepson, Chad Hahn; and my grandsons, Dylan Wright, Duncan, and Reese Fritz, for all the joy you bring to my life.

And to God goes all glory.

REFERENCES

Caldarone, M., & Lloyd-Williams, M. (2004). *Actions: The Actors' Thesaurus.* Los Angeles, CA: Drama Publishers/Quite Specific Media.

Cochrane, L. (1996). *Forgiven and Set Free.* Grand Rapids, MI: Baker Books.

Conroy, P. (2009). *South of Broad.* New York, NY: Random House.

George, E. (2020). *Loving God with All Your Mind.* Eugene, OR: Harvest House.

Gibran, K. (2005). *The Prophet.* Sydney, NSW Australia: Phone Media.

Gill, A. (1995). *God's Promises for Your Every Need.* Dallas: Word Publishing.

Hallmark Editions. (1975). *Look to This Day.* Kansas City, MO: Hallmark Cards Inc.

Karr, M. (2016). *The Art of Memoir.* New York, NY: Harper Perennial.

Kelly, M. (1993). *Life is Messy.* North Palm Beach, FL: Blue Sparrow.

Lee, H. (1999). *To Kill A Mockingbird.* New York, NY: HarperCollins.

Lovric, M. (1993). *Women: An Illustrated Treasury.* Philadelphia, PA: Courage Books.

Phillips, M. B., & Voss, P. (2007). *100 Selma . . . 100 Years.* St. Louis, MO: Reedy Press.

Shurtleff, M. (1980). *Audition.* New York, NY: Bantam Books.

Smedes, L. B. (1984). *Forgive & Forget.* New York, NY: Harper One.

Start, C. (1975). *Webster Groves.*

Verrier, N. N. (1991). *The Primal Wound.* Baltimore, MD: Gateway Press, Inc.

Zondervan. (2002). *The Holy Bible, New International Version.* Grand Rapids, MI: Zondervan Publishing.

ABOUT THE AUTHOR

Catherine Miller Hahn is a Christian, and a retired thirty-five-year teaching veteran of Literature, Theatre, Humanities, Education, and Communication classes at the university, community college, and high school levels in Missouri, Kansas, and Arizona. Catherine has a Bachelor of Arts Degree in Communications and Business from Missouri State University, a master's degree in Theatrical Direction from the University of Kansas, and she completed the

Ph.D. coursework in the Philosophy of Theatre and Film with cognates in Psychology and Shakespeare, also from KU.

Catherine has directed over seventy-five academic, community, and professional theatrical productions. She was awarded Director Emeritus from the Board of Directors for the Prescott, Arizona, Community Center for the Arts.

Some of Catherine's published works can be found in *The Hidden River Cache 2010* and the 2008, 2009, and 2010 issues of Yavapai College Creative Arts Magazine, *Threshold.* She won first and second places for nonfiction in the 2009 Professional Writers of Prescott Contest and first place for nonfiction in the 2010 Hassayampa Writers Club Contest.

Catherine and her husband, Frank, have lived in Prescott, Arizona, since 1993. They share four children, three grandsons, and their terrier mix dog, Molly. This is Catherine's first published book and the first memoir in her series of three.

Additional information can be found at catherinemillerhahn.com.

Made in the USA
Columbia, SC
05 April 2023

14431671R00214